Engineering Archie

Archibald Leitch – football ground designer

Engineering Archie
© English Heritage 2005
Reprinted November 2005,
April 2007

English Heritage is the
government's statutory advisor
on all aspects of the historic
environment
Kemble Drive, Swindon SN2 2GZ
www.english-heritage.org.uk

Design by Doug Cheeseman

Production by Jackie Spreckley at
Malavan Media – creators of the
Played in Britain series
www.playedinbritain.co.uk

Printed by Zrinski, Croatia
ISBN: 978 1 8507491 8 9
Product Code: 50958

Archibald Leitch, photographed in
1924, at the age of fifty nine.

Engineering Archie
Archibald Leitch – football ground designer

Simon Inglis

Instantly Archie – Ibrox Park, Glasgow, in May 1949, where crowds gathered not for a Rangers match but for a speech by the former prime minister, Winston Churchill. Leitch used the distinctive criss-cross balcony design at nine of his other stadiums. By 2005 only three survived in situ; at Ibrox, Goodison Park and Fratton Park. Of those, only the one at Ibrox remains in good order and untarnished by advertisements. Leitch was a lifelong Rangers supporter, and this, the South Stand, opened in 1929, was probably his most treasured commission. Churchill, meanwhile, who used the rally to rail against 'Socialism and Nationalisation', returned to Downing Street in 1951.

Contents

Foreword by Rod Sheard
Introduction – Engineering Archie

1. Glasgow 10
2. Ibrox Park 16
3. Terracing 26
4. Glasgow & Liverpool 34
5. Grandstands 40
6. London 52

7. Grounds
   Introduction 58
   Bramall Lane Sheffield 60
   Ibrox Park, Part One Glasgow 64
   Ayresome Park Middlesbrough 66
   Craven Cottage London 70
   Stamford Bridge London 80
   Anfield Liverpool 86
   Ewood Park Blackburn 90
   Park Avenue Bradford 94
   Valley Parade Bradford 98
   Goodison Park Liverpool 100
   White Hart Lane London 108
   Old Trafford Manchester 114
   The Den London 120
   Leeds Road Huddersfield 122
   Roker Park Sunderland 124
   Highbury London 128
   Hillsborough Sheffield 132
   Tynecastle Edinburgh 136
   Villa Park Birmingham 140
   Dens Park Dundee 146
   St James' Park Newcastle 150
   Selhurst Park London 152
   Twickenham London 154
   Fratton Park Portsmouth 156
   Molineux Wolverhampton 160
   Baseball Ground Derby 166
   Hampden Park Glasgow 170
   The Dell Southampton 176
   West Ham Stadium London 178
   Ibrox Park, Part Two Glasgow 180

   Other commissions 190

8. Legacy 192

   Links 204
   Credits 206

The southern gable of Archibald Leitch's distinctive Trinity Road Stand at Villa Park, Birmingham, built in 1922-24, demolished in 2000.

Foreword
by Rod Sheard, HOK Sport

Of all the buildings in the public realm, stadiums must surely enjoy the highest profile.

Not only can a major stadium accommodate well over a million visitors each year, but the television audience for its events can be measured in the tens of millions. The Telstra Stadium, which we designed for the 2000 Sydney Olympics, was seen by a global audience of over four billion people.

This extreme visibility, combined with the sheer quantity of work Archibald Leitch produced during his lifetime, means that there will be few football fans in the world who have not at least glimpsed a Leitch stadium at one time or another, either on television or in photographs.

And yet this book is the first comprehensive review of his work.

I suspect this is because he worked both as an engineer and an architect, and therefore did not sit completely in one camp or the other.

Leitch was also working in a building genre that was not particularly fashionable. In his day stadiums and football grounds were not given the same civic status as other public buildings, such as town halls or churches. Nor did they possess the scale of other great engineering works, such as bridges or viaducts.

Fortunately, however, the status of stadiums has changed over recent years.

Today they can be regarded as among the most important buildings a city possesses. They can be used to help grow our cities. They help to provide a focus for communities and act as symbols for a nation.

Stadiums can represent glory and failure, elation and misery.

Yet despite their growing prestige, in many ways stadiums have changed little in technical content over the 2,000 years since the Colosseum formed the centrepiece of the Roman Empire.

Archibald Leitch was one of the pioneers of the resurgence of stadiums brought about by the rising popularity of sport at the turn of the 20th century, a popularity that, a hundred years later, shows no signs of waning.

I started my career as a stadium designer 25 years ago and from my very first project, working at Twickenham, to my latest, for Arsenal Football Club, Archie's fingerprints have always seemed to be present.

His output was amazing, especially considering the period in which he worked; no computers, no aircraft to jet him around the country, and, just as importantly, no established body of work upon which to draw.

During my 25 years I have on several occasions had to extend, modify, build around or even demolish Leitch's stands, and in that time I have come to appreciate not only the quantity of his work but also the quality and sophistication in his designs.

I also appreciate that much of his thinking and the issues with which he had to deal are as relevant today as they were a century ago.

Simon Inglis has written and compiled a wonderful study of Archie's life and work, a study which HOK Sport are delighted to have played a part as sponsors.

Rod Sheard was the lead architect for the Galpharm (formerly MacAlpine) Stadium in Huddersfield, winner of the 1995 Stirling Prize for Architecture. His company, the Lobb Partnership, later merged with HOK SVE and has been responsible for a number of stadiums and grandstands around Britain, Europe, North America and Asia. Perhaps the best known are the Reebok Stadium (Bolton), Telstra Stadium (Sydney), the new Wembley Stadium and, also in London, the Emirates Stadium for Arsenal.

Engineering Archie **7**

Introduction

Engineering Archie

Function before form – stairs leading to the upper seats of the McLeod Street Stand at Tynecastle, Edinburgh (b.1914), one of eleven Leitch stands still in use.

Among the many sentiments expressed by critics of football today – its overpaid players, its subservience to television, its high admission prices, to name but three – the one gripe that emerges time and time again concerns the design of modern stadiums.

Why, it is asked, do they all seem to look the same?

The complaint is revealing.

Firstly it reminds us that supporters care very much about the appearance and character of their surroundings; that the experience of attending a football match remains inseparable from the stage on which it is set.

But secondly, it suggests a longing for the grounds of yesteryear; as they existed prior to the publication of the Taylor Report into the Hillsborough disaster of 1989, which abolished the terraces and, in the process, sparked off a revolution that has since seen the construction of nearly 30 new venues in the Football League and Scottish League, plus the wholesale redevelopment of over 40 more on their existing sites.

The last time that football supporters had to live through such major changes to their 'home' grounds was a century ago, between the mid 1890s and the First World War.

And one of the catalysts of that change was another disaster; the Ibrox disaster of 1902, football's first wake up call of the 20th century.

This book is about football ground architecture between Ibrox in 1902 and Hillsborough in 1989, and, more specifically, about the Scottish engineer whose designs came to epitomise the classic look of 20th century football.

That look, moreover, was so readily identifiable because, ironically, so many of his designs looked the same.

When I first started out on my journey around the football grounds of Britain in the early 1980s, I had never heard of Archibald Leitch. Nor, seemingly, had anyone else.

But the more I was able to identify the stylistic similarities found at many of the grounds; the criss-cross steelwork balconies of Roker, Goodison, Ibrox, Fratton et al, and the roof-top gables of Hillsborough, Craven Cottage and Ayresome Park, the more I sensed a common thread. Certain types of steelwork and materials also provided tantalising clues.

Delving further into various club histories – of which there were then relatively few that even mentioned ground developments – Leitch's name started to crop up, here and there. Building records and club minutes added to the evidence, until eventually, in 1983, I was able to build up a list. Even if not comprehensive, I thought it would at least form the basis for any later research I might pursue, if that is, anyone was interested.

As it transpired, football fans *were* interested. More interested than ever I could have dreamed, and in time Archie emerged as something a minor cult figure. In 1987 his two buildings at Craven Cottage, and the South Stand at Ibrox were listed, while, around the same time, the discovery that gave me the most pleasure was that Archie had designed the Trinity Road Stand at Villa Park.

8 Engineering Archie

This was the stand in which I had watched my first ever football match, in April 1962.

The stand then was 40 years old. I was but seven.

Whether the majesty of the Trinity Road Stand was, subconsciously, the reason why Aston Villa became my team thereafter, I cannot honestly say. I certainly wrote several school compositions about Villa Park, and in secondary school took up architectural history with relish. On Saturdays I would visit a cathedral in the morning and a football ground in the afternoon.

Many years later, the 1989 Hillsborough disaster and the subsequent Taylor Report changed everything, for everyone connected with football, and throughout the 1990s I found myself working with architects, engineers, civil servants and safety experts, drawing up design guidelines and standards for the new, tougher era of ground regulation and monitoring, set up under the auspices of the Football Licensing Authority.

In 1996-97 our research culminated in a review of the *Guide to Safety at Sports Grounds*.

Better known as the *Green Guide*, this had first been published to help enforce the 1975 Safety of Sports Grounds Act, itself a response to yet another disaster at Ibrox Park, in 1971.

As editor of the revised *Green Guide* one of my tasks was to follow the paper trail back to the first edition, and thereby come to an understanding of what the standards were and how they had been formulated.

A pattern quickly emerged.

Much of what been considered as best practice, it turned out, had been based on the work of Archibald Leitch.

The dimensions of terracing, for example. The recommendation that crush barriers be installed in unbroken lines between aisles. That those aisles should be sunk in order to deter spectators impeding crowd circulation.

Then there was the geometry of stand design, which dictated the all-important calculation of sightlines; for example the lowering of the first row of terracing below pitch level and the provision of a specifed distance between the perimeter wall and the touchlines.

All these basic rules were there in Archie's work, drawn up, in most cases, before the First World War, yet so often ignored or poorly implemented in so many subsequent designs.

Thus, almost unwittingly, I have spent much of the last two decades following the trail of Archibald Leitch.

This is not to say that Archie was perfect.

As will become clear, as chief engineer to Rangers FC at the turn of the 20th century, Leitch was heavily implicated in the causes of the 1902 Ibrox disaster, a disaster he witnessed at first hand and which must have haunted him for the rest of his days.

Like many an engineer before and since, he was forced to learn from his mistakes.

The majority of his subsequent designs were, moreover, quite utilitarian in aspect. In stylistic terms he put function before form every time, which is why so many of his stands and terraces looked so similar (though also why they were so efficient).

It is also significant that during his entire career he never changed the description of his business on his company letterheads; it remained 'Consulting Engineer and Factory Architect.'

Indeed the industrial side of his work may well have brought in the bulk of his earnings.

We simply do not know.

Apart from one surviving factory in Glasgow – admittedly one of his finest buildings – no non-footballing related records survive.

In fact very little of anything other than his football work survives, which is why the title of this book has a double meaning.

Archie the engineer we know a great deal about from his stands and terraces.

But of the man himself, of his character and personality, all we have to go on are snippets extracted from newspaper reports, letters, and a few, precious family records and reminiscences from his two grandchildren.

In engineering Archie, as it were, from these sources, I hope to have come close to an estimation of the real Archibald Leitch, and the world in which he operated.

I hope also to have corrected errors in previous accounts of his life and work, my own included.

But above all I hope that this account will bring Archie the recognition he deserves, and at the same time help future generations towards a clearer understanding of what an extraordinary social and cultural phenomenon professional football became in the 20th century.

I was one of the millions who watched the game from any number of Archie's stands and terraces.

If you were too, may this book bring back many happy memories.

And if you were not, then boy, did you miss out.

Simon Inglis, March 2005

The Leitch look – typical splayed steelwork supporting the South Stand roof at Fratton Park, Portsmouth.

Engineering Archie **9**

Chapter One
Glasgow 1865–1902

The earliest known photograph of Archibald Leitch, dated 1897. He was then aged 32, with an expanding business and two young children. The prosperity of Glasgow and the British Empire depended upon an army of young professionals like Archie; risen up from humble circumstances, honed by education, driven by a fierce work ethic, but happily able to balance Christian values with commercial nous. The rewards for such men were considerable. Archibald Leitch did very well for himself, and for his family.

It should come as no surprise that the man who designed the best of Britain's leading football arenas during the first half of the 20th century was a Scot.

Nor that he was an engineer.

The Scottish contribution to the early years of professional football was immense. More than that, it was pivotal.

The first professional players were Scots; James Lang of The Wednesday in 1876, John Love and Fergus Suter of Darwen in 1878.

All the great teams of the late Victorian era – Preston North End's 'Invincibles' of 1888-89, Sunderland's 'Team of All Talents' in the 1890s – were built around Scottish talent.

Many an English club was founded by Scots and run by Scots. It was a Scottish draper in Birmingham, William McGregor, who set up the Football League in 1888, and a Scottish team, Queen's Park, whose 'passing game' revolutionised tactics in the 1870s.

As engineers, meanwhile, the Scots were unsurpassed.

James Watt's steam engines, Thomas Telford's canals, roads and bridges, and Robert Napier's iron-clad steamships transformed the very fabric of Britain and its dealings with the world, and in doing so, helped lay the foundations for Glasgow's industrial might during the second half of the 19th century, when it justly earned the tag of 'Second City of the Empire'.

Napier, the son of a blacksmith, used to say that he had been born with a hammer in his hand.

Archibald Leitch might well have said the same.

Archie Leitch was born on April 27 1865, in Comleypark Street, Camlachie, a heavily industrialised district of Glasgow dominated by the Parkhead Forge which, four years earlier, William Beardmore had taken over from the Napier family.

Archie's father, also Archibald, was a blacksmith too, and may well have worked for Beardmore.

If so, he was well placed. There were plenty like him to pick from, and jobs at Parkhead went only to the best of the journeymen.

Archibald senior – the son of a fisherman from Lochgilphead in South Argyllshire – had been one of thousands of Scottish migrants to Glasgow during the 1840s and 1850s. Between 1801 and 1894 the city's population grew tenfold, from 80,000 to over 800,000.

Archie was the fourth of six children, all living in a crowded tenement off Gallowgate, one of the main routes from the east end of the city into the centre.

He must have been a bright boy. In 1876, at the age of eleven, he won a place at Hutchesons' Grammar School, which had just been rebuilt in the Gorbals, on Crown Street.

'The class of children at the school,' reported the Education Commissioners in 1866, consisted of 'not the poorest and most destitute, but mostly the children of respectable labouring people.'

The *Evening Citizen* described Hutchesons' in 1875 as 'a model of severity.' The school itself aimed at 'promoting the intelligence of our working classes'.

Even if Archie did manage to gain a scholarship, his father would still have needed to find extra cash for uniform and books.

But this was the Scottish way. Education mattered. Sacrifices had to be made.

For an inquiring young boy with an interest in practical matters, Glasgow was a tough, though magical city.

Archie grew up in a world of iron and coal, rivets and cogs, boilers and turbines.

In whichever direction he might wander from Gallowgate he could ogle giant vessels rising up in the Clyde shipyards, or steam trains rolling out of the massive North British, or Neilson Co. workshops, both at Cowlairs, or the Glasgow Locomotive Works at Polmadie.

Far more than his peers in the likes of Birmingham or Manchester, he would have seen the fruits of the Empire being carted through the city. Sugar, tobacco, jute and tea.

And in an era when the total tonnage of British merchant shipping was greater than that of the rest of the world combined, the other great Scottish export was of course the Scots themselves.

Engineering, like the army, opened a path to the world, and in Glasgow especially, to the other side of the Atlantic, to the West Indies, to Buenos Aires, and to New York and beyond.

Closer to home, there were other distractions.

On his way to school every morning Archie would have walked past, or even through Glasgow Green, where in 1873 a group of lads calling themselves 'The Rangers' had formed a football club. But even if young Archie had not actually seen the Light Blues in the flesh – they had moved to the other side of the city by 1875 – then there were plenty of others still on the Green, or on the wide expanses of Queen's Park.

Did Archie even play a bit himself?

As we will be forced to concede so often in our tale, alas, we simply do not know.

From Hutchesons' Archie followed a path well trodden by boys of his social class and background. In either 1880 or 1881 he graduated to Anderson's College on George Street (now part of Strathclyde University), where he studied 'science'.

From there in 1882 he joined the engineering works of Duncan Stewart & Co., at their London Road Iron Works, Bridgeton Cross, a short walk from the family's tenement in Gallowgate.

Although Duncan Stewart was best known for its manufacture of sugar making machinery – a major industry in Glasgow at the time – they also produced a variety of bleaching, dyeing and printing machinery, cylinders and presses.

It was an excellent company in which to broaden his knowledge, and his contacts. It also led him, in 1887, to become a draughtsman; a skill that would stand him in good stead for the rest of his life.

But perhaps, like any young man of 22 still living at home, he may also have been restless, because in late 1887 he went to sea, to train as a marine engineer.

Where he sailed over the next three years we cannot be sure. But we know from the few precious reminiscences of his grandchildren that he took frequent voyages overseas throughout his life and had a number of seascapes hanging on his walls. He also had strong links with family and friends in South Africa, and at least some experience of working in India.

In early 1890 he returned to Glasgow however, and we might guess why, because in June 1890 »

▲ **Gallowgate** c. 1910. From his teens until he went to sea in 1887, Archie lived with his parents and two sisters in a tenement above one of the shops on the left.

These new tenements were an improvement on the city's older housing stock. Even so, the rooms were small, the water supply erratic, there were no inside toilets, and foul smells often wafted up from the central close.

None of the buildings shown here remain.

Engineering Archie 11

Glasgow

— Do —	— Do —	— Do —	Lean-to Roof Truss	32'-0" Span, 16'-0" pitch
— Do —	— Do —	— Do —	Columns for Stages	6" & 8" Dia
Australasia Sug. Ref. Co		Melbourne	Plan of F Floor Sugar House	50'-0" × 66'-0"
— Do —		— Do —	Detail Plan of Floor A Sugar House	50'-0" × 66'-0"
— Do —		— Do —	— Do — — Do — B Sugar House	50'-0" × 66'-0"
L. J. Lionarons	Sedatie	Sourabaya	Elevation and Plan of Stages	
— Do —	— Do —	— Do —	Special C. I. Clips for Buildings & Stages	
— Do —	— Do —	— Do —	Lower Plan of Stages &c	
— Do —	— Do —	— Do —	Lean-to Roof Truss over Boilers & Mill House	40 ft Span, 16 ft Pitch
— Do —	— Do —	— Do —	Special C. I. Clips & Shoes	
Australasia Sug. Ref. Co		Melbourne	Detail Plan of C Floor Sugar House	50'-0" × 66'-0"
— Do —		— Do —	— Do — D — Do — — Do —	50'-0" × 66'-0"
— Do —		— Do —	— Do — E — Do — — Do —	50'-0" × 66'-0"
L. J. Lionarons	Sedatie	Sourabaya	Gable Framing for Cooler End of House	64'-0" Span
— Do —	— Do —	— Do —	Do at Mill End of House	64'-0" Span
— Do —	— Do —	— Do —	Arrgt of Sheeting for Roof & Lean-to's	64'-0" Span, 144 ft long
Australasia Sug. Ref. Co		Melbourne	Detail Arrgt of Staircase & Hoist	Staircase 12'-0" Square
Grace Bros & Coy	Cartavio		Proposed Arrgt of Stages	9'-0", 16'-0 & 20'-0" High
L. J. Lionarons	Sedatie	Java	Detail of Stairs	4'-0, 6'-0, 8'-0 & 16'-0" High
— Do —	— Do —	— Do —	Plan of Flooring	
— Do —	— Do —	— Do —	Stairs to Stages & Yaryan Staging & Stairs	
Darley & Butler	Tuticorin	India	Columns for Stages	8"
G. W. MacFarlane & Co for The Hilo Sug. Co		Honolulu	Iron Wharf & Shed	45'-0" × 45'-0"
— Do —	— Do —	— Do —	— Do — with Wood Joists	45'-0" × 45'-0"
Darley & Butler	Tuticorin	India	Roof Sketch & Special Clips	
— Do —	— Do —	— Do —	Arrgt of Stages & Columns	
E. Lloyd Ltd		Sittingbourne	Detail of Staging for Dissolving Tanks	
— Do —		— Do —	Arrgt of Flooring Plates	
Darley & Butler	Tuticorin	India	Framing of Buildings (Wood) for Refinery Plant	
— Do —	— Do —	— Do —	General Outside View of Buildings for — Do —	
L. J. Lionarons	Sedatie	Java	Extension of Buildings	80'-0" long × 64'-0" Span
Darley & Butler	Tuticorin	India	Plan of Flooring & Details	

▲ Soon after his wedding in 1890, Archie was appointed head of the ordering department in the drawing office of **Mirlees, Watson and Co**.

It was a prime job at a respected company. Mirlees, Watson were the city's leading manufacturers of sugar making machinery, at a time when some 80 per cent of all such equipment in the world was made in the Glasgow area.

Shown here is a page from the company's drawing office ledger at the time Leitch was in charge.

All the elements he would later call upon for both factory and grandstand design are here to see; gable framing, details of stairs, columns for stages and sheeting for roofs and lean-to's.

Other entries show lattice girders for Trinidad, a lookout tower for Nicaragua, an iron building for Peru and boiler mountings for Guatemala – all designed to help feed the British mania for sugar products.

But if Archie did ever daydream of these far off places, he would at least have known some of them, having spent three years as a marine engineer from 1887-90.

We know for sure that he spent time in South Africa and India.

12 Engineering Archie

Archie got married. So either it was a whirlwind romance, or perhaps Jessie Black, the dairyman's daughter from just across the Gallowgate, had waited, three long years, for his return.

Archie was now 25; his bride a year younger.

Their wedding took place in St John's Church in the Gorbals. On the marriage certificate Archie described himself as a draughtsman.

Duncan Stewart took him back into their drawing office, but he stayed only eight months and by the end of the year found a more senior position as the head of the Ordering Department of the Drawing Office of Mirlees, Watson and Co.

Once again, this was a high profile company, suggesting that Archie came well recommended.

Like Duncan Stewart, Mirlees, Watson were described as Sugar Machinery Manufacturers – they were indeed the leaders in the field, with a workforce of up to 800 hands – but they also produced a range of engineering products (as described opposite), for clients around the world.

Archie's world by now was probably becoming ever more defined by his work and by his social standing.

He and Jessie set up home in McLellan Street, only a few hundred yards from his workplace on Scotland Street (by Shields Road station). His fellow staff were almost certainly all Protestants, like himself; the sectarian divide in the city between Protestants and Catholics then being quite pronounced.

It is also possible that it was around this time that Archie joined the freemasons. Pretty much every young man of his rank and background did. It was no big deal, and certainly not secret. Indeed it would have been far more of a surprise to discover that he had not been a freemason.

In his later dealings with senior figures in football, membership of the brotherhood would certainly not have harmed his chances of work. But then he was engaged by plenty of football club chairmen who appear not to have had any masonic connections, so it is almost impossible to determine how much or how little it helped.

Archie, the brother, was soon also Archie the father.

He and Jessie had their first child, a son, in April 1891.

Following in the family tradition, the boy was named after his father. On the birth certificate of Archibald Kent Leitch, Archie was now described as 'Engineer's Draughtsman (journeyman)'.

McLellan Street was situated in Kinning Park, which for many years had been the home of that football club we enountered earlier, The Rangers.

Now, they were playing a little further away, but still within walking distance of Archie's house, in Govan, at a ground called Ibrox Park.

Given the train of later events, Archie must surely have become aware of the club and its ground during this period, if he had not been already.

Ibrox Park was then still a new venue, having opened in 1887.

It was one of the best of its kind for the time; holding 25,000 spectators on wooden terraces around a running track, with a small timber and iron pavilion on the Copland Road side.

Maybe Archie even knew the company that had laid it out. Fred Braby and Co. were well known »

▲ The drawing office of the **Clyde Structural Iron Company** on the banks of the River Clyde in Scotstoun, Glasgow, gives us some idea of the environment in which Archie may have worked during his time at Mirlees, Watson and Co.

Over the years Leitch combined on many factory and football-related schemes with the Clyde company, including the Union Tube Works at Coatbridge (*top*), c.1900, and his first ever grandstands, for Kilmarnock and Rangers, both in 1899 (to which we will return).

The company's pattern book included ready made steel-framed designs for factories, drill halls, swimming baths, skating rinks, even market places. They also supplied several of Leitch's football clients with fences and railings.

Much of their work was exported for self-assembly; a sort of giant flat-pack building. One satisfied customer from Rangoon wrote in praise, 'whole work fitted in each other so well... we had no difficulty putting up the ironwork with ordinary native labour'.

Engineering Archie 13

From the Glasgow Athenaeum prospectus, 1898-99: 'The object of the Institution is to place within the reach of the public the fullest and most recent information on all subjects of general interest, whether Commercial, Literary, or Scientific: to provide an agreeable place of resort in the intervals of business; to incite, especially among Young Men, a taste for Intellectual and Elevating Pursuits.' Archie taught classes at various night schools for eight years until 1899. It brought an increase in cash, and confidence.

in Glasgow for this kind of work, and although their small buildings and stands were not as sophisticated as the sort of mechanical and structural designs Archie was used to drawing up on a daily basis, there were common elements; building frames, roofs and stairs, for example.

If Archie did indeed attend matches at Ibrox, he might well have had first hand experience of how crowds behave and inter-relate with their surroundings.

When the ground staged the Scottish Cup Final in 1892, over 26,000 fans managed to gain legal entry, with a further 10,000 forcing their way in by breaking down fences and barriers.

No engineer could possibly witness such a systems failure without at least pondering awhile.

And there were several other sports grounds in the city too, had Archie been that way inclined.

Scottish football might have been a little behind England when it came to the legalisation of professionalism – it was recognised by the Football Association in London in 1885, but not by the Scottish FA in Glasgow until 1893 – and the Scottish League did not form until 1890, two years after the Football League. But there was no doubting that Scottish fans were fanatical to a degree beyond the English.

Attendances at Rangers matches, and at the city's new Catholic club, Celtic, formed in 1888, were often much higher than was typical south of the border, particularly when Rangers and Celtic started up their rivalry in the 1890s. So popular were derby matches between these two clubs that within years of the League forming it became apparent that the more they played each other,

the richer each would become. In 1904 a sceptical newspaper would damn this duopoly by dubbing Rangers and Celtic 'The Old Firm'.

Celtic Park, meanwhile, not far from Archie's former home in Gallowgate, had overtaken Ibrox as the better of the two club grounds, having been expanded in 1892 to hold around 57,000. It also had modern tracks laid down to stage the newly popular sport of cycle racing, as well as the other staple summer draw, athletics.

A third major Glasgow venue was that of Queen's Park, the city's oldest and still resolutely amateur club. Their ground at Hampden Park (not the current site) had the city's first brick pavilion, and held 25,000 spectators.

For their part, also in 1892, Rangers built their first modern stand. Its architect was John Gordon, and its style was one that would become popular in later years; a curved profile roof with a purely decorative semi-circular gable in the centre.

Again, if Archie did take notice of all these developments, what did he think? Was he inspired? Was he critical? Or did he simply see sports grounds as a possible market he might one day consider?

One thing is for sure.

There was no other city in Britain, and therefore the world, in which anyone, regardless of their motives, could visit three such large football venues.

In that sense, it is even less surprising that the man who would eventually dominate the discipline of ground design should not only be a Scot, but a Glaswegian.

But what of Archie the engineer?

After six years in the drawing office at Mirlees, Watson & Co., in 1896 Archie finally broke out on his own, setting up as a 'Consulting and Inspecting Engineer'.

He was by then aged 31. He and Jessie now had two children. A third had died infancy.

They had also moved out of the industrial zone of Kinning Park to the cleaner air of Mount Florida, to one of the many new tenements rising up, on and around Cathcart Road, specifically aimed at young professionals just like Archie.

This was a world away from McLellan Street, or Gallowgate.

There were open fields within walking distance. The rooms were a little larger, and there may even have been inside toilets. Not far away there was Hampden Park, had Archie been interested.

That is, if he had time.

For most of the 1890s, to earn extra cash, he taught at night schools, at the Glasgow Athenaeum (see opposite), at Glasgow School Board classes, and also at the Christian Institute.

His business also seems to have picked up remarkably quickly.

In December 1896 he was made a member of the Institute of Engineers and Shipbuilders in Scotland, by which time he had also moved into new offices at 40, St Enoch Square.

The following February he also applied to join the London based Institute of Mechanical Engineers. (The Institution of Structural Engineers, which might seem the more appropriate body, had yet to be established.)

Archie's application form, which is still held in the Institute's archives, remains an invaluable source of information.

In it he writes that since leaving Mirlees, Watson and Yaryan (as the firm later became known) he had executed several general engineering contracts, and 'was lately appointed Consulting Engineer to the Lanarkshire County Council, Middle Ward'.

But perhaps the most interesting aspects of the document are the names of his proposers and seconders.

They read like a Who's Who of Scottish engineering.

Proposing him as a member was Sir William Renny Watson, the Watson in Mirlees, Watson and Yaryan. This alone should have established his *bona fides*.

Then came Duncan Stewart, his first employer and a major figure in Glasgow circles; Charles Davies, a locomotive engineer; John Robertson, a mining engineer who had worked mostly in Chile, Peru and Argentina, and last, but goodness, by no means least, Sir William Arrol – probably the most prominent engineer of his generation.

Arrol's list of construction credits included bridges in Dundee (he built the second Tay Bridge after the first one collapsed in a storm in 1879), Manchester, Sunderland and Newcastle.

His company was also responsible for Tower Bridge in London, and most famously of all, the Forth Bridge outside Edinburgh, one of the great wonders of the Victorian age, opened in 1890.

Whether Arrol actually knew Archie, or simply signed the form on someone else's say so, is impossible to know.

But for a blacksmith's son from Camlachie, it was an endorsement many of his counterparts would have envied beyond measure.

The Forth Road Bridge was a tourist attraction. It was engineering as spectacle. Engineering as art (and still is).

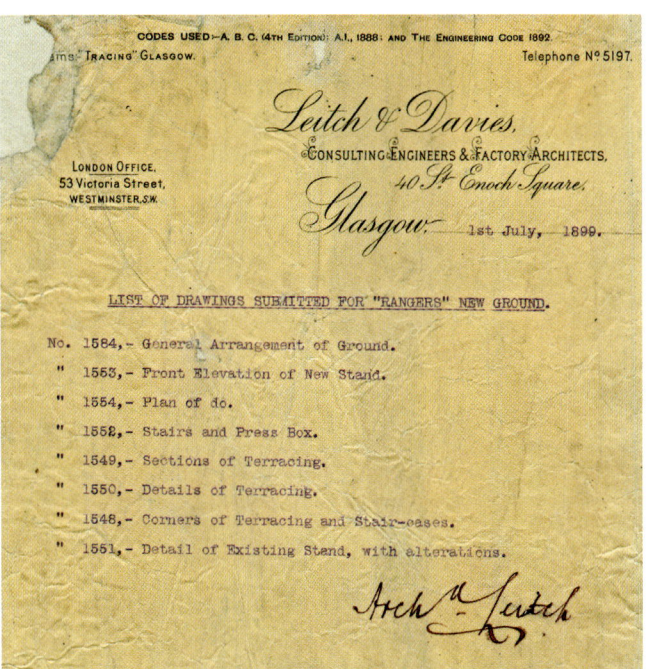

So now Archie was an Associate Member of the Mechanicals, and could put AMIMechE after his name. He also now had a business partner, Harry Davies (*see right*), having perhaps decided that he needed a bit of support in these first few years on his own account.

From what may be gathered from later sources, the partners soon gathered up commissions; a new works for the Stirling Boiler Company in Govan, a contract worth £20,000 overall; the Union Tube Works (£12,000) and the Caledonian Tube Works (1,000), both in Coatbridge, and a chemical works for Alexander Hope Junior in Provanmill (£25,000). Very likely all were in conjunction with the Clyde Structural Iron Company.

And then in March 1899 he had a meeting with a new client.

Their name? The Rangers FC.

▲ Archie submits his first plans for a football ground, in July 1899.

Harry Davies was an experienced civil engineer, probably the son of Charles Davies (who endorsed Archie's application to join the Mechanicals). He had just spent 20 years working on railway construction projects in India.

But whereas he would not remain back in Glasgow for long, for Archie, this one job was just the beginning of a lifetime's passion.

Engineering Archie 15

Chapter Two
Ibrox Park 1899–1902

MR ARCH. LEITCH, M.I.MECH.E.

In their pre-match coverage of the day's big event – the Scotland v. England international at the new Ibrox Park – the *Glasgow Evening Times* of April 5 1902 included this sketch of Archibald Leitch, almost certainly the first time his likeness had been published in a newspaper. Archie was then approaching his 37th birthday. The press was full of praise for his efforts. The Ibrox stand was likely to be full of potential customers representing clubs from both north and south of the border. His other business in factory design was doing well. Rangers were doing well. This was going to be a proud day for all concerned.

Saturday, April 5 1902, was, by all accounts, a typical April day. Sunshine and shadow alternated, with intervals of rain.

Looking forward to the afternoon's showpiece game between Scotland and England at Ibrox Park – the oldest and still by far the most important international fixture on the football calendar – The Scotsman reported, 'Everything possible is being done to have the ground in the best of conditions and a capital match should be witnessed.'

The previous day the England team had checked into the St Enoch Hotel, directly opposite Archibald Leitch's office, and in the morning had enjoyed a short stroll around the town.

For Archie, this was a proud day, and an important one too.

His first grand opus, the new 80,000 capacity Ibrox Park, the largest purpose-built football stadium the world had yet known – London's Crystal Palace held more but was rather less developed – was about to receive the biggest crowd ever to witness a match in Scotland.

All the grandees of the British football establishment were gathered, as were the sporting press. Numerous civic dignitaries were also expected to attend.

To add to Archie's excitement, early editions of the *Glasgow Evening Times* published his portrait (*see left*), and this fulsome report:

"No list of figures can adequately express the magnitude of the work undertaken by the designer and general overseer of such a colossal undertaking.

'Mr Leitch has successfully tackled similar jobs on a smaller scale, such as the ground of the Sheffield United FC, but Ibrox Park is unique in many respects, and the utmost credit is due to him for the very substantial, stable, and artistic laying out of the grounds.

'Mr Leitch is a young man, but he has carried out a work which would be a credit to the most eminent engineer, and he is naturally proud of the new Ibrox, and is happy in the knowledge that nowhere in the universe is there an athletic enclosure of such magnitude or of so compact and perfect a description."

It had taken just over three years to arrive at this momentous day, starting in March 1899. Or perhaps even, many years earlier.

It is of course not compulsory for a football ground designer to like football. But Archie, we can be fairly certain, loved the game and, more specifically, loved Rangers.

His grandchildren recall that he owned shares in the club, and had a tooth mug with the inscription *Good Old Rangers*. Between 1890–97 he and his wife Jessie and their growing family had also lived a short walk from Ibrox, on McLellan Street (near to where Archie was working at the time, for Mirlees Watson and Co., on Scotland Street).

Maybe after work he liked to drop in to the 'Club' restaurant and smoking rooms of 'Honest Tom' Vallance, the former Rangers captain, whose establishment on Paisley Road Toll was a popular haunt for fans of the Light Blues.

But if ever proof were needed that Rangers were Archie's team, it surely lies in the fact that Archie designed the new Ibrox Park without claiming a penny in fees.

Given that he had been in business on his own account for only three years when the work started, and had two young

16 Engineering Archie

children to feed, this was devotion beyond the call of duty.

Nor was it only his time he gave freely. The bulk of the daily responsibility for the ground's design and construction was carried out by his new business partner, Harry Davies, who had just returned to Glasgow after 22 years of major engineering works on the Indian railway network. For Davies, nine years Leitch's senior, Ibrox must have seemed a relatively lightweight diversion.

Leitch and Davies first became involved with Ibrox in early 1899, a watershed year in Rangers' history.

Firmly established members of Scotland's football elite, they were on course that season to win their second League title and their third Scottish Cup final in a row. But Ibrox Park, their home since 1887 – and their third enclosed ground since forming on Glasgow Green in 1872 – was now well out of date.

When first laid out, by Fred Braby & Co., 'contractors for pavilions, stands, barricades and other requisites for football and cricket enclosures,' the first Ibrox had been ahead of its time.

Erected around a running track were timber terraces holding around 25,000 spectators, with an uncovered wooden stand for 1200, and a wooden and corrugated iron pavilion in the north west corner, accessed from Copland Road.

Two developments in 1892 forced Rangers to reconsider their facilities. Firstly, in March that year the ground staged the Scottish Cup Final between Celtic (who had formed as recently as 1888), the club of the city's large Irish-Catholic community, and Queen's Park (formed 1867), Scotland's oldest club, the darlings of the establishment and stalwart defenders of amateurism.

Swamped by over 30,000 fans, Ibrox disintegrated into chaos and the Final had to be replayed.

Three weeks later only 21,000 attended for the visit of England.

The Scottish FA were patently not impressed, for the next four visits by England were all staged at Celtic Park, which, also in 1892, was extended into a 57,000 capacity arena for football, athletics and cycle racing.

Rangers countered by building a new stand of their own that same summer. Designed by architect John Gordon, with 16 rows of bench seats and a curved, gabled roof, it was actually rather fine.

But it was not enough, and by early 1899, as their lease at Ibrox neared its end, and with Queen's Park about to build what they promised would be the city's largest ground, Hampden Park, Rangers had to act, and act fast.

Finding a site proved simple. Land immediately next to the existing Ibrox was available, and a ten year lease was soon sorted.

But how to fund the new ground, and build it within seven months, was an altogether greater challenge.

In early March 1899 *Scottish Sport* reported that after meeting with the club's engineer – then unnamed – the committee had concluded that as they had only £5,600 in the bank, the best way to raise capital was to turn the club into a limited liability company. (Celtic had taken a similar step two years earlier, as had several clubs south of the border, all as a means of financing new stadiums.)

At the first, heated meeting to discuss incorporation, at the Trades Hall on Glassford Street, on March 13, Leitch made what was almost certainly his first public appearance.

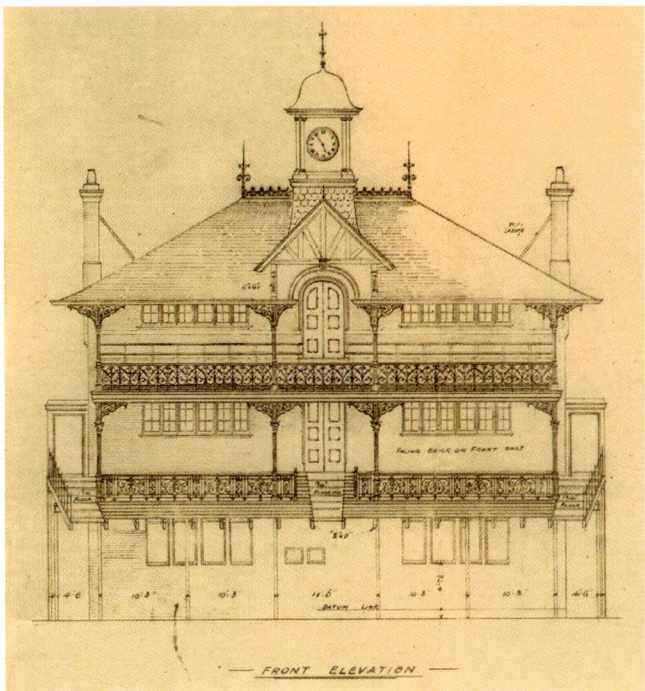

FRONT ELEVATION

Over 400 Rangers members were there, at least a third of whom were reported as being deeply sceptical. Others were just plain obstructive.

According to *Scottish Sport*, Leitch had prepared two schemes for their consideration; one for a ground able to hold 60,000, likely to cost around £10,000, and one expanded to a mind-boggling 140,000, expected to cost in the region of £15,000.

Even in this, his first pitch to a football audience, Archie confidently talked up the numbers, a trait he would exhibit throughout his career (sometimes to almost absurd levels, as we shall learn).

But not everyone was convinced, particularly when they were told that members would receive only one free share each in the new Rangers company. »

Leitch's pavilion at Ibrox had seats for 1,715, dressing rooms for the players and match officials, a boardroom, manager's room and gymnasium. Archie would design further pavilions for Fulham (*see page 74*) and Bradford Park Avenue (*page 97*), before the fashion finally yielded to the more space and cost-efficient solution of a single main stand housing all the required club facilities.

Engineering Archie 17

Ibrox Park

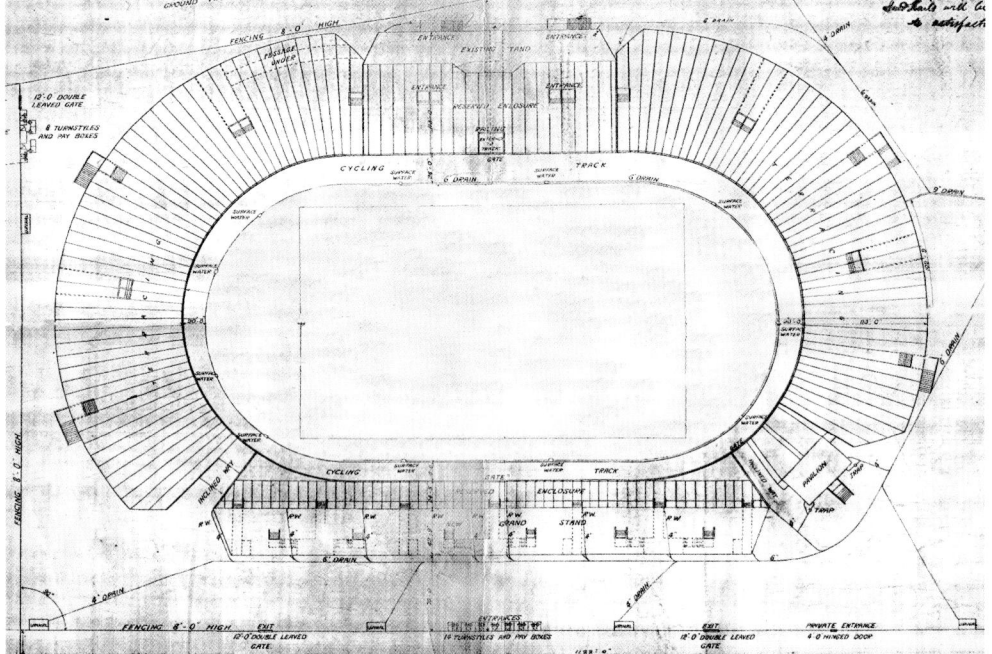

▲ Leitch's scheme for **Ibrox Park** was submitted to the Govan Dean of Guild Court on July 1 1899.

The plan was to lay a new pitch 150 yards westwards from the original Ibrox (whose pitch overlapped the new one in its south east corner) and re-erect John Gordon's stand as a terrace cover on the new north side.

In the south east corner Leitch planned a detached pavilion (see previous page), next to which a stand holding 5,995 seats would fill the south side, with an enclosure for 6,429 in front.

Rangers had only a ten year lease for the new site, so Leitch was keen that the stands could be easily re-erected elsewhere.

In addition he opted to construct timber terraces, supported on steel columns set in concrete, a form of terracing that had been erected two years earlier at Celtic Park, for the World Cycling Championships. (It was also the norm at many of the newly erected American baseball parks, where the system was used for seating, known as 'bleachers'.)

Leitch calculated that the west terrace would hold 35,913, the east 15,218 (because only half the above depth was sanctioned), and the north 14,887. With the pavilion, this gave 79,877 in total.

Never had anyone attempted to build steel and timber terracing on such a scale.

›› Yet two weeks later, at the same venue – with every entrant having to show his membership card to uniformed gentlemen at the door – they were won over.

Two things swayed the doubters. Firstly the committee offered five shares per member, thus soothing a number of malcontents.

Secondly, Archie put on a show.

Today an architect would use a laptop computer to help project his plans.

At the tail end of the 19th century, Archibald Leitch used a magic lantern.

Or, as the *Scottish Sport* described it, he chose to 'exhibit on a screen, a la the cinematograph'.

When at one point during his presentation Leitch mentioned the figure of 100,000 spectators, 'a prolonged whistle' was heard from the assembled members.

One, sitting near the front, was heard to whisper, 'Too big!'

But another, noted the reporter, chimed in, 'It's a football ground we want, not a backyard.'

And so Archie and his magic lantern won the day. With not a single voice raised in dissent, the new Ibrox Park was approved.

Now the real work started.

On July 1 Leitch & Davies sent in the first set of plans to Govan's Dean of Guild Court.

Only a few minor changes were requested. The Borough Surveyor, Frederick Holmes, apparently also told Archie he thought steel treads would be preferable to timber. But Leitch explained that money was tight, and in any case, the terraces were only designed as temporary structures. Rangers might not occupy the site for longer than the ten years of their lease.

Approval was granted 18 days later.

By mid August both the Clyde Structural Iron Company and the timber merchant, Alexander McDougall of Bellfield Sawmills, were contracted. McDougall's price had been £5,280, with a guarantee that red pine would be used throughout.

William Wilton, the Rangers secretary manager – the driving force behind the club's transition to a limited liability company – practically lived on site from then onwards. One of his main concerns for Leitch was that 'the turf should be of the finest'.

But although Harry Davies was there the most, acting as project manager, according to McDougall's foreman it was Leitch himself, a frequent visitor, who practically 'bossed' the job.

Both he and Davies, it was later stated by the foreman, 'seemed all along anxious to keep down costs.'

If so, they failed. From an original estimate of £12,000, the final bill rose to £20,000. Not for the first time would Archie's initial costings prove wayward.

After bad weather delayed the construction, the new Ibrox was ready for its first match, against Hearts, on December 30 1899, by which time half the terracing was complete. On one occasion in its early weeks, fans broke through the ropes and stood on an unfinished section, which, being yet unbraced, started to sway.

Thereafter the workforce grew from 30 to 200 until in April 1900 the new Ibrox Park was completed to Leitch's specifications – as he believed – and to the apparent satisfaction of the Govan Borough Surveyor.

The only significant difference from the original scheme was that whereas the West and North West corner of terracing now extended to the planned depth of 112 feet from the perimeter fence – a total of 96 treads, rising to a height of 37 feet – only half that depth and height was built at the East end.

Had the East matched the West the new Ibrox would have held the full 100,000. As it stood, in its final state, the capacity was 79,877.

At his first attempt, Archibald Leitch had thus masterminded the largest purpose-built football venue the world had ever seen.

Not a bad way to start his career as a ground designer, if indeed that was his intention.

Over the next two years the new Ibrox operated with scarcely a problem, and Leitch soon found himself working for Sheffield United, whose directors had visited for a friendly in April 1900 and, as a result, commissioned him to design a new main stand for Bramall Lane (see page 60).

He had also, in 1899, designed a stand for Kilmarnock (see page 41).

Harry Davies, meanwhile, returned to India in early 1902, perhaps reminded by the harsh Glasgow winters of why he had left in the first place.

Rangers, for their part, were hotter than ever. From February 1898 until the first match of the new century they did not lose a single game. Once settled in their new surroundings the Light Blues won four consecutive League titles between 1899 and 1902.

Yet apart from the ever popular matches against Celtic – their rivals-cum-partners in a Glasgow duopoly soon to be disdainfully dubbed by the press as 'The Old Firm' – the capacity of the new Ibrox was never fully tested, at least, not above 40,000 or so; half the intended limit.

On April 5 1902 that was about to change.

A month earlier, on March 6, Leitch wrote to Frederick Holmes asking him to write a report on Ibrox which Rangers could use to back their bid to stage the forthcoming international against the 'Auld Enemy'. Since Rangers were last hosts in 1892, Celtic had staged the fixture four times, drawing a record 63,000 on the most recent occasion, in April 1900. Now, surely, it was the turn of the new Ibrox.

'Personally,' Leitch wrote to Holmes, 'I have no doubt that everything is in order, still it might be better that both of us should go over the structure in order to have all possible precautions made for the safety of the spectators.'

Holmes duly made his inspection, and on March 8 wrote to William Wilton.

'During the erection of the structure I inspected it regularly, and have also inspected it on other occasions since completion, and my inspection yesterday confirmed the opinion previously formed that not only is the ground suitable in all respects for matches drawing large crowds of people, but that the structure is also perfectly safe for any crowd that can be accommodated on it.

'So far as I am aware the structure has not yet been crowded to its utmost capacity, but some sections of it have, and they have thereby demonstrated, in my opinion, the stability of the whole structure.'

Eight days later Wilton wrote to the Scottish FA offering Ibrox as the venue. In addition to its capacity of 80,000, he wrote, 'a special important feature for the public' was that 'every person on the grounds has an uninterrupted view of the play, with the maximum amount of comfort.

'As an extra precaution,' he added, 'we have placed an order with Messrs P & R Fleming for an iron railing to prevent any encroachment on the field of play.'

Wilton's appeal was successful, but only just. In a ballot amongst SFA delegates, Ibrox beat Celtic Park by just 15 votes to 14.

Not only that, but three days later Ibrox was also chosen to host the year's Cup Final, due to be played three weeks after the international.

In response, Celtic sympathisers decried Rangers as 'wire pullers', suggesting that the voting had been rigged. Such were the rivalries of the day.

But for Rangers, who could now look forward to paying off a large slice of the £9,000 worth of debt they had incurred on the new ground, these were heady days.

As they were for Archie too.

On the great day itself he was there as the turnstiles opened, three hours before the 3.30pm kick off.

As a marching band performed on the pitch, Ibrox filled rapidly. By 2.30pm stewards were posting signs reading 'full' in some parts. In fact, as would later be confirmed, there were 68,114 in attendance, some 12,000 below capacity, but still, as it appeared, more than was comfortable.

Sitting in the stand at 2.45pm, as he later stated, Leitch noticed 'a vacant space on the west terracing... I immediately went round to the back of the terracing where I saw that two of the joists had split. The groundsman was making good or stiffening the joists with the assistance of two joiners. I obtained two constables and directed them to keep the spectators back from the affected part.

Engineering Archie **19**

Ibrox Park

Scotland v England, Ibrox Park, April 5 1902. Before kick off the crowd had burst over the 6' 6" tall perimeter fence. There was no violence. Just a catastrophic breakdown in crowd control, exacerbated by the collapse of dozens of tubular steel crush barriers. Behind the goal, the west terrace appears to be packed solid. At what exact time this, the only known photograph to survive from the day, was taken we do not know. But almost certainly it was very early in the game. Out of shot, high up on the terrace, just to the left, the timber joists in a section close to the uppermost stairway were about to split.

>> 'Afterwards I went round about the ground and saw that there was excessive crushing at all the stairs leading to the western terracing. There was plenty of room for spectators all over the terracings unless near the entrance where the greatest congestion took place.

'This, in my opinion was the reason why visitors not on the terracing tried to get up the stairs. They could see from below the terracing where there was accommodation if they could get up the stairs and get away to the uncrowded places…

'I was outside the western terracing going towards the grandstand when the collapse took place, about 3.40pm.'

It is rarely the lot of an architect or engineer to witness at first hand the catastrophic failure of one of his or her designs.

But on April 5 1902, that was the fate of Archibald Leitch.

Numerous accounts would emerge of what actually occurred at the precise moment when a section of terrace gave way by the stairway in the south west corner.

Some witnesses blamed the fact that, as Scotland were on the attack at just that moment, the crowd had all strained for a view, placing a sudden pressure on the affected area. Others recalled fans in that area stamping their feet.

Certainly a steward insisted that the area was not overcrowded.

What is clear is that before the collapse, a number of failures had occurred elsewhere. (Accidents in crowded stadiums rarely have a single cause.)

Firstly, a sudden downpour sent hundreds of fans piling towards the covered area on the north terrace, creating a crush which toppled the new perimeter railings and forced thousands to spill onto the pitch. Three mounted police managed to keep the touchlines clear so that the match could commence – shades of Wembley in 1923 – but, as the photograph below left suggests, conditions remained far from ideal.

Meanwhile, it would seem that on the western terrace a large number of the tubular steel crush barriers, installed to Leitch's specifications, simply folded under the pressure. This, in turn, caused further surging down the terraces, towards the perimeter.

Amid these wider breakdowns in crowd control, only those in the immediate vicinity were even aware of the collapse taking place.

Eye witnesses spoke later of a loud crack, followed by a sudden falling away, as 80-100 individuals simply dropped onto the steel columns and concrete below. They made barely a sound, disappearing, as one witness stated, 'as if through a trapdoor'.

For a few desperate minutes people fought to escape from the immediate area, pushing forwards and urging those in front to move onto the track. More deaths on the lower terraces occurred as a result.

This was quickly followed by a further, less extensive collapse in the same area as before, sending several more unfortunates into the void.

Yet it was not this which brought the game to a halt, but the influx of more spectators onto the track, as they tried to escape the danger zone.

Only then did a hurried debate take place with the police and SFA representatives. Should the match carry on, or be abandoned?

Twenty minutes later – during which time most onlookers assumed that the police were merely easing the crush on the terraces – play restarted.

20 Engineering Archie

It was a painful choice, but in the absence of any public address system – only in the 1930s would these start to be introduced – the prevailing view was that abandonment might provoke a riot. And if, somehow, the true situation could have been conveyed to the crowd, there was the further risk of fans rushing to the scene of the disaster, thereby hampering the rescue operation.

Another version of events, however, stated that the crowd can hardly have failed to realise the seriousness of the situation, given that a number of bodies and injured people were carried out around the pitch in full view.

Certainly the players were aware. At half time they had had to step over bodies laid out inside the pavilion.

Hardly surprisingly, the second half was a strained affair, the touchlines still being lined by spectators. Yet even the section where the terracing had split did not empty as the game petered out. Mindless of the danger, fans stood within feet of the broken timbers.

And at the final whistle – the match ending in a meaningless draw that was immediately declared null and void – fans chaired the Scottish goalkeeper Doig off the pitch as if nothing had happened, oblivious to the fact that he was clearly in tears.

In the minds of football's critics, of which there were many who despised its rampant commercialism and its hold upon the masses, the mere fact that the match lasted the full ninety minutes was repeatedly cited as evidence of the crazed mentality of fans, so intent on their precious game that no amount of human suffering in their midst could divert their attentions.

Back at the scene of the collapse meanwhile, there could be no hiding from the awful truth.

The dead and injured lay piled up in a bloody tangle – a sight Leitch must have seen at first hand – as ambulances and doctors flocked to the scene.

Those who had not been killed instantly on hitting the ground were horribly mangled or gashed on the steel supports and corrugated fencing as they fell.

Others survived the fall, only to be crushed under the weight of people above them. One man hung suspended for several minutes, head down, his foot caught in the steelwork, until he was rescued.

Even hardened doctors and ambulancemen were shocked at the level of injuries.

A young boy sobbed, 'Mother, mother, ye tell't me no to come to the match, for I'd be killed.'

His mother was not the only one. Several other witnesses came forward in the disaster's aftermath to say that they always suspected the terracing, and that those Rangers fans 'in the know' avoided its upper reaches. The lower tiers, where if anything the crowd had been packed more densely, all withstood the pressure.

For Archibald Leitch, the day which had promised so much had descended into hell.

But of his impressions of the actual event, we have only these few, matter-of-fact words, recorded during his subsequent interview as part of the investigation.

'I assisted some of the injured and afterwards went towards the grandstand where I met the Borough Surveyor and Chief Constable. I returned to the scene of the accident and saw Mr McDougall there. I spoke to him.

A number of artists tried to depict the scene at Ibrox for the national press. This photograph, from a popular London weekly, *The Sketch,* was more graphic than most however, showing how the timber joists at the uppermost part of the terrace had snapped in the south west corner, and how corrugated fencing was torn down to reach the victims.

He said he did not know what to attribute the accident to unless overcrowding.

'I was terribly upset at the occurrence and went home.'

What he talked of privately with his wife Jessie that night, we can only imagine.

Twenty five people died as the result of the disaster (plus another from his injuries 18 months later). At least 516 more were injured, of which, according to *The Scotsman,* 24 were 'dangerously injured' and a further 168 'seriously injured'.

In total, 587 would later receive compensation. »

Ibrox Park

Ibrox's south western terrace, on the Monday after the disaster. Note that the crush barrier in front of the void remained upright, suggesting that the collapse was caused not by a surge or swaying, but rather by localised weaknesses in the joists, seventeen of which gave way. The void measured 70' 6" x 11' 6". If it had been full to capacity, based on Leitch's own calculations of 16" width per person on each 14" tread, around 530 people would have occupied the affected area at the time the collapse occurred.

» In the immediate aftermath, the nation's newspapers were filled with graphic accounts of what had occurred. Two mournful poems and various artists' impressions were published, together with chilling photographs of the scene, taken two days after the disaster.

There were wider concerns too. As noted in *The Sketch*, assuming that crowd movements had been to blame, 'This same "sway"... came perilously near to causing a similar disaster at the great lacrosse match witnessed by the Prince and Princess of Wales during their recent tour of the Colonies.'

It also warned that 'the most stringent regulations for the construction of Coronation Stands are now likely to be enforced.'

(Scheduled for June 26, though postponed because of King Edward's health, until August 9, the Coronation had spawned the construction of dozens of small temporary stands for parades around the country.)

But in stark contrast to current practice, there seemed to be no rush to apportion blame. An appeal fund set up by the Lord Provost of Glasgow instead announced that 'The committee is most hopeful that with the facts authoritatively ascertained, litigation will not be resorted to by any sufferer.'

The Scottish FA gave the most; £3,000 initially, plus a further £2,000 later.

Archie gave ten guineas.

As for Rangers, they wanted to donate £1,000 – their share of the match receipts – but were advised not to until the question of liability was determined. (They were not insured, but then no sports clubs were at this time.)

But once it became clear that the club would not be held liable, William Wilton – who had the highest profile and therefore bore the bulk of public criticism – devoted his customary energies into a frantic bout of fund raising. In total the separate Rangers appeal raised a further £4,000.

And although it was assumed, and even announced in the Glasgow press, that an official inquiry would soon follow, as would have been the case in England, in fact under prevailing Scottish law the only mechanism under which an inquiry could take place was if the deaths had occurred in the course of industrial employment or occupation.

Clearly they had not (and the law would not change until 1906, partly as a result of the disaster).

But there was another route towards determining what had occurred, and why, albeit one which promised no-one any great satisfaction.

On April 15, Alexander McDougall, the timber merchant responsible for supplying and erecting the Ibrox terracing, was charged with culpable homicide.

His crime? That he had, contrary to his contract with Archibald Leitch, signed on August 8 1899, used for certain bearers or joists, 'wood of an inferior quality of yellow pine instead of red pine of the best quality' and that, furthermore, instead of fitting the joists in the specified manner of long and short lengths alternately – that is, 'broken-banded as was proper and tradesmanlike' – had made them all short instead.

In another time, in another place, had a public inquiry been

22 Engineering Archie

set up, McDougall might not have had to endure what seemed tantamount to a show trial. In other circumstances the spotlight might well have fallen on the person with overall responsibility for the design and construction of the terracing.

But on July 8, at the High Court of Justice in Glasgow, it was Alexander McDougall who stood accused in the dock, and not Archibald Leitch.

Even so, Archie's reputation was now firmly on the line.

All of Glasgow was agog with the trial, and in the close circles of engineering and construction, there would almost certainly have been as many individuals against Archie as for him. His association with Rangers, whom many in the sporting world decried for their arrogance and ambition, would also not have helped.

Haunted by the sights he had witnessed at the disaster scene, Archie can hardly have endured a darker period in his life.

McDougall's trial took three days and called on 80 witnesses, of whom Leitch was not surprisingly the most prominent for the Crown prosecution.

And yet at times it seemed as if Leitch himself was the accused.

For the defence Thomas Shaw KC made it clear that McDougall was being scapegoated in the absence of a public inquiry.

The Crown's case, he said, 'was as flimsy and insubstantial as Mr Leitch's design.'

But as would be expected, entering the witness stand on the afternoon of the first day's proceedings Leitch insisted, 'I attribute the disaster wholly to bad timber.'

In his evidence – the transcript of which runs to 49 pages – Leitch told of numerous occasions in which he caught McDougall's men using inferior wood to that specified, and had ordered its replacement with red pine. In November 1899 he had written to McDougall to complain, without receiving a reply.

The trouble was that as soon as the joists were covered by treads, it was difficult to detect what kind of timber had been used.

'Therefore a great deal of reliance had to be placed on the integrity of the contractor.'

The joists that had broken in the collapse, he said, were all in short lengths rather than being long and short alternately. They were also, crucially, all in yellow pine.

And on this point – the relative merits of red and yellow pine – much of the next two days' proceedings concentrated.

McDougall's foreman claimed that Leitch had not only seen but approved the use of yellow pine, just to get the job done. However, if McDougall had used yellow, which he admitted he had, why had he billed Leitch only for red?

But did it make any difference? For the prosecution, two joiners who had studied the structure said they had never seen such poor quality yellow pine used as joists.

Another described the yellow pine as fitted as totally unsuited for joists. It was more the sort used for making boxes.

Several witnesses, including Leitch, also gave the results of various tests, comparing the strength of red and yellow pine. Two tests showed red to be capable of bearing four or five times the weight of yellow.

But witnesses for the defence dismissed these calculations entirely. There was good quality yellow pine and poor quality red pine. What mattered more was the cut, the numbers of knots and the level of sap in each length.

Leitch was also quizzed in detail on his calculations of the likely loadings the terracing would support. Had the ground been across the Govan boundary, in Glasgow, stated one witness, the terracing would not have met minimum load bearing standards.

Certainly Leitch's explanations were unconvincing on this arcane aspect – to the layman at least – of engineering design, suggesting he had used dead loads rather than live loads in his calculations.

Nor, it was argued, had he allowed a sufficient factor of safety. Leitch said he used a safety factor of five. Various defence witnesses insisted this should have been 10-12 with live loads.

But his most awkward moment came at the end of his cross examination by Thomas Shaw.

The court heard that morning from William Wilton that Rangers had already asked John Gordon – the architect of their original main stand at old Ibrox in 1892 – to work out how much it would cost to strengthen the terracing, by adding more intermediate joists

Shaw now produced a letter, marked 'Strictly Private', written by Leitch to the Rangers chairman James Henderson on June 19 1902.

In this letter Archie complained that if it were known that the club had employed another architect it would be tantamount to a vote of no confidence in Leitch and might seriously jeopardise the Crown's case against McDougall.

Much to Archie's discomfort, Shaw read out the letter, and then asked, 'Do you regret writing that letter?'

Archie flashed back, 'I regret having it read here.'

That this riposte provoked laughter in the court hints at Leitch's tone (a tone that would be echoed in a non-related court hearing we will come to later, in Chapter Five, and from which, together with one or two other direct quotes, we may perhaps deduce Archie to have possessed a cool demeanour and a dry wit. He often seemed to provoke laughter.)

Thus concluded Leitch's evidence.

The defence called two star witnesses.

The first was Sir Benjamin Baker, an imposing figure with a huge walrus moustache. He was the designer of the Forth Bridge no less, one of the great engineering wonders of the age.

Leitch's designs were, said Baker, 'very unusually light', especially when one compared them to the Coronation stands being built at the time. In fact he had never seen a structure so dangerously light for such a purpose. 'I would not approve of it for a moment.'

He also believed there was no appreciable difference in strength between red and yellow pine *per se*, each sample being variable according to the cut.

But he added, 'I don't blame the engineers because they are absolutely misled by these fictitious strengths of timber.'

The prosecution then produced Baker's own book, published in 1870, in which he stated that red pine was stronger.

The second day concluded with the defence's next celebrity witness, Sir William Arrol, who announced himself to the court – as if they did not know – as the contractor of the Forth Bridge.

Possibly the most illustrious engineer of his age (his company »

Engineering Archie 23

Ibrox Park

» also helped build London's Tower Bridge), Arrol knew of Leitch, if not personally then by name. Five years earlier he had been a signatory to Archie's application to join the Institute of Mechanical Engineers.

But he too dismissed Leitch's designs, as did a local civil engineer, Carl Bonn, who thought Leitch's design showed 'lamentable insufficiency'.

According to Bonn's calculation the terracing could bear only 26 lbs per square foot, and it should have been 190 lbs. He also pointed out that bolt holes had been drilled in some of the joists, not by McDougall, but in order to fix the corrugated fence at the back, and other rails and barriers around the stairways. Not all these holes had been used, which alone would have reduced the strength of the joist by 20 per cent.

And so, on the morning of third day, the trial came to its climax.

The late Victorian and Edwardian periods, it should be recalled, witnessed a catalogue of inventions and technological advances, from underground trains to aeroplanes, from telephones to moving pictures.

Hardly a week went by without reports of an accident or mishap somewhere in the western world. In the few years either side of the Ibrox disaster there would be tram accidents in Highgate, Swindon and Mansfield; a Metro fire in Paris, an explosion at the Woolwich Arsenal, a fire on a suspension bridge in New York.

In France spectators were killed watching a motor race. Others were killed in an airship crash. A year after Ibrox 15 people died in a rail crash in Glasgow.

The machine age was a dangerous age, and professional football, its greatest diversion, was less than twenty years old.

Perhaps the jury understood the risks that novelty brought. More likely they took the side of the scapegoat. They needed just 30 minutes to reach their verdict, and it was unanimous.

'We find that that Mr McDougall's substitution of yellow for red pine in no way contributed to the disaster. Not guilty.'

Was Archie furious at this outcome? We shall never know.

But it certainly left some serious issues hanging in the balance.

They were best summarised in a *Glasgow Herald* editorial.

On the question of red or yellow pine, it commented, 'It has been laid down as an axiom that in the multitude of counsellors there is safety. That may be so, but apparently the multitude had better not consist exclusively of experts.'

But a graver point was this.

'Does the Ibrox disaster... not point to the necessity for some very drastic regulations for the construction of huge arenas required for the patrons of football? Surely modern skill and science should be equal to the production of something quite as stable as the ancient Roman circus.'

That indeed was the crux of the matter. The question was, who would take up the challenge?

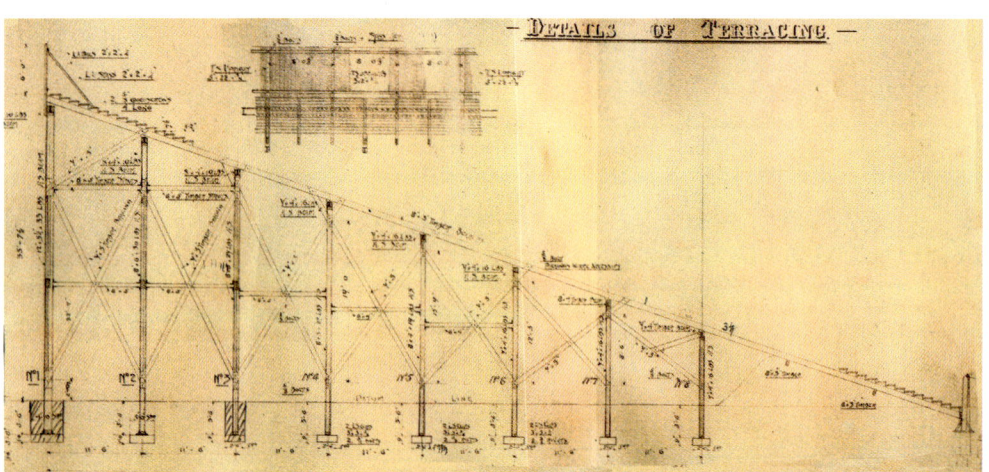

Leitch's original but fading drawings of the Ibrox terracing. Measuring 112' deep and 37' tall at the rear. Its steel columns were laterally spaced 12' 1" at the rear. The lower plan shows two bays. At the point where the disaster occurred the joists were set 4' apart. Various defence witnesses said that the number of joists should have been doubled or even tripled to bear the expected live load of spectators.

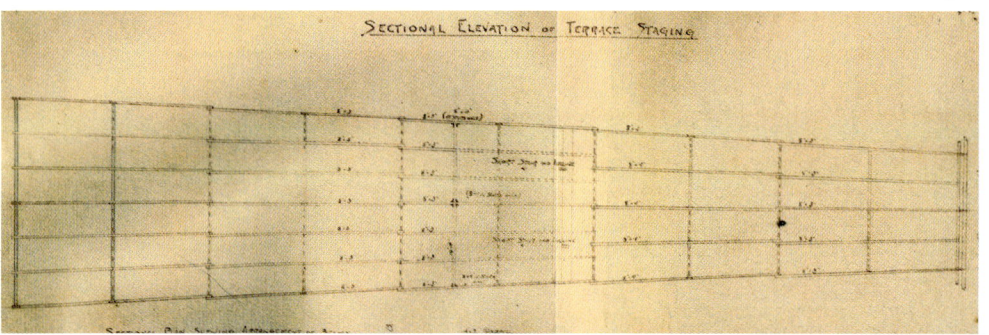

Strictly private

Jas Henderson Esq
Pollokshields

40 St Enoch Square
Glasgow

19th June 1902

Dear Mr Henderson

Ibrox Disaster

Nothing but extraordinary circumstances would have constrained me to write you re the above, and it is therefore only on account of my having heard that you and your fellow Directors have appointed Mr Gordon to superintend the Reconstruction at Ibrox, that I have thought it advisable to give you my views on this decision, providing and assuming it to be correct.

Apart altogether from personal considerations, it seems to me that when this decision (if true) is known, it will seriously prejudice the case of the Crown v. McDougall. I suppose I will be the Chief Witness for the Crown, and if I am to appear as having been thrown overboard by the 'Rangers' it will certainly have a disheartening effect on me, and an equally encouraging effect on McDougall.

You and the other Directors know full well that McD will employ every means to blacken and damage my character, as he has already done, and if in this laudable endeavour he is to obtain the assistance of the 'Rangers', unsolicited, it will be no matter of surprise if the verdict goes in his favour.

In being a witness for the Crown, I am equally the principal witness for the 'Rangers', and even as a matter of policy, I think it most injurious in the interests of the Club, to do anything in any shape or form, which can be twisted into a favourable opinion of McD, and an unfavourable one of myself.

I think I am not unreasonable in asking you, therefore, to refrain from any action prejudicial to me.

Again from a personal point of view, this appointment, (if correct) practically amounts to a vote of no confidence in myself. Why should you condemn me unheard? Have I not done my duty? I have no reflections personally. I did everything I was entitled to perform, and in numerous instances did far more than my duty, all with a view to disinterestedly advance the welfare of the Club.

A decision such as this cannot be otherwise than most disastrous to my future prospects here and elsewhere.

Is there no considertion due for the free services rendered, for the interest displayed with a single eye for the Club's welfare, and last tho' not least, for the absolute honesty of act and intention which has characterised every transaction between the 'Rangers' and myself?

Is there no consideration for the use of my money which the Rangers had, nor for the fact that up till now, I have never received a single penny towards my professional fees? Have I ever pressed you for money? Have I not time and again freely and unasked used my credit for the 'Rangers' benefit?

I regret having in any way to speak for myself in this manner (it is not natural) but I have experienced so much trouble that you will bear with me at this time.

I need hardly say what unutterable anguish the accident caused me, surely the most unhappy eyewitness of all.

I can only conclude by assuring you that I can and do conscientiously assert and solemnly declare that no action or word of mine contributed towards the accident, and that apart from those who suffered sad bereavement, and even including these, no one has suffered more than I have.

This is a critical time for me, and it might be well if we could have a free talk over the matter with a view to a general arrangement and trusting you will take this letter in the same spirit in which it has been written

I am Yours faithfully

Arch. Leitch

◀ It is said that the engineer Sir Thomas Bouch was 'a broken man' when he died ten months after the collapse of his recently completed Tay Bridge, during a violent storm on the night of December 28 1879.

Seventy-five rail passengers were killed in the disaster, which had been caused by Bouch's failure to take into account wind pressure.

Until that fateful night, wind factors formed no part of a bridge engineer's routine calculations, so Bouch was hardly alone in his omission.

Nevertheless, unable to bear the guilt, he withered away, watched helplessly by his family and friends.

The Ibrox disaster of 1902 was Archibald Leitch's very own Tay Bridge. And unlike Sir Thomas, he had been there to see it happen.

Leitch was, we may deduce from a number of sources, a self confident fellow. Ambitious too.

But he was also a family man who knew what it was to grieve. In 1894 he and Jessie lost their second child in infancy. Later in life two other daughters would die at a young age.

So would the Ibrox disaster make or break Archie?

Perhaps the outcome of this letter to the Rangers chairman – the one read out in court to his acute dismay – would provide the answer.

Engineering Archie **25**

Chapter Three
Terracing

If there was one element of the British football ground which distinguished it from most other 20th century stadiums built overseas – at least those outside northern Europe – it was the absolute predominance of the terrace. And for a simple reason. Two people could stand where one could sit. Archie's clients demanded capacity, and while the crowds turned up willingly in their millions to take advantage, who could gainsay them?

Under the circumstances it would have been perfectly understandable had Rangers FC dispensed with the services of Archibald Leitch following the events of April 5 1902.

And sure enough, if we are to believe Archie's plaintive letter to the club chairman, James Henderson on June 19 1902 (*see previous page*), they were about to do just that, by re-engaging the architect, John Gordon, whom they had employed in the early 1890s, prior to Leitch's first involvement with the club.

But whether Archie's letter touched a raw nerve, or whether John Gordon was minded (or persuaded) not to stymie the standing of a fellow professional, the fact is that following the receipt of his letter, Rangers not only retained Leitch as their consulting engineer, but continued to do so for the next 30 years or more.

Had it been otherwise; had Rangers dropped him in 1902, Leitch's budding career as a football ground designer might well have ended, there and then.

Football may have been thought of as a big business.

But it was a small world.

So was this just another case of members of the same Glasgow tribe sticking together? Should we perhaps suspect a Masonic closing of ranks?

Possibly. But unlikely. The Rangers' board were businessmen first and foremost. Sure, Archie had done all that work and not pressed the club for his fees, suggesting that he must have loved the Light Blues. He was, after all, still at an early stage in his independent business career and had a family to support.

But there were plenty of other engineers in town, cut from the same cloth as Archie. Who amongst the ranks of the Protestant professional classes of Glasgow would not have wanted to work for the mighty Rangers?

No, the man must have had something to have kept his place in the Ibrox firmament.

And he must also, surely, as an engineer, have been absolutely determined not to walk away from the problem in hand.

That is not the engineer's way. Not the true engineer.

And so, with Rangers giving him a second chance, in the months and years that followed Archie's 'unutterable anguish', it was the engineer in him which sought to banish his demons by coming up with a solution.

The challenge? A practical and economical way of building a terrace large enough, solid enough, and well managed enough to safely contain the heaving masses of Britain's rising football mania.

A solution that was based on calculation and experience.

A solution, in other words, that was engineered.

There is a tendency, in today's post-Hillsborough world, to look back on the packed football terraces of the 20th century as somehow wild and primitive places of gathering.

To see them as symbols of an uncaring industry that would rather spend pounds on players than pennies on roofs, or stewards, or proper toilets or refreshment facilities.

To see the man on the terrace as fodder for the ambitions of vainglorious directors; the pumped up butchers, bakers and candlestick makers of the nation's football club boardrooms.

And there is indeed a grain of truth in all those assertions.

Yet it is also true that the football terrace as it would evolve in the years immediately following the Ibrox disaster, and how it would appear thereafter for most of the rest of the 20th century, was a considerable advance on what had existed before.

Let there be no doubt.

Compared with the terraces, or more accurately, viewing slopes, to be found at most Victorian grounds – with their cinder and gravel banks, muddied earth, wooden barriers nailed together and thumped randomly into the ground – the newly improved football terrace of the Edwardian age was a symbol of modernity.

Regular steps, measured risers, solid footings, fixed steel barriers, designated aisles, and, best of all, reasonable sight lines – all these elements which would later be taken for granted, or, just as often, badly executed by poor designers – were, when they first appeared in the early 1900s, seen as bringing great benefits for the ordinary football fan paying his sixpence.

What is more, they were the product of the labours of Archibald Leitch.

The man who described himself at Ibrox in April 1902 as 'surely the most unhappy eyewitness of all' was in fact the man who designed the modern football terrace.

Archibald Leitch could have walked away from football and stuck to his factory work.

Instead, he sat down at his drawing board.

▲ As at Ibrox, as in any branch of engineering, wherever a weak link exists, one can be sure that it will be found out.

The barely legible caption reads: 'Scene of the terrible catastrophe which happened at **Owlerton** (*now called Hillsborough*) during the replayed Cup Tie (Second Round) between Wednesday and Wolverhampton Wanderers on January 14 1914, when a retaining wall at the Penistone Road End collapsed, injuring more or less severely 75 people. The game was stopped while the injured were removed, but was resumed afterwards. Wednesday won 1-0.'

The writer was Teddy Davison, the Wednesday goalkeeper who kept a comprehensive record of his playing career and later managed the club. His counterpart in the Wolves goal fainted when he saw what he thought was a corpse and was unable to carry on playing.

'It is only through such accidents that we arrive at anything like perfection,' commented the *Sheffield Independent*. 'There will no doubt be a complete overhauling of the arrangements at Hillsborough.'

Engineering Archie 27

Terracing

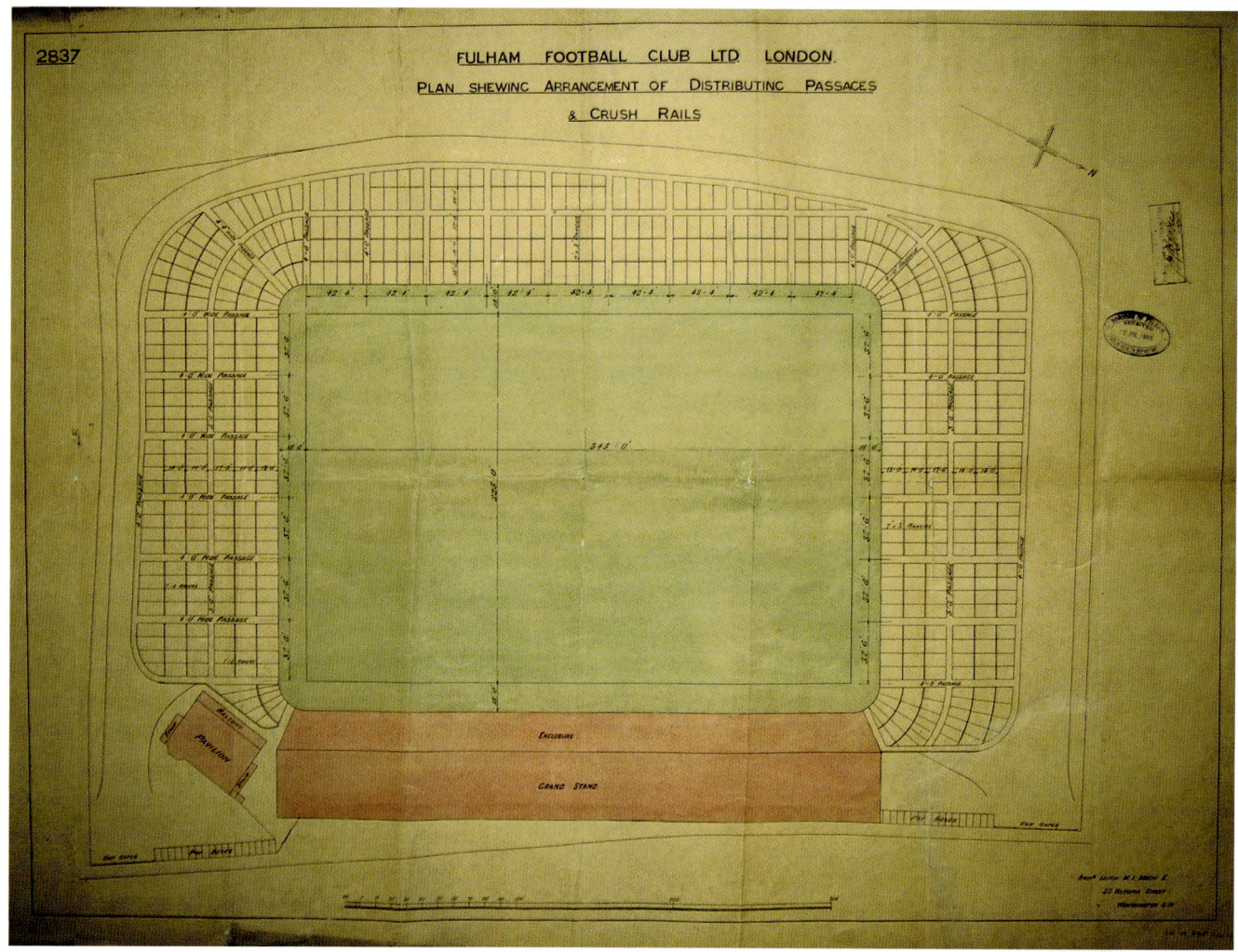

▲ Dated 18 July 1905, Archibald Leitch's plan for Fulham's new ground at **Craven Cottage**, west London, illustrates his more engineered approach to terrace design following the mistakes of Ibrox, using a system of distributing passages and 'crush rails' fixed equidistantly between sunken aisles, each four feet in width.

With relatively few modifications to radial gangway routings, this layout of terracing would be accepted as standard practice for the rest of the century.

Indeed had all grounds adopted the continuous barrier layout there may well have been far fewer casualties over the years. Instead, many clubs and engineers persisted in ignoring Leitch's model by failing to provide adequate circulation routes and by tolerating staggered gaps between lines of barriers.

Moreover in the absence of statutory controls they continued to do so, even after Leitch's model was effectively enshrined in the *Guide to Safety at Sports Grounds*, first issued in 1973.

(That guide, incidentally, recommended radial gangways of a minimum 1.1m width. The 1997 revised version extended this to 1.2m, or four feet. Just as Leitch specified in 1905.)

Hawthorn, Blackburn.]
EWOOD PARK, THE HOME OF THE BLACKBURN ROVERS.
This famous enclosure has the reputation of possessing one of the finest playing pitches in the First Division of the League.

◀ This view of **Ewood Park**, Blackburn, reproduced from *The Book of Football*, published in 1906 (see *Links*), shows the typical viewing slope of the late Victorian, pre-Leitch era. Consisting of timber rails placed fairly randomly on an earth bank, such slopes cannot have been easy to stand on in a full crowd, particularly in wet conditions. In the far corner stands the players' pavilion, a common feature at grounds before dressing rooms and other club facilities were integrated into main stands. This photograph was taken a year before Leitch was hired by Blackburn Rovers to design just such a stand, on the Nuttall Street side. Leitch went on to replace the Riverside Stand (*on the left*) in 1913 (*see page 93*).

◀ The 1902 Ibrox disaster took place just as Queen's Park were starting the final phase of their vast new **Hampden Park**. Their engineer, Alexander Blair, decided to equip the solid banks of terracing with barriers made from concrete posts and one-inch diameter wire ropes (*shown left in 1920*), arranged in such a way that they formed three sided pens, each designed to hold up to 80 fans.

As Archie was living a short walk away at the time he would almost certainly have noted this novel arrangement with interest. But he was clearly not convinced.

Shown left in 1924 the terraces at **Villa Park** are in the process of being upgraded from earth and cinder treads with timber rails and footings, to the Leitch standard of concrete treads and risers, fitted with rigid steel, purpose-built crush barriers and sunken gangways.

Each of the new barriers was designed to Leitch's patent, as shown overleaf.

Engineering Archie **29**

Terracing

Nº 4453 A.D. 1906

Date of Application, 23rd Feb., 1906—Accepted, 10th May, 1906

COMPLETE SPECIFICATION.

"An Improved Method of Constructing the Terracing and Accessories thereof in Football and other Sport Grounds."

I, ARCHIBALD LEITCH of 30 Buchanan Street, Glasgow, Consulting Engineer, do hereby declare the nature of this invention and in what manner the same is to be performed, to be particularly described and ascertained in and by the following statement:—

This invention which relates to the terracing provided around football, cricket, and other sport grounds for the accomodation of spectators, has for its object the improvement and simplification of the construction of such terracing and its accessories, so that such construction admits of ready removal of any of its parts for renewal or repair when necessary.

The invention is illustrated by the accompanying drawings.

Figure 1 is a side elevation of a portion of terracing as constructed under my improved method of carrying and shewing and securing the crush rails of such terracing, whilst Figure 2 is a front elevation of Figure 1. Figures 3 and 4 are details of construction hereinafter referred to.

In carrying out the invention in lieu of piling the ground as ordinarily practiced I provide a series of rakers or bearers a which form the main support of the terracing and are spaced at suitable distances apart and set at the angle or rake it is desired to give the terracing. These rakers or bearers are sunk beneath the surface of the soil b and have secured to them by angled clips c or brackets c of wrought or other iron or steel runners d which form the front face of the steps of the terracing, the clips c being secured to the rakers and runners respectively by bolts e and f. These runners d rest upon the rakers a and are checked as at g in Figures 1, 3 and 4 to embrace the rakers a and so provide against the possibility of longitudinal motion of the runners d, whilst taking the strain off the bolts e, f, in the clip c, the space between each runner being filled in with earth as shewn, and the rakers a thereby completely buried.

The simplicity of the construction of terracing in the manner above described will be readily apparent and the advantages attending the use of rakers or bearers placed as shewn and described, instead of piling the ground, are great, as should subsidence of the soil take place at any particular part of the terracing no great excavation is necessary, the space left between the bearers or rakers a and the soil b due to subsidence being made up by the insertion, beneath the affected bearers or rakers, of more soil or other suitable support, whilst the handiness and strength of the method of supporting the runners d forming the steps of the terracing is obvious.

This construction of terracing lends itself with advantage to the carrying of the supports or standards for the crush rails usually provided on such terracing. These crush rails and their carrying standards as constructed and arranged under this invention comprise standards h or carriers of tee, angle or other section of iron bent as shewn at their upper parts and having their lower ends bent at suitable angles to form feet to enable them to be secured to the rakers or bearers a by bolts i, or the lower ends of these standards may, instead of being bent for said purpose, have secured to them as shewn at Figures 1 and 2 angled plates or brackets j of wrought or other iron or steel the foot or sole portion of said plate being secured to the rakers a by the bolts i. These

[Price 8d.]

standards are further stayed each by one or more angle or other iron stays k secured by bolts l and m respectively to the upper part of the standard or rail carrier h and to the runners d as shewn at Figures 1 and 2. The crush rails consist each of a tube o, or a wooden bar, supported upon the upper end of the standards or carriers h and is held tightly thereon by a clip n embracing the tube and secured by bolts to the flat web of the tee or other iron standard or carrier h, the clip being formed as shewn so that when the rail or bar rests upon the upper surface of the standard h a space is left between said surface and the feet of the clip in order that when the bolts are tightened up the clip effectually clamps the rail or bar upon the standard h. By thus dispensing with the necessity for forming a hole in the standard in which to secure the rail, the original strength of the standard or carrier is maintained.

By the arrangement above described, i.e., securing the crush rail standards h to the rakers a a support or carrier is provided for the crush rails which is capable of resisting great pressure upon it, as the weight of the spectators, in addition to the buried rakers a, augmented in strength by the runners d, must be lifted before the standards can be overturned.

Where the terracing is formed of concrete or similar solid material the crush rail standards are bolted down into the concrete or like material instead of to rakers or bearers.

I am aware that clips for securing rails to standards have been previously used and I make no claim to this feature alone, but only to the combination in connection with crush rails for terracing as described.

Having now particularly described and ascertained the nature of my said invention and in what manner the same is to be performed, I declare that what I claim is:—

(1) The method of constructing the terracing and accessories thereof of football, and other sport grounds, substantially as hereinbefore described with reference to the drawings annexed.

(2) In the construction of terracing, the provision of rakers or bearers arranged as described and of runners secured thereto, substantially as and for the purpose set forth.

(3) In the construction of crush rails for terracing in football and other sport grounds, the method of carrying and securing the standards and of carrying and securing the rails thereto, substantially as and for the purpose set forth.

Dated the 20th day of February, 1906.

ROBERT BROWN,
Of the Firm of Robert Brown & Co.,
26 Renfield Street, Glasgow,
Agent for the Applicant.

Redhill: Printed for His Majesty's Stationery Office, by Love & Malcomson, Ltd.—1906.

▲ Having tried out his ideas at both Craven Cottage and Stamford Bridge, in 1906 Leitch applied for his first football-related patent, No. 4453, 'An Improved Method of Constructing the Terracing and Accessories thereof in Football and other Sport Grounds.'

To readers of a certain age, the patent application's diagrams will be instantly recognisable.

Patented Leitch Crush Barriers were installed, in their thousands, at hundreds of football, rugby and other sports grounds between 1906 and the 1960s.

Indeed they became so ubiquitous as to be almost invisible.

As can be seen, Leitch envisaged the use of timber 'runners' (or footings). But we know that from 1908 onwards he was using concrete instead. He even devised a proprietary form of wooden 'moulding box' to help with their construction.

First trialled at Goodison Park, Everton, he also, cannily, made sure that when the work was complete the boxes were sold on to Manchester United – at half price – for the preparation of terracing at their new Old Trafford ground.

30 Engineering Archie

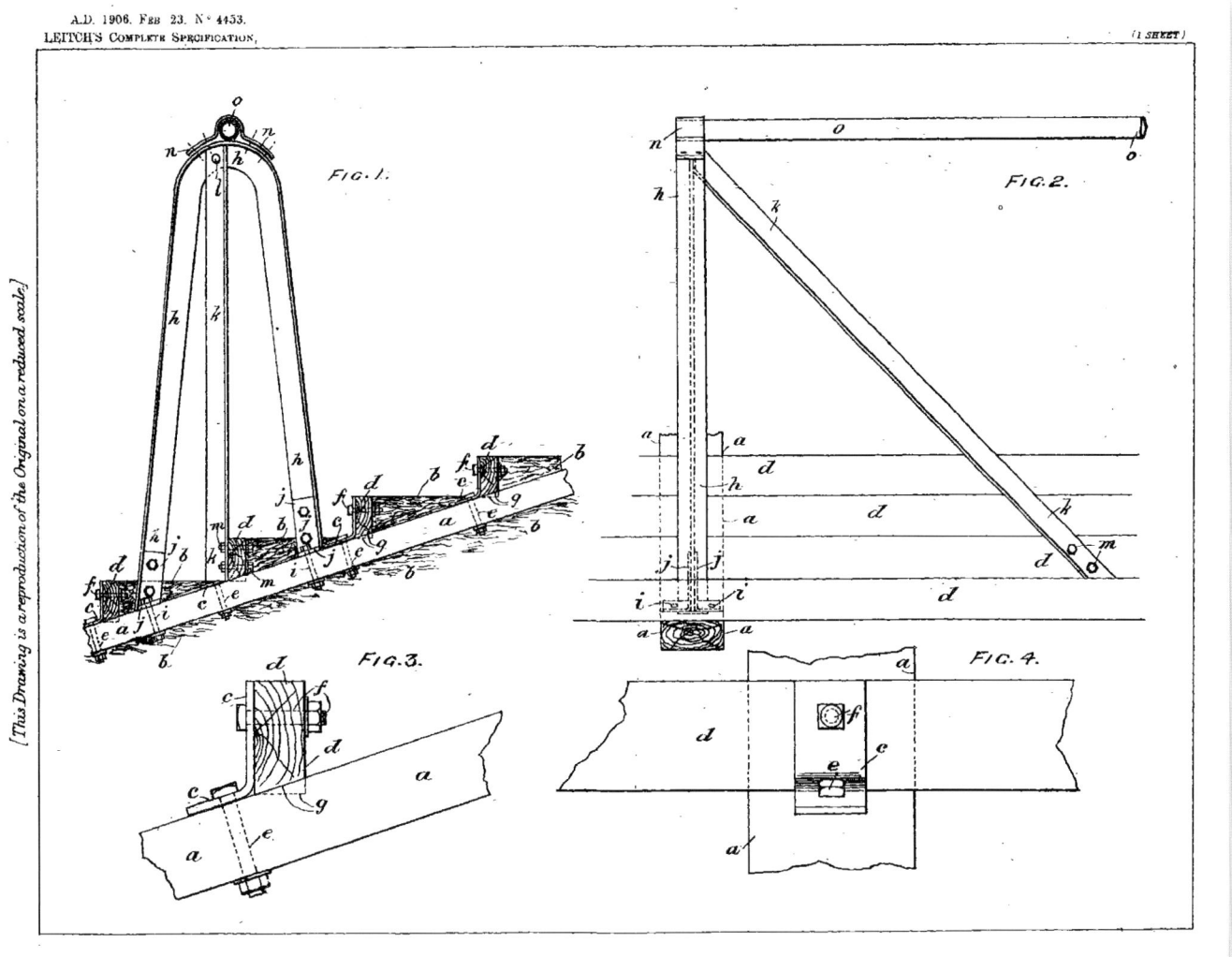

But although Leitch's barriers proved extremely successful – and perhaps moderately profitable in terms of royalties for the ten years that the patent applied – Leitch's method for fixing the barriers did not, ultimately, prove necessary.

As he himself anticipated on page two of the patent application, concrete foundations obviated the need for such a system.

Leitch barriers remained in common usage until at least the mid-1970s, when load testing became obligatory, although surviving examples may still be spotted at smaller grounds today.

They did suffer from one inbuilt fault, however. The tubular 'crush rails' were prone to internal rusting, which meant they lost strength without any visible signs; a characteristic only revealed by tests conducted under the auspices of the Taylor Report into the Hillsborough disaster.

As it was this disaster which led to the abolition of terracing, Leitch's work may thus be said to have been born of one disaster, in April 1902, and consigned to history by another, in April 1989, almost exactly fifty years after his death.

Engineering Archie **31**

Terracing

◀ Workers from Humphreys of Knightsbridge, the contractors with whom Leitch often worked, lay terracing in front of the main stand at **Selhurst Park** in 1924, allowing us a rare glimpse of Leitch's patented system of rakers and risers in mid-construction.

Might those steel units stacked up on the right be the 'moulding boxes' referred to earlier?

Notice also that the front row of terracing lies below pitch level, in fact to a depth of 2' 8" (810mm). This was a standard Leitch feature, designed to offer two main benefits.

Firstly, it limited the height of the terrace, and therefore of the structures behind, thereby reducing the cost of stand construction, with no sacrifice in capacity.

Secondly, the fact that the pitch sat above the level of the first row of spectators made for better sightlines all round.

A third, less significant benefit, in some locations, was that the outflows of the pitch drains were more accessible, and therefore easier to maintain.

The stand shown in mid-construction is still extant at Selhurst Park, 80 years later, albeit much modifed and reclad (see pages 53 and 153). The terraced enclosure shown here, meanwhile, was reprofiled and fitted with seats in 1979.

◀ Heavyweight Jack 'Miracle' Hobbs – from down the road in Shepherd's Bush – gets into shape for his first bout in three years at **Stamford Bridge** in 1953.

Terrace steps formed a regular part of the footballer's training routine. One drill was to run up and down the banks carrying army rucksacks, filled with weights.

But even if his exertions were more posed than punishing, Hobbs' photo-opportunity gives us an opportunity to see a typical Leitch terrace in detail.

This one was originally laid out in 1905, but because the banking was raised in such a hurry, subsequent settlement required the terrace steps to be patched up on a regular basis.

The section shown here has clearly been recently renovated, with new concrete footings (clipped to the rakers underneath), and fresh gravel and cinders on the treads.

It will also be noted that the barriers are staggered between aisles, leaving gaps through which crowds could surge.

As seen on page 28, Leitch's terrace layout for Craven Cottage used continuous barriers. It is likely that Stamford Bridge was, when first completed, the same, as they were designed at the same time.

The suggestion is therefore that Chelsea (and indeed the majority of clubs) either settled for staggered layouts in order to reduce costs when renovations were carried out, or that Archie himself decided to allow the practice.

The earliest known debate on barrier layouts came in 1924, in a report by the Government's *Committee on Crowds* (to which we will return in Chapter Six).

Based on fairly circumstantial evidence, surprisingly the report favoured the Hampden wire rope and penning system, and added 'we do not attach any importance to the question whether the barriers are continuous or intermittent'.

In the 1970s that advice changed, in favour of continuous barriers. But until after the Hillsborough disaster, it was rarely implemented.

▲ Although its origins were the slopes of the very first stadium at Olympia in the 7th century BC, the football terrace was very much a phenomenon of the 20th century.

The terrace was no place for the weak, for the old, or, as this image of **Ibrox Park** from the 1920s would suggest, for women. Only in later years would females be seen on terraces in any number.

Nor should we forget that while major accidents were rare – Ibrox was the worst affected, suffering two fatalities in 1961 and 66 in 1971 on an exit stairway, as well as 1902 – many unreported injuries occurred on a routine basis

And yet, and yet, on the vast majority of occasions, the terrace was a largely self-policed and, at least until the darker days of

the football hooligan from the 1960s onwards, a place of joy and comradeship. When it failed, it failed because of poor design, or more often, poor management.

Indeed the great irony of the British football terrace was that just as, in the aftermath of Hillsborough, experts finally came to agree on how best to design and manage them, they were abolished.

Engineering Archie 33

Chapter Four
Glasgow and Liverpool 1902–15

ARCHIBALD LEITCH, M.I.Mech.E.

The well-known Football Ground Expert. Engineer for the reconstruction of the Spurs' Ground.

Archibald Leitch wins a rare mention in a club publication – Tottenham Hotspur's souvenir booklet to mark their entry to the Football League in 1908. Archie's client list during the thirteen year period between the Ibrox disaster and 1915 included eight clubs who won either the League Championship or the FA Cup (or both). Clearly the stigma of the disaster had little or no effect on business. The period also marked Archie's departure from Glasgow.

Archibald Leitch's entry into the world of football coincided with a period of extraordinary change in the horizons of ordinary men and women.

As a number of historians have remarked, most notably Asa Briggs, a spate of inventions and innovations in the late 1890s would create the foundations of what we now term the 'leisure industry' (an oxymoron on par with another creation of the period, the 'industrial park').

In 1896 alone, the year Archie first set up in business, Marconi gave his first demonstration of radio waves. The first modern mass market newspaper, the *Daily Mail*, appeared on the streets and, in London, the first moving picture show drew packed audiences for a run that lasted eighteen months. Between 1908 and 1914 over 3,500 cinemas opened in Britain. Gramophone records brought music to one's hearth.

Also to appear during the period leading up to the First World War were motor cars and aeroplanes, while rather more within most people's budgets, a new generation of electric trams and motorised buses would, in addition to the more widespread use of bicycles, allow a freedom of movement hitherto unknown.

All good news for a stadium builder.

In our own lifetimes we have grown accustomed to creeping modernisation. Just think of how telephones have changed in the last twenty years, for example. Yet they are still telephones. We have never known life without them.

Whereas for Archie's generation, this sudden onrush of innovation, of so many mechanical and electrical benefits, in such a short space of time, would transform everyday life in a way that we can scarcely imagine.

This was the context in which Archie now set about designing the first purpose built football grounds of the new century.

In that sense, Ibrox had been a Victorian calamity, a leftover from the 19th century.

Archie's own world of work was changing too.

In addition to the arrival of a telephone and a typewriter in his office, in factory design – over a century after the start of the industrial revolution – iron was being replaced by precision made, standardised steel elements; beams, stanchions, stairways, balustrades and so on, all employed by Leitch in his industrial and football work.

Amongst the products being turned out by the new processes were of course his own patented crush barriers.

His grandstand for Sheffield United, built in conjunction with the Clyde Structural Iron Company in 1901 – they would later become known as the Clyde Structural Steel Company – was said to be the first in Britain to have electric lights installed.

In subsequent stands he would lay on telephones and telegraph offices within the press boxes, and underground hot water boilers to serve the dressing rooms.

Perhaps most radically of all, only a year after the timber-induced nightmare of Ibrox, Archie started work on Glasgow's first reinforced concrete building, the Sentinel Works (*see opposite*).

34 Engineering Archie

When working in steel Archie also pushed the boundaries. His first double-decker appeared in 1907. Two years later his giant stand at Goodison Park was dubbed the 'Mauretania Stand'.

Archie's press exposure increased too, as advances in print technology allowed newspapers to print more photographs and illustrations. Thus Archie was able to publicise his work, and help spread his name, by providing sketches and descriptions of each new ground to the likes of *Athletic News*, *Lotinga's Football Weekly* and *Football Chat*.

Several of these images are reproduced later in the book.

The game of football itself went through what can best be described as acute growing pains during this period.

The audience certainly showed no signs of waning. As soon as Leitch's new patented terraces were ready they were being tested to the limit. Some, like those at Stamford Bridge in London, started to break up, having been terraced before the banking had had a chance to settle.

Amid this manic drive to expand and to compete, numerous clubs, Archie's clients among them, were hauled up before the Football Association, to explain their less than transparent financial dealings. Several directors with whom Archie dealt ended up being suspended as a result.

As CB Fry, the gifted amateur footballer and cricketer put it in 1911, 'In football it is widely acknowledged that if both sides agree to cheat, cheating is fair.'

This cheating manifested itself on and off the pitch; in the form of match fixing scandals, violent play, under the counter payments and the poaching of players. »

▲ Football grounds have often been likened to cathedrals. But as Calvin Coolidge, later to be the US President, also remarked in 1916, 'The man who builds a factory builds a temple.'

Archie may well have scoffed at such a notion. And yet, the only one of his factories known to have survived *is* a temple in its own way; a temple to modernity, to efficiency, to light, and above all, to concrete.

Indeed, some may consider the **Sentinel Works**, in Jessie Street*, Polmadie, Glasgow, built between 1903-05 for the Alley and MacLellan Engineering Co., to be Leitch's finest work. So fine that it is now listed Category A (the Scottish equivalent of Grade 1).

Not least, it was the first ferro-concrete building in Glasgow.

It is also now the third oldest surviving in Britain as a whole, and the oldest Leitch structure too.

There is, it must be said, a question of accreditation. Certain records credit Brand & Lithgow as architects, with Leitch as engineer. Yet the drawings are in Leitch's name only, and Brand & Lithgow's previously known works were generally on a smaller scale. Nor are there any records of them working in reinforced concrete.

Also, the Sentinel Works is built using the Hennebique System, the same form of reinforcement Leitch used to build his first concrete grandstand at Anfield, a year later.

But in the context of this book, surely the most intriguing aspect of this wonderful, though now sadly derelict building, is that it might easily be a grandstand. The proportions are certainly similar.

We cannot help but ask, therefore, does the assured façade of the Sentinel Works offer a tantalising glimpse of how Archie might have embraced modernism in his stand designs, if only he had found a client adventurous enough to have given him full rein?

*That Archie's wife was also called Jessie appears merely to have been a coincidence, though one that no doubt caused much mirth in the Leitch household.

Engineering Archie 35

▶ The **Leitch family** gather for the Golden Wedding anniversary of Archie's parents, Archibald and Agnes, in 1905, at their retirement home in Rothesay, on the Isle of Bute.

Perhaps reflecting his growing position within the family, Archie stands in the centre, flanked by his sisters Margaret and Agnes.

His wife Jessie sits at the front, alongside his ageing mother.

Archie and Jessie had four children by this time (a fifth having died in infancy), although none were present when this portrait was taken. They had also recently moved into a semi-detached suburban villa in Maxwell Drive, Pollokshields, their first proper family home.

This was to be Archie's busiest year in football, working on both Stamford Bridge and Craven Cottage simultaneously. He cannot therefore have spent too much time at home in Glasgow.

▲ A further sign of prosperity came in 1906 when Archie moved offices to **No. 34 Argyle Arcade**, at 30 Buchanan Street. The arcade entrance is visible in this 1904 view, between the two hanging globe lights on the right (above the back of the horse-drawn wagon).

To the right of the entrance to the arcade – itself a beautiful structure, built in 1827 – was Miss Cranston's famous Tea Rooms. Did Archie take clients there, or perhaps Jessie, for tea and cakes?

(A boutique occupies the premises today, and the street is pedestrianised.)

Argyle Arcade would remain the Leitch company's Glasgow address until Archibald Kent Leitch, who lived in London, closed it in 1939 following Archie's death.

❯❯ A new generation of wealthy businessmen was taking an interest in the game, several of them brewers, who were quick to see the profits to be had from attracting thirsty fans to grounds built near their pubs.

Quite a few of them had their fingers burnt. All were larger than life characters.

Leitch found himself increasingly occupied in London, serving the ambitions of a number of such individuals, all anxious for their new ground to be the one that the FA would choose as a new Cup Final venue, to replace the woefully inadequate – if vast – Crystal Palace.

In west London, in 1905, Archie ended up designing stadiums for two competing chairmen at the same time; one a leading building contractor, the other a speculative house builder.

In Blackburn in 1906 a cotton magnate hired Archie to build a stadium fit for his expensively assembled team.

In Bradford in 1907 a mill owner confounded all logic by starting up a professional team in a city which already had one. Archie designed a new ground for him too.

The Manchester brewer John Davies, who had taken over his local club, Newton Heath, and turned them into Manchester United in 1902, hired Leitch to build him a lavish new stadium between 1908-10, and in doing so saddled the club with debts that took 41 years to pay off. Virtually every week Davies had to throw money at the club just to keep it afloat.

So if, in his gloomiest moments following the Ibrox disaster, Archie ever wondered if he would work in football again, it was these monied individuals – blinded by ambition and seemingly losing all business sense the moment they crossed the threshold of their clubs – who kept him busier than he might ever have dreamed.

Of course he was not alone.

In 1902, a month before the Ibrox disaster, Archie applied for full membership of the Institute of Mechanical Engineers.

Again, his application form tells us what else he was up to. In addition to ongoing factory work he was now acting for three local councils, and also, intriguingly, for the Kroonstaad Corporation in South Africa – this was shortly after the Boer War – and 'for several principalities in India'.

Leitch stated, 'I employ about 30 hands in my office.'

But there could be no doubting who 'bossed the job'.

Leitch's energies appeared to be boundless. He seemed to write and sign most of the correspondence with all his client clubs. He was forever attending board meetings.

On occasions, as in his dealings with Arsenal in 1913 (*as revealed overleaf*) and Hearts in 1914, he clearly took on too much and the job suffered.

He must also have spent a good deal of his working life on trains, particularly the overnight sleeper between Glasgow and London, where his attentions were increasingly drawn after 1905.

This may have been the chief factor in the next upheaval in his life; his decision in around 1909 to move the family from Glasgow to Blundellsands, on the Crosby coast just outside Liverpool.

Another motive was no doubt the steady downturn in Glasgow's economic fortunes after the turn of the century. The engineering and shipping boom by then was well and truly over. Whereas Liverpool, and Manchester, newly enriched by the ship canal, appeared to offer a factory architect richer pickings.

As did all those English football clubs, with money to burn.

After working with Liverpool and Everton it is also possible that Archie took a shine to the city.

Certainly the new Leitch home in Blundellsands, which they named 'Inverclyde' to remind them of home, was a considerable step up the property ladder.

Only six years after leaving a tenement in Cathcart Road he and Jessie were now neighbours with stockbrokers, lawyers, a knight of the realm even.

But as his fortunes fared even better on Merseyside, this large suburban villa would turn out to be only a stepping stone to yet another move, six years later.

As it did for so many successful Scottish men of Archie's generation, London called.

▲ A celebratory meal, if not, it would appear, much of a party mood, before the opening of Manchester United's **Old Trafford** in February 1910.

The photograph is one of a set taken to mark the opening of what was effectively the first true football stadium of the 20th century, as opposed to an updated ground.

(Others from the set appear on the cover and on page 118.)

Archie (*second from the right*) had worked long and hard to secure this contract – which totalled £60,000 in value, his largest yet – setting up an office in Manchester for the duration.

Sitting next to Archie in the corner is 'Honest John' McKenna, the Irish chairman of Liverpool who was about to be elected President of the Football League, a post he would hold for 26 years. Over the years McKenna attended a number of Archie's openings.

By this time Archie was also living in Liverpool.

Engineering Archie 37

Glasgow & Liverpool

▶ A unique and fascinating insight into Leitch's working methods and the procedures of the day appeared in Arsenal's match programme on December 21 1963, shortly after the 50th anniversary of Highbury's opening. It was written by a first hand witness, Alfred Kearney, an employee at Leitch's Manchester office. After his spell in London Kearney returned to the north west where he took over the tenancy of Leitch's Liverpool office in Dale Street.

Constructing Highbury's North Bank in 1913 (*below*). Note the grid of raker beam and footings in place, ready for the barriers to be fixed. As we learnt in the previous chapter, a Leitch terrace was no mere hump, but a designed piece of engineering. The view from the same angle (*opposite*) was taken in August 1933, when Arsenal were at the height of their powers. The Leitch stand on the far side (*see page 128ff*) was replaced by the current East Stand in 1936.

"This is an inside account of the alarums and excursions, in 1913, when the Arsenal football ground was being made. In those days we clinked golden sovereigns in our pockets, bought cigarettes 20 for 6d, and I believe Arsenal's big signing of the time was George Jobey. Times have changed.

In about 1908, Archibald Leitch, a consulting engineer and commercial architect, who had his office in Glasgow, had created a practice in Scotland for the building of football grounds. Rumours of likely similar happenings in Lancashire and Yorkshire caused him to move his practice to Manchester, the Glasgow office being maintained for other work in the shipyards.

I joined the firm as second assistant and 'battle' commenced. The main objective was to capture and consolidate the market for the Manchester United ground at Old Trafford, one of the few grounds constructed inside a symmetrical perimeter wall and originally laid out for 100,000 spectators, but shortage of money caused only part of the plan to be carried out for about 70,000 spectators.

The business sprouted and the chief assistant was called back to Glasgow and I was promoted to chief assistant and designer.

Mr Leitch's time was taken up chasing likely financiers to support various works that might be influenced our way, and at this time you might say that probably about only half a dozen football clubs in the country were really solvent; Woolwich Arsenal being one of the 'others'. He spent a long time in London at Stamford Bridge, Tottenham, etc., and during 1911-12 began to bring back, from his London journeys, large-scale Ordnance plans of some of the London sites on which to plan and lay-out a new ground for 100,000 people. The purpose was to provide a Cup Final ground to replace Crystal Palace.

Most of these schemes were found to be too expensive and special considerations were necessary, not the least of which was the proximity of an Underground station, and so the last site to be considered, and planned, was the area south of the London College of Divinity bounded by Avenell Road, Highbury Hill and Gillespie Road.

I was made head cook and bottle-washer of the project and on a Friday early in 1913, Mr Leitch informed me that interested people had come to terms and that the job was to proceed forthwith, and I was ordered to London immediately.

I asked about drawings and specifications and was told that I would have to do them on site as the ground was to be ready for opening in the coming September. It was at this stage that I found out that it was to be the new home of Woolwich Arsenal, then tottering at Plumstead, and that the people behind the scheme were Messrs Henry Norris and William Hall who, I discovered, had done a lot of dwelling-house building in the Fulham district, Mr Norris then being Mayor of Fulham.

Monday morning saw me getting into what was probably a two-cylinder Renault taxi at Euston with my rods, poles and perches, plus personal luggage, and later being deposited on the pavement in Avenell Road outside a forbidding brick wall which, at that time, ran the whole length of Avenell Road on the westerly side.

I felt rather like, as the catch line in pantomime had it in those days, 'The only one saved from the wreck'.

I found a large timber entrance gate on which I pounded as I had not been told who to contact, and I was very grateful when it was opened by two representatives of Messrs Humphreys Ltd, Civil Engineers of Knightsbridge, who were just installing the builders' hut. They looked after me and after a couple of days I found some very fine accommodation in Sotheby Road, and I discovered that the area around was a theatrical quarter, being an off-shoot from the Finsbury Park Empire.

I was all set to start and as hardly anything had been planned, except a small perspective which I had put together for my own diversion, the job was just in my head and in my hands.

The first move I made was to get down to the LCC Engineer's Office (then in Spring Gardens), to see if they would pass my plans piecemeal, preliminary to the building committee's monthly meets. They agreed and we were off. I had one foot at Highbury and the other in Spring Gardens, rushing each drawing I got passed, back to the site and fixing up the setting out with the foreman.

The first plans were to get the pitch laid out. Remember there were no bulldozers or mechanical diggers. It was all navvies, picks, spades and barrows. The College end was six foot higher than Gillespie Road and the first job was to take a line across the centre of the pitch dug into the Aubert Park, and have the spoil wheeled to the other end to level out the pitch space. We then started to form the embankment at the other end.

Then a bombshell dropped.

The hang-over of the Victorian era still clung to Highbury, although the city VIP's had more or less left their villas and coaches and horses, etc. The

38 Engineering Archie

suburbanites were still feeling superior however, and a bright boy in Highbury Hill started a petition to get the Islington Borough Council to put a stop to this 'vulgar project'.

It appeared that we hadn't a chance, but Mr Norris pulled some strings behind the scenes and I was able to get on once again.

Tons of material were required for forming the embankment and news of the 'tip' soon went round. Dozens of people brought us stuff from all over London and the yellow London clay, dropping from the carts, left the streets and roads all around Highbury dyed yellow for many weeks.

More trouble started when we wanted to build the high brick retaining wall at the College end, when the LCC Office 'passed the buck' and referred me to an out-of-date Parish Council office in Holloway Road, where two or three old gentlemen of the 'father to son' type of ancient officials of officialdom were in charge.

They did not know the difference between a retaining wall and a retaining fee – so now what? Once again Mr Norris came to the rescue and told me to forget them, and I did.

Then another bombshell. We commenced building a high boundary wall abutting Highbury Hill back gardens, when we received a solicitor's letter threatening an injunction because we were over the building line.

It was a trick because we were not over the line, but we could not afford to be held up so we pulled the wall down and rebuilt it six foot further in on our own side.

So another threat was dealt with.

At the Gillespie Road end we needed an entrance opposite the Tube station, so two houses were bought and pulled down, giving us a good passage and leading to a large area where turnstiles and exit gates could be constructed to feed out up to the 'Spion Kop'.

So we progressed: everyone but myself becoming more pessimistic and depressed, wondering whether the chaos could be got ready.

Mr Norris, who was later to be knighted, was a tough nut; testy and a one-way man – his way. I did not let him worry me for I was too busy, but all the staff of Messrs Humphreys Ltd gave me wonderful co-operation and, although it wobbled on numerous occasions, the job went on.

In those days anything incongruous was referred to as 'a proper Fred Karno's' after the music hall Crazy Gang of those days, and so this title was tacked on to our project at Highbury.

Time was getting on and looking to the future we began to plan the position of the exit gates and turnstiles. The latter were delivered but we could not get the pay boxes ready for the opening.

A week or so before September, I got the contractors to supply me with hundreds of feet of rough timber and many carpenters who, at danger points, made rails and passages guiding people into the turnstiles and out to the exits.

Offices, dressing-rooms, bathrooms, etc., were roughly ready. Baths were in position but were not connected to supplies and drains. A couple of army field kitchens were brought in for heating water and the contractors' handymen were really first class.

Even the players and officials of the club fell in with the spirit and treated it like a picnic, working hard here and there and getting a wonderful kick out of everything they did. They worked like Trojans.

As 'D' Day neared, Mr Leitch, possibly thinking that discretion was the better part of valour, made himself scarce and on the week previous to the opening he could not be found. The testy Mr Norris did everything to find him, without success, and was beside himself, for although the ground was a hive of activity we were not really ready.

About 11.00 am on the Saturday morning of the opening, things looked grim, for the exit gates were still open and carts were hanging around, going in and out on their various business, and Mr Norris almost threw in the sponge and insisted on taking myself and Humphreys' representative to lunch at a very large Italian restaurant next door to Finsbury Park gates.

I gave instructions that all exit gates were to be closed, for a sprinkling of people were coming along to see what was happening, but on returning from lunch, I found the exit gates were still open and hundreds of people were lining up at the entrances four or five deep in Avenell Road.

I rushed in and arranged for all the exit gates to be closed and then the spectators came in. I shall never know why they did not just walk in the exit gates and gate crash without paying, but it says much for the sportsmen of those days that they did not.

Thank goodness the weather kept fine and the match was played – the crisis was over.

I stayed on for four or five weeks helping with the completion until a proper clerk of works and foreman were appointed to take over for the finishing arrangements."

Henry Norris – the 'tough nut' whom Leitch worked for twice, at Craven Cottage in 1904-05 and Highbury in 1913. Norris was later at the centre of one of football's greatest scandals, the promotion of Arsenal to the First Division in 1919 (see page 129).

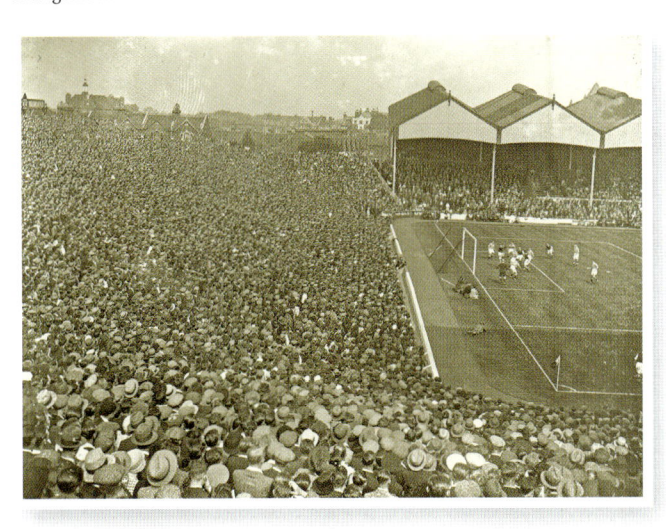

Grandstands

Chapter Five

Grandstands

On January 25 1905 Archibald Leitch made his first recorded public appearance in London, as an expert witness in a case brought by the London County Council against Fulham FC, under the London Building Act 1894.

The case was a petty one, mainly concerning which tier of local government had the right to approve certain types of building.

Fulham considered their stand (*illustrated below right*) to be a temporary structure and as such had gained approval from Fulham Borough Council. The LCC, however, deemed it to be a permanent building, and therefore one that came under their jurisdiction. They also considered the stand dangerous and had repeatedly ordered its removal.

Leitch was already designing a replacement for Fulham, so could not lose either way. But in his opinion, according to a report of the hearing in the *Daily Telegraph*, the stand in question was a structure, not a building.

'A structure was a skeleton... the roof was no essential part of the structure.'

The report added that Leitch 'had tried in vain to get from the LCC a definition of a building,' a comment which provoked laughter in court.

He was then asked by the LCC's barrister, 'What would you call the grand stand at Epsom?'

Showing the same dry wit he displayed in the Ibrox case three years earlier Leitch replied, 'I should call it a grandstand.'

The barrister then asked, 'You practice in Glasgow, I believe.'

'That,' interposed the magistrate, amid more laughter, 'is obvious.'

London during the Edwardian period was full of cocksure Scottish engineers; busy on railways, viaducts, bridges, docks, roads and tramways. It was the same right across the Empire.

But until Leitch there had never been such a thing as an engineer who specialised in grandstands.

In fact, before Leitch we know the names of very few individuals who designed stands at all.

Thomas Verity, architect of the pavilion at Lord's in 1890 (still extant), was better known for his theatres. Thomas Muirhead designed pavilions at Old Trafford and The Oval, also in the 1890s. But these were hardly grandstands.

There were also numerous contractors who specialised in the type of basic timber and iron pavilions and stands that could be seen at sportsgrounds all over Britain during the late 19th century. One such was Fred Braby & Co. in Glasgow, who laid out the original Ibrox Park in 1887.

Otherwise, only one man can truly be said to have been a grandstand architect, and that was the prolific John Carr of York (1725-1807). Among a long list of buildings for which he was responsible, including The Crescent at Buxton, were four grandstands, all at racecourses; at Knavesmire, York (1755) – the lower arcade of which survives – Beverley (1769), Doncaster (1776) and Nottingham (1777).

After Carr, other architects may have designed the odd one or two grandstands at a local level.

But only Archibald Leitch made it his business on a national scale.

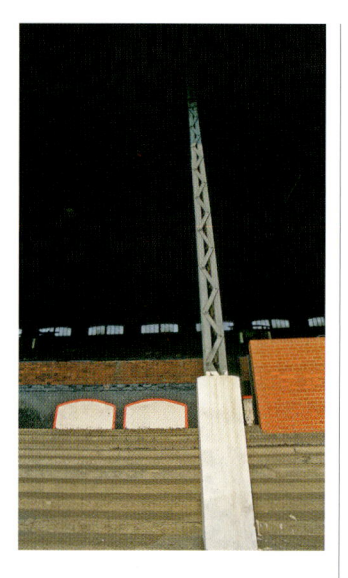

Archie's Column – a tapering lattice column at Fulham's Craven Cottage, still playing a supporting role a century after its erection in 1905. Borrowing from his experience of designing industrial sheds, Leitch used lattice steel throughout the stand's columns, girders and trusses to speed up construction and reduce the cost of materials.

Fulham's problematic stand (*right*) built by Robert Iles of Walham Green in 1903, was typical of the stands commonly seen at Victorian sports grounds. (Presumably Iles already had the four stands lying idle – perhaps left over from the Coronation – and simply bolted them together to form a whole.) After the hearing at which Leitch gave evidence, the magistrate fined Fulham a token 10s, plus 4s costs, for a technical breach of planning procedures. Fumed *The West London and Fulham Times*, 'A more wicked waste of ratepayers' money cannot be imagined.' The London County Council was now down £100 in costs. 'Poor Public!' concluded the newspaper.

40 Engineering Archie

▲ Archibald Leitch was by no means the first designer of sports grounds to place a pedimented gable on the roof of a grandstand.

Britain's urban and surburban sports clubs and municipal parks were awash with similarly ornamented stands, pavilions, lodges and gatehouses.

This two-sided stand belonged to the Leeds Cricket, Football & Athletic Company at **Headingley**. With 2,000 seats on its football side, and 1,000 facing the cricket pitch, it was designed in 1890 by Smith & Tweedale (architects also of the Grand Arcade, Leeds, 1897).

Stands of this two-sided type were relatively rare, so it can be no coincidence that Leitch would find himself designing a more modern version for a rival Yorkshire club, Bradford, in 1907 (see page 95).

Headingley's stand catered only for general spectators. Club members and players all congregated in a much grander pavilion alongside. This separation was a cricketing tradition which permeated football in its earliest days. Leitch himself designed three pavilions with adjoining stands, at Ibrox (1899), Craven Cottage (1905) and Bradford (1907).

▲ This, the main stand at the new **Rugby Park** in Kilmarnock, Ayrshire, was almost certainly the first stand ever built to a design by Archibald Leitch.

Opened on the day of Killie's First Division debut, against Celtic, on August 26 1899, the stand was constructed by the **Clyde Structural Iron Company** of Glasgow, with whom Leitch had already worked on various factories and industrial buildings. He was also working with the company that summer on the construction of the new Ibrox Park for Rangers.

As can be seen there were no players' facilities within the stand (there is no gate leading onto the pitch). These were still housed in a separate pavilion.

Nor was there mention of Leitch in any of the reports of its inauguration (which was followed a week later by the staging of a Highland gathering at the ground).

A possible explanation for this lies in what Leitch himself stated at the court case involving Fulham in 1905.

As reported opposite, he said 'The roof (of a stand) was no essential part of the structure.'

This suggests that while Archie may well have been responsible for designing the base of Kilmarnock's stand, he left the steelwork details to the draughtsmen of the Clyde Structural Iron Company.

If this was indeed the case, then it must also follow that several of the other stands he subsequently worked on with the same company – especially those at Ayresome Park (see page 66) and Park Royal (page 190), which were virtual clones of the Rugby Park stand – were very much collaborative designs.

In other words, that their characteristic roofs and gables may not have been his work at all.

But whatever Archie's level of involvement in this 'exceedingly handsome' structure, as described by the *Kilmarnock Standard,* the experience would certainly have given him an inkling of what was to follow in his stand building career.

After delays caused by a joiners' strike, workmen were still feverishly completing its construction on the morning of its opening.

The stand was extended in 1914 and extensively remodelled and re-roofed in 1961.

Engineering Archie **41**

Grandstands

THE CLYDE STRUCTURAL IRON CO., LTD.

GRAND STAND
Supplied and erected at Newcastle, to seat 5000 persons.

DESIGNS AND ESTIMATES FREE ON APPLICATION

ESTABLISHED 1834.

SOLE CONTRACTORS FOR THE NEW STAND AND GROUND FOR THE CRYSTAL PALACE FOOTBALL CLUB
To the Designs of ARCHIBALD LEITCH, Esq., M.I.Mech.E.

HUMPHREYS LTD.
ENGINEERS AND CONTRACTORS
KNIGHTSBRIDGE, LONDON, S.W.7

Specialists in Design and Construction of Iron, Timber and Composite Structures.

TEMPORARY STANDS FOR ALL PURPOSES ON HIRE

Recent Contracts completed include Stands for:—

TOTTENHAM HOTSPUR
AYLESBURY
BLACKBURN ROVERS
DULWICH HAMLET
MANCHESTER CITY
MILLWALL
BEERSCHOT, ANTWERP
CHARLTON ATHLETIC
ALDERSHOT COMMAND
ARSENAL
BARNSLEY
COVENTRY
HUDDERSFIELD TOWN

SOUTHEND
BROMLEY, KENT
CHATHAM UNITED SERVICES
MANCHESTER UNITED
UXBRIDGE R.A.F.
GILLINGHAM
EBBW VALE
WAKEFIELD TRINITY
OXFORD UNIVERSITY
TWICKENHAM (New Stand in course of construction).

FOR ESTIMATES AND PARTICULARS APPLY—

HUMPHREYS LTD.
KNIGHTSBRIDGE, LONDON, S.W.7.

Telephone: KENSINGTON 6447 (3 lines).
Telegrams: HUMPHREYS, KNIGHTSBRIDGE, LONDON.

▲ The two contractors with whom Leitch most often collaborated were the **Clyde Structural Iron Co.** (see also previous page) and **Humphreys** of Knightsbridge.

Although Leitch was not involved in the design of the stand shown above in 1905, at **St James' Park, Newcastle** – the job went to another Glasgow engineer, Alexander Blair – the photograph is a reminder of how much the construction business at this time still depended on manual labour and horsepower.

Humphreys' advert from 1924 (right) lists eight clients for whom we know they worked alongside Leitch. So close was this relationship that in certain instances, even when the stands' drawings clearly emanated from Leitch's office, it is hard to distinguish which party designed which element within a ground.

For example, were Humphreys more responsible than Leitch for the specification of multi-span roofs at Old Trafford in 1910 (see pages 114ff) and Highbury in 1913 (pages 128ff)?

The exact authorship of the East and West Stands built at Twickenham during 1927-32 (see page 154) is also unclear. Neither was ever accredited to Leitch, yet they appeared to be carbon copies of a standard Leitch double-decker.

One characteristic of Humphreys' long, and obviously committed involvement with football and sport in general – until the 1950s at least when they ceased trading (or were taken over) – is just how often they had to battle to get paid.

At Charlton Athletic Humphreys ended up having a representative on the board after the club defaulted, while Manchester United overstretched themselves so much to build Old Trafford in 1910 that it was not until 1951 that Humphreys' final debentures were paid off.

42 Engineering Archie

▲ Construction work at two of Archibald Leitch's Yorkshire grounds in the years shortly before the First World War.

At **Leeds Road, Huddersfield**, Leitch laid out a new ground on an existing site, with Humphreys as the lead contractor and the Clyde Structural Iron Company erecting the usual lattice steelwork.

Shown here in November 1910 are (*top left*) workers fitting wooden supports for the bench seats on the upper tier, and (*above*) the reinforced concrete base of the stand nearing completion.

As we read in Chapter Four, Leitch was an early exponent of this new wonder material, and from his first use of it in a football context, at Anfield in 1906 (*see page 89*), until 1914, seemed to prefer concrete to steel for the stand structure itself (although he always specified steel for the roof).

An example of his proficiency in the use of concrete is the South Stand at **Hillsborough**, **Sheffield** (*above right*), where, working to the limits of the material at the time, in 1914 he designed a 4" slab for the seating deck (*see page 132*).

Not all his experiments were as successful. At Huddersfield, for example (*top right*), where the pitch had to be relaid after only one season, Leitch fitted an adaptation of his standard crush barriers around the inside of the perimeter fence. The idea, which he patented in 1910, was for the tubular hand rail to double as a pipe, supplying water for pitch irrigation.

He first trialled the system at Manchester United's Old Trafford in 1910, his most ambitious ground to date. Within a year it was described as 'practically useless.'

Engineering Archie **43**

Grandstands

Messrs The Directors of　　　　　　　　　　36 Dale Street
The Everton F C Ltd　　　　　　　　　　　　Liverpool
　　　　　　　　　　　　　　　　　　　　　31st March 1909

Gentlemen

　　　　　　　　New Grand Stand & Terracing

The following is the List of Tenders received for the steel work of Structure, Roof and Boarding and Seating of same:– The names are placed according to Estimate, the lowest offer first.

Contractors	Time	Price
Clyde Structural Iron Co. Ltd., Glasgow	4 months	£5,687 14 3
Blakeley & Co., Liverpool	4 –do–	£5,804 10
F Morton & Co. Ltd, Liverpool	16 weeks	£5,928 9 3
Wood & Co. Ltd Edward, Manchester	18 –do–	£6,111 - -
Pearson & Knowles Ltd, Warrington	17 –do–	£6,186 2 4
Bruce & Still Ltd, L iverpool	18 –do–	£6,225 3 4

Estimated cost　　　　　　　　　　　　　£5,784 5 –

The Lowest offerer is a first class firm, who can give you satisfactory work. They have executed most of the latest Grand Stands in the country.

The next firm who could be relied upon to work satisfactorily in a big undertaking such as this is F Morton & Coy Ltd of Liverpool, and as suggested by me to Mr Kelly and Mr Cuff, I put myself in communication with them, considering that as they are a local Firm, and anxious to secure the order, you might be disposed to give them a preference.

The result of my interview was, that if they obtain the order at the estimated price, they will in addition to what is specified, give the whole of the Steelwork an additional coat of paint after erection, and also paint the whole of the Timberwork of the Roof 2 coats of approved colour. They are not busy and will concentrate all their energies on the work.

As they are a local firm, of worldwide reputation, and with their works most convenient for inspection, and as they have offered what is practically equal value, I beg to recommend that their offer be accepted.

Should you however take the view that the lowest offer be accepted, then I have no hesitation in recommending that the Tender of The Clyde Structural Iron Coy be accepted.

Awaiting your further instructions

Francis Morton & Co. Ltd., Bridge & Roof Builders of Liverpool, leave their stamp on one of the columns of Leitch's Bullens Road Stand at Goodison Park in 1926, still in use today. The company provided the steelwork for a number of Leitch's clients, starting – as we see from this correspondence – with Everton's Main Stand in 1909 (*see pages 100ff*), the largest Leitch had designed up till then.

44 Engineering Archie

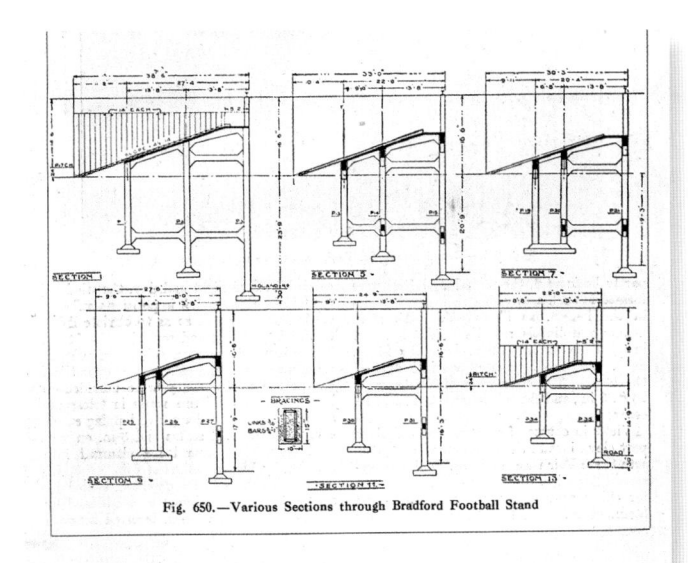

Fig. 650.—Various Sections through Bradford Football Stand

◀ While Everton went for steel in 1909, Leitch was already using ferro-concrete elsewhere, for example at his Sentinel Works in Glasgow (see page 35), in 1903, and at Everton's neighbours at Anfield, in 1906 (page 89).

These diagrams, reprinted from *Cassells Reinforced Concrete* (1913), show Leitch's sectional drawings for the Midland Road Stand at **Valley Parade, Bradford**, in 1908 (page 99).

Each of the stand's structural members varied in form and scale according to the changing geometry of the site, which was both on a slope and tapering in plan.

Other Leitch stands using ferro-concrete were at Leeds Road, 1910 (page 43 and 123), Roker Park, 1913 (page 125) and Ewood Park, 1913 (page 93). In each case, however, and at Valley Parade too (in 1951), the structures were demolished some years before their steel framed contemporaries, mainly owing to structural defects arising from the then experimental nature of the material.

Indeed of the eleven Leitch stands currently in use, only two concrete examples survive, at Anfield and Hillsborough.

Apart from its uncertainties as a material, at least in the early 1900s, another drawback of concrete was the time it added to construction schedules.

For that reason, apart from Leitch's North Stand at Hampden Park (see pages 48 and 172ff) and of course the Empire Stadium at Wembley – completed, famously, in 300 days in 1922-23 – steel remained the norm in football stand design until at least the 1960s.

Shown left is the steelwork for Leitch's double-decker East Stand at **White Hart Lane, Tottenham**.

Fifty seven days after this photo was taken in July 1934 the stand was opened. At the time Archie was virtually retired and living not far away in Cockfosters, so this is where he would take his grandson to watch matches.

The East Stand remains in use today, having been re-roofed and much altered since the 1980s (see page 112).

Engineering Archie **45**

Grandstands

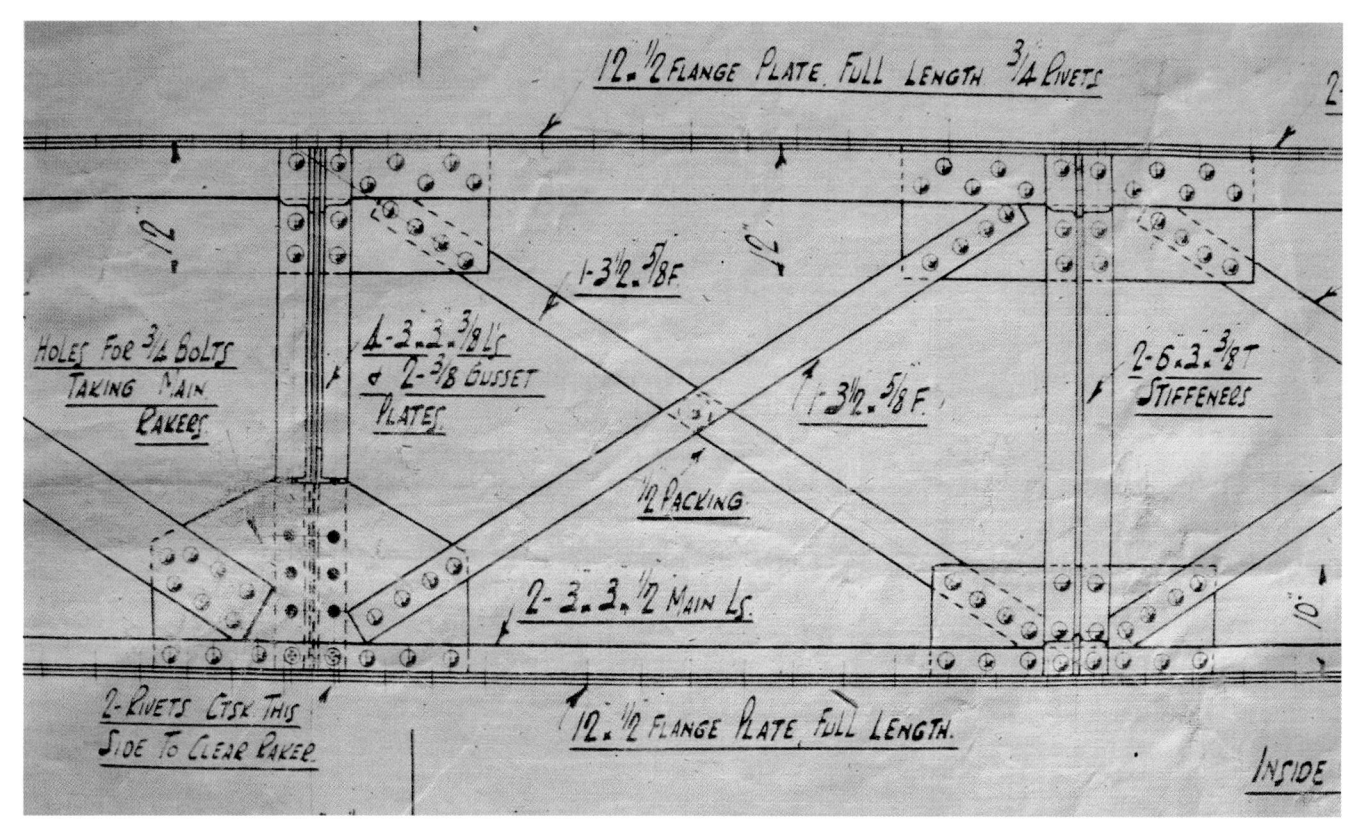

Leitch's trademark balcony truss – a feature of all his steel-framed double-decker stands – appeared first at Bradford Park Avenue in 1907. These drawings, however, relate to Goodison's Bullens Road Stand, built in 1926. Although highly distinctive, the design was purely functional. The inclined ties work in tension, the vertical struts in compression, while the protruding lateral restraints (marked 'outrigger' on the section, right) act as a lateral restraint for the top boom, which formed the handrail for front row spectators.

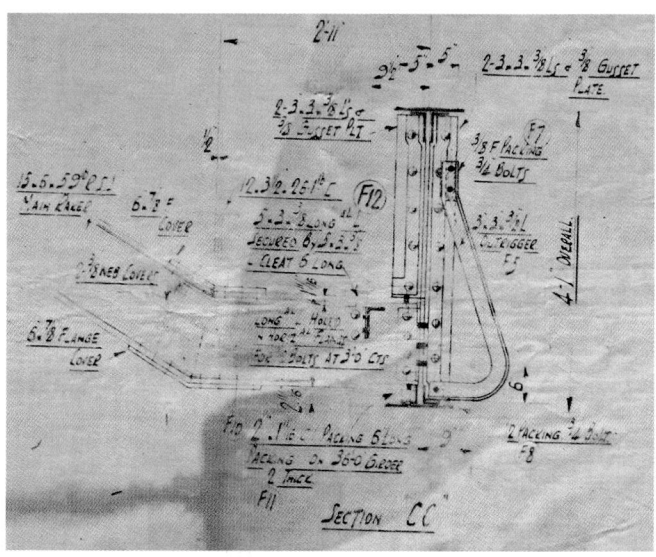

In the post war period spectators became accustomed to seeing Leitch balconies painted in a variety of club colours. As far as can be ascertained, however, the majority were originally painted a dull shade of matt green. At some locations, for example Twickenham (*page 155*) and the Baseball Ground (*page 168*), the timber backing was also painted green. Only one club ever chose to cover their Leitch balcony as a design statement, and that was Aston Villa, whose curved wooden panelling added a genuine extra dimension (*page 144*). Alas, in modern times, another, much less welcome development has been for the balconies to be covered by advertisements, as is the case at Fratton Park (*page 159*).

▲ The classic Leitch balcony truss on the **Bullens Road Stand** (*top*) still looks out over Goodison Park today, a feature instantly familar to football fans all over the world.

Backed by timber boarding, the criss-cross detailing is a perfectly expressed example of riveted steel structural design. Its robust form may follow function, yet, when extended to the full length of a grandstand, some 300-350 feet long, it appears both traditional, and modern at the same time.

Also shown is a section from the Main Stand at **Roker Park** (*above and page 126*), displayed proudly, if somewhat incongruously, in the car park of Sunderland's Stadium of Light, where its surprising bulk and height, 1.25m tall, can be truly appreciated.

Of the 17 Leitch stands featuring this balcony, four survive: at **Fratton Park** (*above*), at Ibrox Park (*pages 180ff*) and at Goodison Park (*page 104ff*) where in addition to the Bullens Road Stand there is a refined version at the Gwladys Street End, built in 1938, in which sheet steel replaced the timber backing and inclined stays. Spurs' East Stand was similar.

Engineering Archie **47**

Grandstands

▶ Minutes of the Wolverhampton Wanderers FC, February 24 1925:

'Write Mr Leitch that Sec. have seen the representative of the Bennet Furnishing Co., (who) informed him that the second screw in the back upright of the seats is not necessary, but my directors think otherwise. Would he please give his opinion.'

Archibald Leitch brought a lot of business to Bennet of Glasgow, makers of tip-up wooden seats in the days before plastic seating took over from the late 1960s.

Indeed Bennet seats proved so robust that some have lasted over 70 years, for example at Goodison Park (*see page 106*), and possibly even longer at Craven Cottage (*page 77*).

One factor in their success was that, providing the iron brackets were kept in reasonable condition, a club's in-house chippy could repair or replace the seats or seat backs with relative ease.

Unless bench seats were specified to save money, Leitch designed his seating decks with seat widths of 18 inches, which was three inches more than the standard set by train and omnibus companies. That same measurement – 460mm – is still used today, albeit as a minimum.

For other comparisons between Leitch's specifications and those of modern stands, see page 194.

THE NEW STAND .. at .. HAMPDEN PARK.

Architects:
ARCHIBALD LEITCH AND PARTNERS,
London and Glasgow.

JAMES D. BENNET LTD.

121 AVENUE STREET,

GLASGOW, S.E.

If you contemplate building a New Stand or Re-Seating an old one, we are at your service for the supply of

STAND SEATING

In one of our Stock Designs or to Architect's Specification.

RECENT CONTRACTS:
Hampden Park - - Queen's Park F.C.
Goodison Park - - - - Everton F.C.
Ninian Park - - - - Cardiff City F.C.

THE NEW STAND SEATING.

Contractors:
JAMES D. BENNET, LTD.,

Telephone:
Bridgeton 3497-3498.

Telegrams:
Scholastic, Glasgow.

WOLVERHAMPTON WANDERERS FOOTBALL STAND

300 TONS OF STEELWORK.

The illustrations indicate the new roof covering recently erected over south terraces at the Wolverhampton F.C. ground, and same affords valuable cover for approximately 12,500 spectators. The very large span girders supporting the roof at the front enable an almost unobstructed view of the playing field from any position in the stand.

Quick access and egress to and from the terraces is gained by means of the distributing corridor which is provided under the terrace for the full length of the stand.

Architects and Engineers :
ARCHIBALD LEITCH & PARTNERS, LONDON.

The erection of this Stand was carried out during the playing season, with very little inconvenience to the Football Club.

The view on left was taken from the rear and top step of the terrace and shows the two other stands erected by us to the architects' instructions.

Rubery, Owen & Co Ltd

LONDON:
Imperial Buildings
56, Kingsway, W.C.2
Telephone : Holborn 6306-7

DARLASTON, SOUTH STAFFS.
Telephone : Darlaston 130 (P.B.X.)
COVENTRY - Britannia Works, Paynes Lane
Telephone : 60051-2

BIRMINGHAM, 3 :
Lombard House
Great Charles Street
Telephone : Central 8134-5

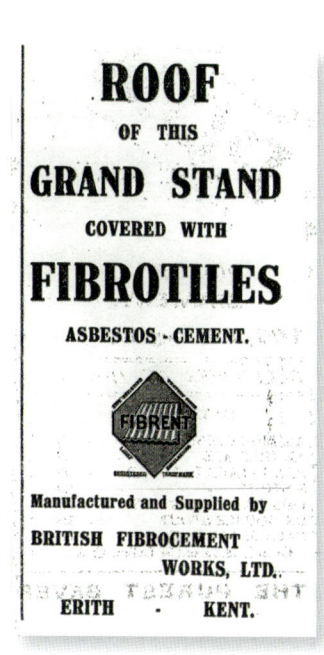

ROOF OF THIS GRAND STAND COVERED WITH FIBROTILES ASBESTOS - CEMENT.

Manufactured and Supplied by
BRITISH FIBROCEMENT WORKS, LTD.
ERITH - KENT.

Raising the roof at two Leitch grounds: Selhurst Park, south London in 1924 (*above*) and Molineux, Wolverhampton in 1935 (*left*).

Engineering Archie **49**

Grandstands

If you had a Leitch stand, naturally you wanted to show it off. Posing proudly here are: (*top left*) Bradford City and their Midland Road Stand in 1910; (*top right*), Tottenham Hotspur and their West Stand in 1950; (*above left*) League Champions Everton and their Main Stand in 1939, and (*above*) Portsmouth and their South Stand in 1954.

50 Engineering Archie

Not a logo in sight – four post-war teams put Archie behind them. They are: (*top left*) Liverpool, in front of their Main Stand in 1967; (*top right*), Sheffield Wednesday in front of their South Stand in 1973; (*above left*) Scottish League Champions Rangers in front of their South Stand in 1959, and (*above right*) Sunderland, in front of their Main Stand in 1969.

Engineering Archie 51

Chapter Six

London 1915–1939

Archibald Leitch was aged 70-71 when this photograph was taken, c.1936. He had only recently withdrawn from daily involvement in the business, but could not resist going up to Sunderland to present a wrist watch to Lady Raine, the wife of the local MP, who performed the opening ceremony of the club's Clock Stand in September 1936. Since starting in the business in 1899 Leitch had completed at least 46 individual stands and pavilions.

Archibald Leitch was well versed in the art of salesmanship and public relations. He had to be in order to win so much work.

A week before the opening of Crystal Palace's new ground at Selhurst Park in August 1924 (see opposite), Archie, a representative from the builders, Humphreys of Knightsbridge, and the Palace chairman Sydney Bourne, invited the press to what the *Croydon Times* reporter described as 'an excellent luncheon' at the Wilton Arms Hotel in Thornton Heath.

His counterpart, 'Nestor' of the *Croydon Advertiser*, offered the following report of the speeches.

'Called upon for a few words, Mr Leitch began by quoting from Macbeth that "this is a sanguinary business".

(Whether Archie meant the business of building a football ground in the midst of strikes and materials shortages, or simply public speaking, is not clear.)

"I am not a speaker but a Scotchman," he said, and then proceeded to prove he was both.

He asserted that when finished Selhurst Park will be the largest football ground in London, and it was up to the public to give the directors the support to complete their work.

They were not providing luxuries; the directors had not the resources of clubs like Aston Villa, but to encourage them he mentioned that one of the biggest clubs in London were in much the same position as themselves only a few years ago and yet to-day they had more money than any other club in London.

And he knew what he was talking about as he had designed the ground for the club.'

(That club was Arsenal.)

'Mr Leitch referred to the unexpected difficulties which he and the contractors had met and which accounted for the unfinished condition of the ground.

They had, however, done their best and he asked for the indulgence of all.'

(With all parties possibly a little worse for wear by this stage, a conducted tour of Selhurst Park then took place.)

'Walking round the ground with Mr Leitch it was easy to be seen that he is immensely proud, and justifiably so, of his handiwork.

"Look," said he, "on the stand and terraces already completed we can easily accommodate 20,000 spectators and every one will have a clear view.

"But to get a real idea of the immensity of the ground you must come up here," he said, and we all climbed to the top of the bank backing on to Whitehorse-lane.

And then we realised that Mr Leitch's words were no idle boast, but that Mr Sydney Bourne's dream of an ideal home for the Palace is coming true.

In his mind's eye Mr Leitch already visualises a cup final tie or international game being played at Selhurst Park and some of us may live to see his optimism realised.'

Almost every ground Archie had worked on in London had been similarly extolled. In 1904 he predicted Craven Cottage would be a likely venue for Cup Finals. He said the same of Stamford Bridge in 1905 and Highbury in 1913.

Selhurst Park, he told the press, would ultimately be enlarged to hold 80,000 spectators, and perhaps even more...

Briefed by Archie, 'Tityrus' of *Athletic News* wrote of Selhurst Park, 'I wandered round this place until fatigue overtook me, but it was evident that there was space for 100,000 people with the site fully equipped.' »

52 Engineering Archie

▶ Opening day at Crystal Palace's **Selhurst Park** on August 30 1924. As children peep through gaps in the fence, a solitary bobby keeps the queues in order.

A week earlier Archie had told the press that the ground might one day be capable of holding the FA Cup Final. But surely everyone knew by then that since the opening of **Wembley Stadium** the previous year that was never likely.

Not at Selhurst nor indeed at any of the capital's club grounds.

Archie was a fierce critic of Wembley. Of course that may have been because he had not been consulted on its design.

But just as likely he was angry because the stadium suffered from so many technical flaws. A great opportunity had been missed.

Five months earlier, in March 1924, the Home Office published the findings of a special committee (see Links), appointed to study the shambolic events surrounding the opening of Wembley; the occasion of the infamous 'White Horse' FA Cup Final, when 200,000 people had overwhelmed the stadium in April 1923.

Only by a miracle had no-one been killed in the crush.

Chaired by the former Home Secretary, Edward Shortt, the committee included Frank Pick of the Metropolitan Railway, the Chief Constable of Lancashire and the Secretary of Yorkshire County Cricket Club.

Its brief was to look into the issue of crowds, transport arrangements and other matters relating to the safety of the public 'at athletic grounds'.

The members visited five club grounds, including three by Leitch, namely Ibrox Park, Roker Park and Villa Park.

Yet despite Leitch's 25 years in the business, yet again he was not consulted.

Maxwell Ayrton, the architect of Wembley, was however.

For those who recall the old stadium's foibles, this extract from Ayrton's evidence (which was not published and would therefore not have been seen by Leitch) explains a great deal:

Q. You told us that prior to designing the stadium you visited the Hampden Park Ground?
Ayrton. No, Mr Williams the consulting engineer visited it.
Q. So that you really had no data when you designed the thing? (*Wembley Stadium*)
Ayrton. That is so.
Q. You simply designed it out of your head?
Ayrton. Very largely.
(*A discussion follows on the interpretation of what is a stairway and what is a gangway.*)
Q. As far as I can see you really did not go to the people who had practical knowledge in designing, and of great crowds at sports arenas, when you set to work to design the stadium at Wembley?
Ayrton. We had the advantage of many discussions with the Football Association who know a good deal about these grounds.
Q. But the designing of the buildings turned a great deal upon practical experience, as represented by actual dimension?
Ayrton. Yes.
Q. And you had no actual dimensions; you simply put these down out of your head?
Ayrton. And from the various stadiums that I saw.
Q. What did you see before (*you designed Wembley*)?
Ayrton. The only one which I actually saw before, I should think, was the Chelsea ground.
Q. Just that one ground?
Ayrton. Yes.

Engineering Archie 53

London

▲ Family man – the **Leitch family** pose in the studio, it is thought, whilst staying at their summer house in Cliftonville, around 1920.

Archie was now aged 55, and, despite the uncertain state of the nation's economy, was about to embark upon a hectic decade of football ground work.

By then his 29 year old son, **Archibald Kent Leitch** (*right*), was in the family business. In 1927 he became a partner. But only in the 1930s, when his father turned 70, would he assume full control.

Standing behind Archie and his wife Jessie are daughters Nancy (*left*) and Jessie. An older daughter, Jeannie, had died at the age of 22, two years earlier. Tragically, Nancy, who studied art, also died young, at the age of 29, in 1933.

As Archie Jnr did not marry until 1938 – he lived with his parents until the age of 45 – and had no children, Archie had to be content with just two grandchildren, upon whom he doted. These were the son and daughter of Jessie, whose marriage in the Scottish Presbyterian Church of St Columba, in Pont Street, Knightsbridge, was one of the social highlights of north London's large Scots community.

Archie always had a twinkle in his eye, his grandchildren would later recall. He could fill a house with laughter.

» As it happened, the ground's highest ever gate would be 51,482.

But then Archie did like to talk the talk. It had been the same ever since his first magic lantern presentation in front of the Rangers members in March 1899.

As his fellow countryman JM Barrie famously had one of his characters declare in 1908, 'There are few more impressive sights in the world than a Scotsman on the make.'

Archibald Leitch and his family left their home just outside Liverpool during the early months of the First World War.

Judging by the size and location of the house to which they now moved in London, business was better than ever.

Etruria House in Lonsdale Road, Barnes, overlooking the River Thames – formerly the property of a member of the Wedgwood family (hence its name) – was yet one further step up the ladder for the blacksmith's son from Glasgow.

Archie had got this far, we can only assume, from his wider success as a consulting engineer and factory architect.

It was surely not as a result of his earnings from football.

Archie invariably charged clubs five per cent of his fees, out of which he had to pay his everyday business and staff costs.

But with no more than one or two significant football commissions on the go at any one time, plus ongoing routine works for his regular clients – such as Chelsea, Tottenham, Fulham and Everton – this would surely not have been sufficient to deliver him to such pomp in Barnes.

Besides, there would be no football work at all for the company between 1914 – when the war brought a sudden halt to work at Villa Park – and his first post war commission, in 1921, for Dundee.

Not only that, but after only five or six years in Barnes, during the early 1920s the Leitch family moved once again, to an even grander house in the north London suburb of Southgate.

By that stage the pace of football related work had picked up again, and the 1920s would see Archie re-engaged by Tottenham Hotspur (who were now effectively his local club), plus a number of new clients, including Newcastle United, Portsmouth, Wolverhampton Wanderers, Derby County, Southampton and, perhaps surprisingly, the English Rugby Union at Twickenham.

In 1927 he was also called in to oversee the modernisation of Hampden Park, whose wire rope barriers were now conceded to be obsolete. The Leitch patented barrier had finally won the argument, once and for all.

As mentioned earlier, a major disappointment for Archie had been his lack of any involvement in the new Wembley Stadium.

But he compensated for that by working on the two grandstands that, Craven Cottage apart, would represent the pinnacle of his career; the Trinity Road Stand for Aston Villa, completed in 1924, and the South Stand at Ibrox Park for Rangers, opened in 1928-29.

Yet even these two considerable buildings appeared to arouse very little interest from outside the narrow confines of the local and football press.

By contrast, when the respected London architect Claude Ferrier designed a new West Stand for Highbury, in 1932, the architectural press gave it detailed coverage. Similar attention attended the opening »

54 Engineering Archie

▲ Football man – **Archibald Leitch** (*back row, far left*), now aged 62, lines up with the leading football administrators of the day.

Tellingly, he was the only non-affiliated individual present.

The occasion was a meeting of the all powerful **Football League Management Committee** in Newcastle in mid August 1927.

Newcastle United had won the League title that May, and, as was often the custom, hosted the committee's pre-season meeting.

Leitch's presence was hardly a coincidence.

He had, since 1921, been advising Newcastle on various improvements to their St James' Park ground (*see page 150*), and was at the time in the midst of prolonged efforts to persuade United's landlords, Newcastle Corporation and the City Freemen, to relax certain planning restrictions on the site.

In addition to various directors and officials from St James' Park, the group was made up of several of Leitch's past and present clients.

These included Everton's Will Cuff, who was also Leitch's family solicitor (*middle row, third from left*), and in the front row, Fred Rinder of Aston Villa (*far left*), William Hall, formerly of Fulham, now with Arsenal (*second left*), and Arthur Dickenson of Sheffield Wednesday (*second from right*).

Also in the front row was the indefatigable, chain-smoking Charlie Sutcliffe (*third from left*), a former referee and solicitor from Burnley who was once dubbed 'football's dictator' but whose funeral in Rawtenstall in 1939, three months before Leitch's, was filmed by Gaumont British News.

It is unimaginable today that a club architect or consulting engineer would be considered so much a part of the football industry's ruling hierarchy.

But Leitch had worked with many of these individuals for years, and shared not just their love of football but also their powerful work ethic and sense of Christian duty. These men were from the old school of football administration.

Of the 22 First Division clubs that would kick-off the 1927-28 season two weeks after this group picture was taken, 16 had, at one time or another, been clients of Archibald Leitch.

Engineering Archie 55

London

▲ 'The stadium has carried the day against the art museum, and physical reality has taken the place of beautiful illusion.

'Sport merges the individual into the Mass. Sport is becoming the university of collective feeling.'

Hannes Meyer, the Swiss architect and Director of the Bauhaus in the late 1920s had clearly never been to a British football ground.

The physical reality of a typical Leitch ground during the inter-war period had much to commend it, but of 'beautiful illusion' there was little, at least not for players Tom Jackson and Billy Walker, scrubbing down in Leitch's Trinity Road Stand at **Villa Park** in 1927 (*top left*).

True, in the boot room of the South Stand at **Ibrox Park** (*above left*) the individual did rather merge into the mass, but the collective feeling in the dressing room of the South Stand at Portsmouth's **Fratton Park** (*top right*) was more cup of tea than university,

And as for stadiums v. art museums, Blackburn Rovers' boardroom at **Ewood Park** (*above*) fitted out by Leitch, was regarded as the acme of good taste in 1908.

So maybe Leitch's stadiums did carry the day. But it was the workaday they evoked the most.

of Arsenal's East Stand, by Ferrier's partner, William Binnie, four years later (which replaced Archie's original stand at the ground, built in 1913).

In that respect, therefore, it may be said that despite the qualities seen at Fulham, Aston Villa and Rangers, Archie never rattled the doors of the architectural establishment.

Not even the Sentinel Works gained any press.

But whether this lack of recognition bothered Archie or not, it was understandable.

If the Sentinel Works had demonstrated his ability to work in new materials, in a fresh and modern guise, the truth is that none of the many stands he designed after the First World War were especially innovative.

Both the Trinity Road Stand and the South Stand at Ibrox were undoubtedly handsome.

But compared with many of the swooping concrete and cantilevered stands being built elsewhere in the world – in France, Italy, Germany, even Argentina – they took no risks.

Of course a designer is only as good as his or her client, and British football clubs were, and remain, exceptionally cautious and financially driven. Claude Ferrier and William Binnie were fortunate in that respect to catch Arsenal at the time they did.

And it must also be conceded that neither Ferrier or Binnie won any further commissions as a result of their work for Arsenal, admirable though it was.

And so Leitch, and from the mid 1930s, increasingly his son, carried on, right up until the very last stand the company designed – the North Stand at Chelsea, in 1939 – pretty much repeating the same patterns of work.

Archie and Jessie made their final move in 1935, to a brand new semi in Cockfosters, at the end of the Piccadilly Line in north London, just round the corner from their daughter Jessie, her husband and their two children.

Archie called the new house 'Braehead', as it sat at the top of a hill. Fittingly, its frontage was dominated by a standard Tudorbethan pedimented gable, just like the ones he used to put on his grandstands.

Archie, the grandchildren would later recall, was a man full of life and laughter. He and Jessie always had dogs. There always seemed to be excitement when he came home from one of his many trips. From one such trip, to the Caribbean they think, he came home ill after a fall on board ship.

Archibald Leitch died in his bed at Braehead on April 25 1939, two days short of his 74th birthday.

He was buried in the family plot in East Sheen, along with his two daughters, Jeannie and Nancy.

A brief notice appeared in the journal of the Institute of Mechanical Engineers. It stated that Leitch was a consulting engineer and a factory architect.

There was no mention of football grounds, and no other obituaries have been found.

Twentieth century football's designer-in-chief died a forgotten man.

After his death, Archibald Kent Leitch carried on the business for a further ten years. But the outbreak of war, and its aftermath, virtually ended the prospects of any meaningful work in football.

There were a few jobs in the late 1940s; routine work for Millwall and Fulham. The North Stand at Stamford Bridge also needed finishing off. But it was a poor stand, and would be demolished in 1976. Archie Junior also submitted plans for a stand on the riverside terrace at Craven Cottage in 1950. But it proved too expensive for the club and was dropped.

The last listing for Archibald Leitch and Partners appears in 1955. It is believed Archie Junior retired the following year.

The company therefore operated for exactly 60 years.

Archie Leitch, wrote his old friend, the Spurs director and journalist, George Wagstaffe Simmons, in 1946, 'possessed a fertile brain, allied with an almost uncanny perception of the possibilities of sites.'

Fertile brain? Uncanny perception?

No Scot, no engineer, could wish for higher praise.

Archie is introduced to the Duke of Gloucester at the Football League's Jubilee Banquet, at the Dorchester Hotel in May 1938. Many old friends and clients were there, including Will Cuff of Everton, Fred Rinder of Aston Villa, Morton Cadman and Charlie Roberts of Tottenham, and Ernie Edwards of the *Liverpool Echo*. This is the last known photograph of Archie. Eleven months later he was dead.

Engineering Archie 57

Chapter Seven
Grounds

Narrow minded – the transfer gate leading from Portsmouth's Fratton End terrace to the enclosure of Leitch's South Stand. At some grounds thousands of fans were able to change ends at half time via such transfer gates.

The twenty-nine grounds featured in this section represent the main sports-related commissions carried out by Archibald Leitch's company in England and Scotland during the period 1899-1939.

Not counting terraces and basic terrace covers, Leitch was responsible for at least 46 individual stands and pavilions in England and Scotland, and possibly as many as 51.

Of the total, twelve structures (eleven of them stands) survive in one form or another as of early 2005, the oldest two being the Stevenage Road Stand and pavilion at Craven Cottage, Fulham, both completed in 1905.

Although Archie's son, Archibald Kent Leitch, carried on the business after his father's death in 1939, no new clients or substantial football-related works were secured after 1945, and, as mentioned earlier, the company ceased trading in around 1955.

The entries are presented in chronological order, beginning at the date either when we know Leitch first became involved with the particular client, or, if not known exactly, when his first stand or terrace for that client was completed. An exception to this approach is Leitch's work for Rangers, which is divided into two periods to provide greater clarity and a sense of context.

In several instances Leitch's work was carried out over a concentrated period of one or two years, such as at Anfield, Dens Park and Fratton Park. At others Leitch's services were engaged on a regular basis on a broad range of ground-related matters, most of them fairly mundane. In particular the company carried on working for Rangers, Fulham, Chelsea, Everton, Tottenham, Sunderland, Wolves and Derby for periods spanning from 10-40 years.

Inevitably the level of data that survives for each ground is variable.

Rangers, Manchester United, Wolves, Aston Villa and Hearts maintain comprehensive archives, all of which have proved invaluable. Manchester United and Arsenal also have excellent club museums.

Other club records have been traced to private collections.

But many clubs have simply destroyed their early minute books, correspondence and archives, or lost them to fire, negligence or even theft.

Local authority building and planning archives have yielded a surprising number of Leitch plans, particularly in Glasgow and London (under the auspices of the London Metropolitan Archive, where the records of the London County Council are kept).

From various libraries, agencies, public and private collections we have also unearthed a wealth of photographic material, although again this has tended to be more comprehensive in the larger cities.

Individual club historians have proved a rich source of archive material and knowledge, as have the National Football Museum at Preston and the Scottish Football Museum at Hampden Park.

All are to be thanked for recording and conserving such a key part of Britain's popular cultural and architectural heritage.

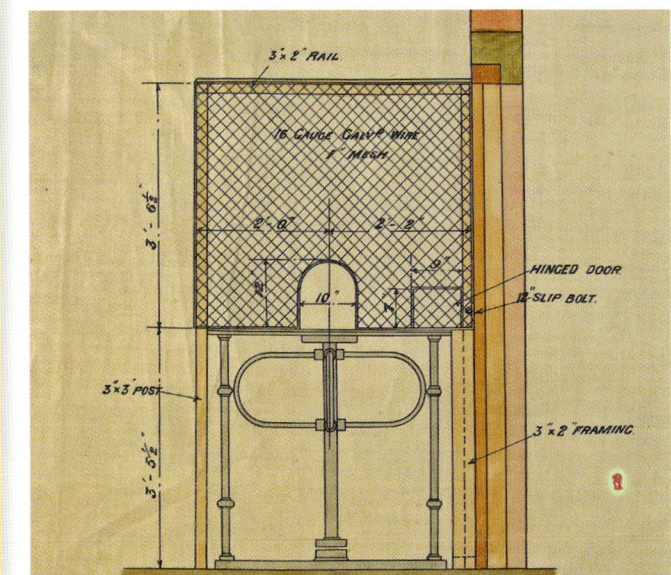

▲ Archibald Leitch had regular dealings with a number of suppliers and manufacturers, but none were more crucial to the management of 20th century football grounds than the products of the Salford engineers, WT Ellison & Co.

Their **Rush Preventive Turnstile**, invented in approximately 1895, was fitted to a huge number of sportsgrounds, swimming pools, piers, zoos, parks, gardens, exhibition halls, ferry terminals and even public toilets. (For an account of their development see *Played in Manchester*, the first book in the *Played in Britain* series).

This Ellison advertisement from the 1937-38 *Athletic News Football Annual* lists 23 of Leitch's clients in English and Scottish football.

▲ Three hours before kick-off, **Arsenal** supporters queue outside Leitch's turnstile block in Avenell Road, Highbury, in August 1936 (*top*). Once through the gate they would enter a dark, enclosed passage such as the one shown above, extracted from Leitch's drawings for Anfield in 1906. WT Ellison & Co. claimed that each Rush Preventive turnstile could process 4,000 entrants per hour, or 3,000 if change had to be sorted.

The heavy metal clunk that accompanied each turn of the spindle brought immense relief – after all that interminable queuing you were in! But also a tremor. You were about to enter what JB Priestley memorably described as 'another and altogether more splendid kind of life.'

Engineering Archie 59

Sheffield United

Grounds

Bramall Lane, Sheffield 1900–01

Football's surge in popularity during the late Victorian period coincided with the advent of mass produced colour postcards. As one of the leading teams of the early 1900s, Sheffield United were ripe for commercial exploitation. This was one of several so-called 'Write Away' postcards produced by Raphael Tuck & Sons of London. Frank Reynolds, the artist, also worked for *Punch* and the *Illustrated London News*.

Having established his credentials at the highest possible level of Scottish football, with Rangers, Archibald Leitch won his first commission south of the border in December 1900.

At the time, more prestigious clients than Sheffield United could hardly be imagined. The Blades had won their first League title in 1898, only nine years after the club's formation. A year later they won the FA Cup.

Their chairman was Charles Clegg, chairman also of the Football Association, and in Bramall Lane – purchased from the Duke of Norfolk in 1899 for £10,134 – they possessed one of Britain's best known arenas.

First laid out for cricket in 1855, in 1863 it had become Yorkshire's county headquarters. Football was first played there in 1862. Bowls, tennis, cycling and athletics followed later. In 1878 the ground made history by staging the first football match played under electric light, an event drawing an estimated 20,000 crowd, the largest gathering ever to see a game outside of Glasgow.

Bramall Lane also staged England's first ever home international played outside London, against Scotland in 1883. A year later it then claimed the largest crowd yet to have attended a cricket match, at least officially, when 20,700 attended a game against the Australians in 1884.

But by the time Leitch was called in, it was evident that the winter game was by far the more profitable.

As we learned in Chapter Two, Leitch – then in partnership with Harry Davies – first made contact with United in April 1900, when they visited his recently completed Ibrox Park for a friendly.

Six weeks later he wrote to the club offering to prepare a 'General Plan of Stand Accommodation' for Bramall Lane. Whether he wrote to other clubs in a similar vein is not known. But the letter certainly proved timely, because the following November United's mainly wooden football stand, located on John Street, directly opposite the recently completed cricket pavilion, was badly damaged by fire. According to the *Sheffield Telegraph* the stand, though barely five years old, was 'not a thing of beauty'. Nor did its internal arrangements 'conform to present ideas'.

United contacted Leitch and Davies soon after, and in March 1901 their first designs were approved. As became his usual practice, Leitch took the added precaution of having a large model, six feet long, made up to impress the directors. (Alas not one of these has survived.)

He also invited the same Glasgow firm with whom he had worked on his first football commissions, Kilmarnock and Rangers (as well as several factory buildings) – the Clyde Structural Iron Company – to tender for the steelwork. They won the contract with a price of £1,929 15s 1d.

The remaining construction work added a further £3,000 to the bill, but this was well within the club's means, given their ongoing success, and included other works carried out at the same time, such as the removal of the cycle and athletics track and various other improvements to the terracing.

The John Street Stand at Bramall Lane, photographed from the cricket pavilion. Behind the stand lies St Mary's Church, b.1830, and still extant.

As illustrated above, Leitch's first stand in England was a straightforward, though tidy design, with covered seating for 3,800, and an enclosure in front for 6,000 standing spectators on 25 rows of terracing.

Of course its most eye catching feature was its prominent roof-top press box, in which up to 60 seats on four rows were provided.

But the stand was also said to have been the first in the United Kingdom 'to be lighted by electric light'. In addition, a 100 yard warm-up track was provided underneath the seating tier.

One idea which did not catch on was the provision of separate players' tunnels for each team (seen above on either side of the white sight screen).

While this arrangement was known in the cricket world – at grounds where amateurs and professionals often had separate changing rooms – it was hardly common in football, and would eventually be superseded by a single, central tunnel in 1923.

Otherwise, the stand, which opened in September 1901, represented an admirable calling card for Leitch's new line of business, and would often be featured in the press. For example, in 1902, shortly after United had won the FA Cup a second time, the ground staged a Test Match against Australia, followed in 1903 by another visit by Scotland for a football international.

Alas for Sheffield, also that year Yorkshire decamped to Headingley where they have remained ever since. But cricket continued to be played at the ground until 1973, and although Leitch's stand was badly damaged by bombs in 1940, its core survived until finally replaced by a new stand in 1996.

Engineering Archie 61

Sheffield United

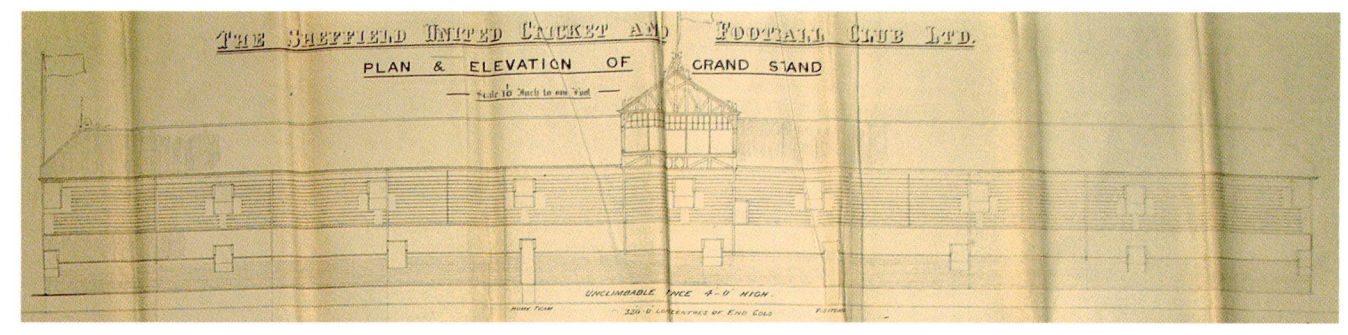

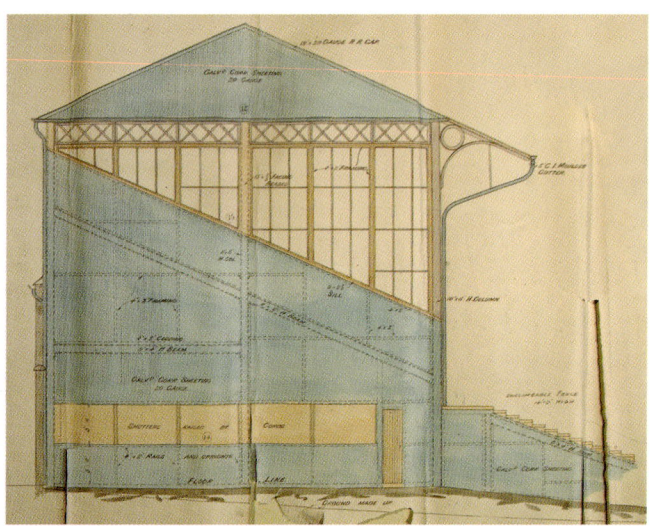

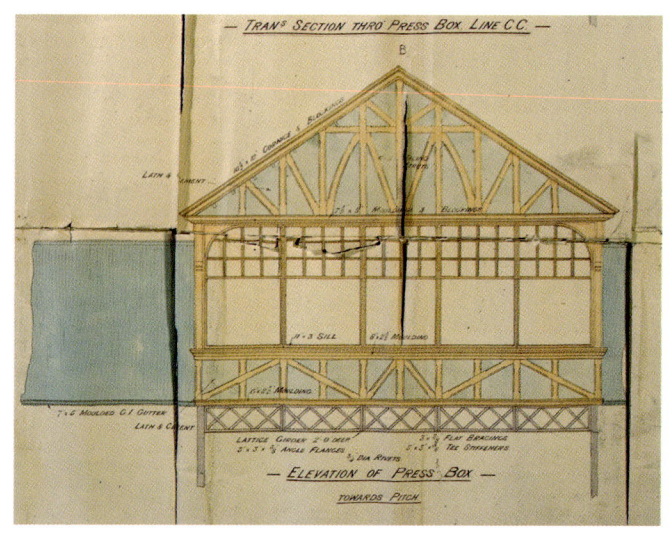

▲ These creased, flaking drawings of the **John Street Stand**, submitted in early 1901 and now preserved in the Sheffield City Archives, are typical of the draughtsmanship emanating from Leitch's office in the pre-1914 period.

The stand's specifications were as follows: 330 feet in length (on a grid of 7' 6" centres) x 36 feet wide x 33 feet high to the eaves. Materials used were to be iron framing and 'strong wood covered in corrugated iron'.

There were 13 pay boxes, eight WCs and four urinals for males, and just one WC for females (a not untypical ratio for the period).

Interestingly, a note from Leitch's office attached to the plans, referring either to the stand enclosure or to another area of the ground which Leitch was also asked to improve, confirmed that the steppings were to be constructed in steel and concrete, rather than iron and wood, as previously proposed and rejected by Sheffield Corporation. This, it should be noted, was still several months before the Ibrox disaster.

The press box, its pediment dressed in lath and cement mock-Tudor detailing, and accessed via a narrow staircase at the rear of the stand, was 47 feet above ground level at its highest point. Though such confined, elevated boxes would scarcely be allowed under modern fire and safety regulations, they were common enough during Leitch's time, and would remain in use at some grounds right up until the 1980s.

The roof-top position was favoured originally, it is thought, not only to provide a clear view over the pitch (although in reality the window frames often proved a barrier to decent vision), but also because a higher vantage point made the release of carrier pigeons easier in the days before telephones.

▶ Bramall Lane in 1933, with Leitch's **John Street Stand** on the right, facing the cricket pavilion. Even though the ground extended to nearly 12 acres, and there was room enough for a large bowling green and practice pitches behind the Shoreham Street terrace (later the Kop), there was never quite enough space to divide the site into two distinct cricket and football areas, as at Yorkshire's two other first class grounds, Headingley (see page 41) and Bradford (page 95).

This resulted in a ground that was neither fish nor fowl. The concrete terracing made for uncomfortable accommodation for a cricket audience, while football fans could view properly from only three sides of the pitch – an unnerving experience, particularly for visiting teams.

When Bramall Lane recorded its highest ever attendance of 68,287, for a match against Leeds in February 1936, thousands of fans were forced to watch from the cricket pavilion side. However, as a heavy mist descended, many surged forward, over the cricket pitch, to get closer to the touchline. Yet there was no disorder. As the *Sheffield Telegraph* reported, 'What a disciplined race we are. On the Continent or in America, folk would have not been so orderly.'

Orderly or not, there was only one other ground of this type in Britain, and that was Northampton's County Ground, finally vacated by the football club in 1994.

At Bramall Lane it was football that prevailed. A stand built in front of the cricket pavilion finally gave United a conventional four sided ground in 1975. But in the process it robbed Sheffield, and British sport generally, of one of its most eccentric and historic arenas.

Leitch's John Street Stand after a German air raid in December 1940. Although the stand was largely restored, the magnificent press box survived only in a truncated form.

Rangers

Grounds
Ibrox Park, Glasgow Part One 1902–28

For all parties concerned, the repercussions of the April 1902 disaster were severe.

For the Scottish FA, their initial offer of £3,000 to the Appeal Fund – donated in the hope of staving off litigation – left them with only £22 in the bank.

For Rangers, £9,000 in debt and facing the mammoth task of not only rebuilding their terraces but also their scarred reputation – for greed, for appearing to cut corners, and, as far as the Catholic half of the city was concerned, simply for being Rangers – the challenges were immense.

To recap briefly, at the time of the disaster they had just recorded their fourth League championship in a row. Though less successful in the Cup, they were still the dominant force in Scottish football. But to pay for the reconstruction of Ibrox Park they had to put all twenty two players up for sale, at a stroke paving the way for Celtic to overtake them as Glasgow's leading club.

Although they won the Cup again in 1903, not until 1911 would the League trophy return to Ibrox.

As for the potential income from England internationals, that evaporated with the opening of Hampden Park in 1903.

For Archibald Leitch, his retention by Rangers after the disaster – following their initial approach to architect, John Gordon – offered a vital step towards his rehabilitation.

The first evidence that Archie was back in favour is a set of revised plans dated July 30 1902.

Surprising as it may seem, under these plans two thirds of the controversial wooden terracing would remain in use for the next two years. Only the rear section of west terrace, where the collapse occurred, was dismantled, reducing the depth by four bays from 112 feet to 50ft.

All remaining sections were meanwhile strengthened by the addition of intermediate joists, in pitch pine – a tacit admission that perhaps Leitch's critics had been right to question his original design, though hardly an outright rejection of the system *per se*. (In fact, similar terracing would be found at football grounds around the world for much of the 20th century, particularly in South America, even in recent years.)

But even if the strengthened sections were now perfectly safe, in the interest of public relations they could hardly stay.

Thus once Rangers had negotiated the purchase of the site, in 1904, for £15,000, the inevitable process of raising solid embankments began in earnest, helped considerably the fortuitous excavation of a railway cutting alongside Ibrox at the same time.

Terracing the banks with patented Leitch barriers cost a further £15,000, meaning that from their original estimate of £12,000 in May 1899, the new Ibrox had cost Rangers nearer £45,000.

Although they wore royal blue, as shown on this postcard published by Valentine's of Dundee, Rangers were nicknamed the Light Blues. This was to differentiate them from the Scottish national team, who play in dark blue. The name Rangers was chosen from an English rugby annual by Moses McNeil, one of four brothers from the Gare Loch area who founded the club on Glasgow Green in 1873.

Ibrox Park in 1910, with the roof that John Gordon designed for the old Ibrox in 1892, re-erected over the north terrace. Notice its curved gable, a feature echoed by Leitch in several of his later stands.

64 Engineering Archie

▶ This early 1920s view of Ibrox Park – note the name marked out in chalk on the back of the west terrace – shows how the ground evolved from 1904 onwards.

The most significant change was of course the raising of solid earth embankments, thus extending the ground's footprint at either end. Before this Rangers had considered selling some of their spare land for tenements. (Incidentally the tenements seen behind the east, or so-called 'Rangers End' were built on the site of the earlier Ibrox Park.)

Both side stands and the pavilion (*in the top right hand corner, and below right*) were otherwise as Leitch laid them out in 1899.

On the left is the **North Stand**, the front section of which was salvaged from the old Ibrox Park.

On the right is the **South Stand**, Leitch's own design, which featured a roof top 'telegraph and press box' similar to the one he would provide for Sheffield United (*see page 61*).

Unfortunately no detailed images of this stand survive – it was replaced by another Leitch design in 1928 (*see page 181ff*) – but from the plans we find that it had bench seats for 5,715 spectators, with a steel frame and corrugated iron roof; clearly a less developed building than was the pavilion.

Note how much spare land there existed between the back of the South Stand and the unmade roadway behind (now Edmiston Drive). Its replacement would fill that entire space.

As the years went by Leitch increased Ibrox's banking, so that the capacity crept up from around 50,000 in 1907 to nearer 83,000 by the early 1920s.

By then Glasgow could boast the world's three largest football grounds; Ibrox, Celtic Park and Hampden Park (neither of which, contrary to earlier accounts of his career, Archie had worked on, although he was subsequently engaged at Hampden in 1927).

But despite the more robust nature of Ibrox Park, there were frequent signs that in one crucial respect the lessons of 1902 were not heeded, either by Rangers, or any of the country's other clubs.

Rush Preventive Ellison turnstiles may have assisted in the control of admissions. But there was still no real attempt to limit numbers on a calculated basis. Gates were simply shut when no further fans could be squeezed inside.

Rangers thus found themselves targeted only three years after the disaster, when another crush occurred during the traditional New Year, or Ne'erday match v. Celtic.

The *Glasgow Star*, admittedly a newspaper sympathetic to Celtic, said of Rangers' attitude, 'The money's the thing.'

Yet in truth Celtic were no different. Income was invariably put before safety at every ground in the country. Solid banking and Leitch's patented barriers and terraces may therefore have represented a useful advance. But without regulation, or applied crowd management techniques, the nation's football grounds continued to be fraught with potential risk.

Other than the concrete perimeter wall, which replaced the iron railings installed for the ill-fated international in 1902, and some minor differences to the detailing, the Ibrox pavilion was much as Leitch designed it in 1899 (*see page 17*). One player from this period recalled how long the climb up the steps to the dressing rooms seemed after a hard game.

Engineering Archie 65

Grounds

Ayresome Park, Middlesbrough 1903–37

After the court proceedings which followed the Ibrox disaster in 1902, Archibald Leitch must have wondered if his short-lived career as a stadium builder had come to a premature end.

His regular business continued to flourish. Indeed in 1903 he started planning perhaps his finest industrial building to date, the Sentinel Works in Glasgow (see page 35). But apart from the John Street Stand at Bramall Lane, completed in 1901, Rangers were then his only clients from the football world.

Yet if Leitch was tainted by Ibrox in some circles, as surely he was, the directors of Middlesbrough had no such qualms.

Besides, they were in fix.

Although the club were by then well established – having formed in 1876 and turned professional in 1899 – shortly after Christmas 1902 they were give notice to quit from their existing home at the Linthorpe Road cricket ground. This was half way through their debut season in the First Division.

Finding a site was no problem. Boro had already started preparing a new ground at Ayresome Park, which they planned to complete by 1904. But now they had just eight months to complete the task.

In January 1903 Boro invited tenders for the ground construction. Whether Leitch spotted the advertisements, or whether he was already working for the club, is not known. What is clear is that the resultant stand was straight from the pattern book of the firm with which Leitch often worked, the Clyde Structural Iron Company of Glasgow.

Boro had specified a stand measuring 75 yards long, to seat 2,000 spectators, costing no more than £1,750. Leitch and Clyde were able to supply one 92 yards long for £1,521.

Fitting out the stand with the usual dressing rooms, offices, a gymnasium and billiard room – the latter apparently *de rigueur* for professionals of the day – added further costs, as did the dumping of thousands of tons of spoil to form the banking on three sides. Also, opposite the new stand, the club's existing stand from the cricket ground was re-erected, joist by joist, slate by slate, thereby taking the total cost to just short of £12,000, for a total capacity put at 33,000.

Hardly surprisingly the new stand was not quite finished in time for the official inauguration on September 12 1903, a League match against neighbours Sunderland, watched by 30,000.

But it was an undoubted success. 'Every enclosure was filled with an eager throng,' reported the *Evening Gazette*, 'and thin lines of smoke told of the consumption of much tobacco.'

For reasons unclear the opening ceremony was performed by a Londoner best known as a pioneer of electric trams, James Clifton Robinson. (If Leitch did attend, the two would surely have found much to discuss. The Sentinel company for whom Leitch was also working at the time built steam powered lorries.)

Middlesbrough, meanwhile, were about to go off the rails. As the initial rush of enthusiasm subsided and the team looked certain to drop into the Second Division – which would have

Building a new ground is one thing; filling it, another. Having spent nearly £12,000 on Ayresome Park in 1903, Boro were so desperate for success that in February 1905 they paid neighbours Sunderland a record breaking £1,000 for centre forward Alf Common. The rest of the football world was aghast.

severely hampered the club's ability to pay its debts on the ground – they lavished £1,000 on Sunderland's Alf Common.

This turned Boro into pariahs, and sparked off investigations that culminated in eleven of their twelve directors being suspended for illegal payments. Subsequent probes then led to the new chairman, a local Tory politician, being banned for bribery in 1911.

Boro were not alone in their waywardness. Football then was as venal a business as ever it would become. Moreover the club did manage to find an even keel and by 1912 not only pay for Ayresome Park's construction but also purchase the site.

For Leitch Ayresome was also of great significance. Though hardly a work of great sophistication, it was his first complete stadium, purpose built for football. Nor could he have wished for a better showcase than the First Division, most of whose members were in the process of upgrading or moving to new grounds.

Back in Glasgow, in 1903 Leitch moved his young family to a detached villa in Pollokshields, one of the city's better suburbs.

Clearly, despite Ibrox, his confidence had not diminished.

Leitch often provided exquisite sketches of his company's ground proposals, although there is nothing to indicate that he was ever the artist. This example, dated August 1903, is the earliest known, and the only one in colour. The artist may not have been a football fan, because the twelve yard line illustrated here was replaced by the penalty area as we know it today in 1902.

Engineering Archie 67

Middlesbrough

▶ 'Well Saved Williamson' reads the caption on this postcard, showing Boro keeper Tim Williamson in action against Small Heath, two weeks after Ayresome Park's opening in 1903.

Originally Boro's **North Stand** had ten columns supporting its distinctive barrel roof. These were reduced to four (*see below right*) before the ground hosted three matches in the 1966 World Cup.

In its final decade seemingly every surface at Ayresome Park was decked in red, including the Leitch patented crush barriers at the Holgate End, whose cover was added in 1937 (*see opposite*).

Another familiar feature of the North Stand was its semi-circular roof gable, which, unusually, was glazed, suggesting that it may have been intended to house an elevated press box (as was provided when the Clyde Structural Iron Company built a similar stand for Newcastle United two years later). Leitch himself echoed the semi-circular gable at Liverpool in 1906.

For many years Boro's gable was covered by an advert for McEwan's 80/- beer (*also shown on the back cover*). This was one of 1300 items auctioned before the ground was demolished in 1995 and is now on display, along with other Boro related memorabilia, in the Ayresome Park pub, on Albert Road, close to the former ground.

68 Engineering Archie

▲ This second pen and ink drawing of **Ayresome Park**, dating from 1936, was drawn by the Leitch company's regular artist of the period, who signed himself simply as 'Macdonald'.

It illustrates Leitch's scheme for two major additions.

At the **Holgate End** a cover was erected at a cost of £2,714, while a new two-tier **South Stand** (to replace the original Linthorpe Road stand), added a further £13,047.

Both were constructed by Dorman Long and Co., who more recently played a major role in the construction of the dramatic roof of the new Wembley Stadium.

As can be seen, the South Stand (see also page 197) was a rather more prosaic structure, typical of Leitch's low budget stands of the period. Indeed Boro historian Eric Paylor (see Links) has noted that Dorman Long had wanted to erect a clock on the stand roof (as there was on Sunderland's new Clock Stand, also built by Leitch and completed the previous year). But the directors baulked at the extra cost of £110.

The South Stand was opened by the Football League's now ageing stalwart, Charlie Sutcliffe, in September 1937. If Leitch, then aged 72, also attended, this may well have been the last stand opening before his death in 1939. By this time his son, Archibald Kent Leitch, was running the business.

Ayresome would subsequently record its largest ever crowd of 53,802 in December 1949.

The East End was finally covered, and seated, for the 1966 World Cup, by which time the capacity had dropped to 42,000. In 1995, when the ground was vacated, the limit was 24,211.

Housing now occupies the site, but the ground is suitably commemorated by a delightful series of artworks dotted around the estate, as shown on page 201.

Engineering Archie **69**

Fulham

Grounds
Craven Cottage, London 1904–50

The Bible tells us that no man may serve two masters.

But in the years 1904 and 1905 Archibald Leitch did just that, by somehow managing to work for two powerful, strong-headed men who were not only near neighbours but also deadly rivals.

Much is made in modern times of the influence and might of wealthy football club chairmen.

But it was no different in Archie's day, and in some ways the chairmen with whom he had to deal exerted more influence than their modern counterparts in that, by their actions, they created and shaped the very map of British football.

No more so than in London, and in particular, in west London.

Fulham Football Club had been playing at their Craven Cottage ground on the banks of the River Thames since 1896. It was a pleasant enough location, if hardly promising in terms of its access to public transport or in the density of its local population.

In other words, it was not an obvious berth for an aspiring professional football club.

In 1903 the club built its first stand at the ground; the odd looking temporary stand which soon became the subject of a legal case in which Leitch was eventually called as a witness (see page 40).

The exact sequence of events is not clear, but it would seem that in early 1904, while the argument over the stand's licence was first brewing, Leitch was invited down to London to draw up plans for the modernisation of Craven Cottage.

Fulham's dominant director at the time, Henry Norris, was the same age as Leitch, and had risen from humble origins to amass a fortune as a speculative house builder in the area. He also wielded considerable clout in local affairs, becoming Mayor of Fulham in 1909 and gaining a knighthood in 1917.

Football historians have generally cast Norris as a bully.

But Craven Cottage would not have existed today without him.

Leitch's first scheme for Norris (see opposite), dated May 1904, was for an 80,000 capacity ground which Norris intended to put forward for use as a Cup Final venue. But although this was Archie's first venture in London football circles, the resultant plans were hardly impressive.

Meanwhile, also in 1904, a few miles away, another building mogul, Gus Mears, had bought a large and well established athletics ground called Stamford Bridge.

Like Norris, Mears' intention was to turn his ground into London's finest sporting arena.

Mears was in a much stronger position, however. He owned his site, whereas Fulham were only tenants. Also, Stamford Bridge was next door to both a railway and an underground station.

By contrast, Craven Cottage was decidedly not well connected.

As the months passed and Leitch's plans for Craven Cottage

Actually Fulham were founded in 1879, but, like this cartouche on the Stevenage Road façade, that is but a detail. More important is that the stand and its adjacent pavilion, built in 1905, are the oldest football works of Archibald Leitch still extant, and the only ones in England to be listed. Fulham's 6.3 acres of riverside real estate have, for the last 20 years been 'a block of flats waiting to happen'. But in 2004 the ground's future was at last assured. Contrary to all expectations therefore, this is a story with a happy ending.

Fulham 'façadism' revealed, as a record 41,000 crowd gathers to see the club knock out the mighty Manchester United from the Cup in 1908. Note the undeveloped plot to the left. As revealed opposite, had things worked out differently the scene above might well have been reversed.

70 Engineering Archie

appeared to be faltering, Mears offered an obvious solution.

He invited Fulham to become tenants of the new stadium he was planning at Stamford Bridge.

The offer made perfect sense. Mears had the site and the space. Norris had a club, albeit then only a Southern League club of no great rank. But a club with a local following and good prospects.

At least one member of the Fulham board was in favour of accepting the offer, even though Mears was proposing a fairly hefty rental of £1,500 per annum.

But Norris was unwilling to play second fiddle to another man's ambitions, which left Mears two options; either to sell Stamford Bridge for a quick profit or, to carry on with his plans and form his own football club to play there.

He decided on the latter, and thus was born Chelsea FC.

Whether Mears was already in contact with Leitch by the time he made this decision is not clear. But Archie was certainly working for Mears by at least December 1904 because work on the new Stamford Bridge commenced soon after.

We also know that in late January 1905 Leitch attended the court case concerning Fulham's stand. Also, that within days of the hearing the *West London and Fulham Times* reported that Fulham had obtained a 99 year lease on Craven Cottage and that redevelopment would soon start there too.

Thus between January and September 1905 Leitch found himself working on two major stadium projects within a few miles of each other, and for two club chairmen who were now in direct competition.

Not a bad way for an aspiring engineer from Glasgow to get noticed on London's emerging »

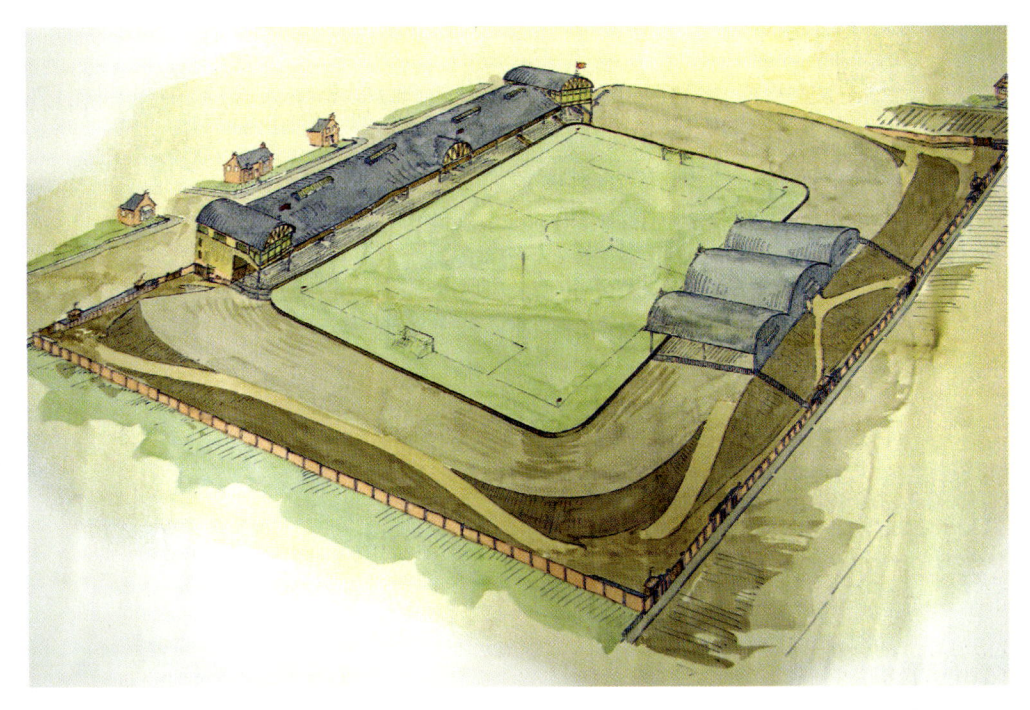

▲ Dated May 21 1904 this hand tinted, almost cartoon-like drawing, was the Leitch company's original design for the new **Craven Cottage**.

From a stylistic point of view it is unlike any of Leitch's other sketches, and may well have been the effort of an office junior.

Other, more precise sections (not shown) show a stand with wing pavilions on stilts, as seen above; for directors at one end, press at the other. An odd notion indeed.

Another drawing gives the capacity as no less than 80,000.

But here's the twist. These hitherto unseen drawings are not for the site we know today as Craven Cottage, but for one directly opposite, bounded by Stevenage Road, Woodlawn Road, Kenyon Street and Greswell Street.

So, what was the story?

In September 1904 the *West London and Fulham Times* reported that although Fulham were now intent on the scheme above, had gained approval from the London County Council, and were offering shares in the enterprise, they were not getting the desired response.

'Fulham tradesmen have proved themselves very, very poor sportsmen,' commented the newspaper, which appeared to be a mouthpiece for Norris.

As was his way, Norris therefore tried a bit of pump-priming.

In November it was 'rumoured' that this new ground was likely to replace Crystal Palace as the venue for Cup Finals (frankly, an absurd notion, given its scale and location).

Yet a month later more 'rumours' had it that Fulham would, after all, move to Stamford Bridge the following season, because Fulham were 'a little disgusted' by the poor support shown by tradesmen in the Craven Cottage area.

Yet ony a few weeks after that – during which time Fulham, and Leitch, had appeared in court over the licensing of their temporary stand (*see page 40*) – it was revealed that a 99 year lease for the existing Craven Cottage site had been secured and redevelopment was to start in the summer.

Of the scheme above, no more was heard. Until shown here.

So, was Norris serious about this alternative site? Or, as a property developer, did he merely conclude there was more profit to be made from building houses on it, as indeed happened? (Harbord Street now runs through its centre.)

Or, was he merely hoping to stymie Mears' own plans for a rival club at Stamford Bridge?

With Norris it is hard to tell.

Still, it is a colourful sketch all the same, and probably just as well that it never left the drawing board.

Engineering Archie 71

Fulham

football circuit, if a potentially fraught strategy all the same.

Stamford Bridge we will come to in the next section.

As for Craven Cottage, the Clyde Structural Iron Company were again hired to provide the steelwork. Construction started in early May. By late August 150 men were working day and night, right up to the opening match.

As the ground had been in use for nine years by that stage most of the banking – raised using excavations from the Shepherd's Bush underground – was already in place. These banks were now terraced and fitted with a type of crush barrier Leitch would patent the following year (see pages 28-31).

But the main effort focused on the pavilion and a 5,000 seat stand – virtually a carbon copy of the one already designed and approved for Stamford Bridge – and the stand's ornate brick frontage.

If this frontage's style was at the behest of Norris, who was, after all, a house builder, it was certainly a major task to complete in the time allotted. (It was also in distinct contrast to the stripped modernity of Leitch's recent Sentinel works, see page 35.)

Nor was it cheap. The new Craven Cottage cost £15,000, compared with the £12,000 Middlesbrough had paid for a new ground built from scratch.

But it was rather fine all the same and was opened on September 2 1905 in front of a 20,000 crowd.

Two days later, the new Stamford Bridge opened in front of a mere 6,000, which must have put a smile on Norris's face.

But not for long.

From 1906 onwards, Chelsea's attendances would shoot up, outstripping those of Fulham every single season until the present day.

Henry Norris had backed the wrong horse, and he knew it.

In 1910 in an attempt to bring instant First Division football to the Cottage he took over Woolwich Arsenal and tried to merge them with Fulham. But that strategem failed, and so he abandoned Fulham and hatched a plan for a stadium elsewhere in the capital.

It was called Highbury, and its architect would be Archie Leitch.

Thus the football map of London was carved out by one man's ruthless ambition.

No chairman today has anything like that level of power or influence. Though if you were the designer of two of his grounds, you would hardly complain.

72 Engineering Archie

▲ Club photographers, Moyse of Putney High Street, captured this panoramic view of Fulham's **Craven Cottage** for *The Book of Football*, published in 1906.

'No Southern League club of recent years has made such rapid progress,' read the accompanying caption. 'Even those who knew the playing field at Craven Cottage a year ago are astounded at the wonderful transformation that has been made.'

Intriguingly, Leitch's corner pavilion, known ever since as the Cottage (*far right*), has yet to have its verandah added, even though it formed part of the original plans.

It may also be noted that although the rooftop gable's timber detailing has not altered since 1905 (*see page 1 and back cover*), the voids under the pediment suggest that Leitch may have allowed for the creation of a press box. This however never materialised.

(The original 18th century Craven Cottage, incidentally, after which the site was named, was located roughly where the central part of the stand was built.)

Moyse's photograph offers an early view of what would become Leitch's standard form of terrace layout, with sunken aisles and lateral gangways, just discernible amid the crowds on the Riverside terrace (*left*) and far Hammersmith End. (*For the plans, see page 28.*)

The Book of Football certainly thought the terraces 'quite perfect'.

Note the trees lining the rear of the Riverside Terrace. These were all that remained of the woods which occupied the site until Fulham's arrival in 1894. Only one, a plane tree, survives today in a corner of the Putney end, the sole tree to be found within a senior football venue anywhere in England, and now, happily, the subject of a preservation order.

Leitch claimed that the new Craven Cottage would hold 60,000 on its three sides of open terracing, plus 3,000 in the enclosure and 5,000 seats in the stand.

In fact, despite very few changes to the ground over the next fifty years, the highest ever gate was 49,335, for the visit of Millwall in October 1938.

According to the *The Book of Football*, when the site was first being cleared by Fulham, a tunnel was discovered, leading to Barnes, on the opposite side of the river.

Though unlikely, if true it was soon submerged under six feet of soil, dumped on the site to raise the pitch above the high tide level.

Engineering Archie 73

Fulham

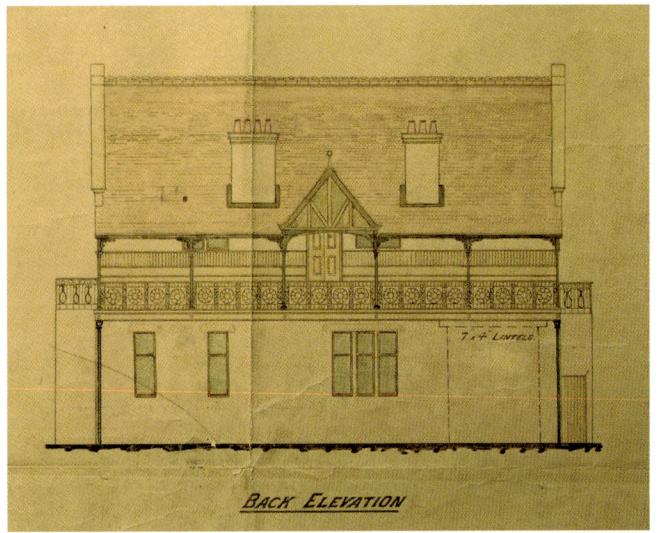

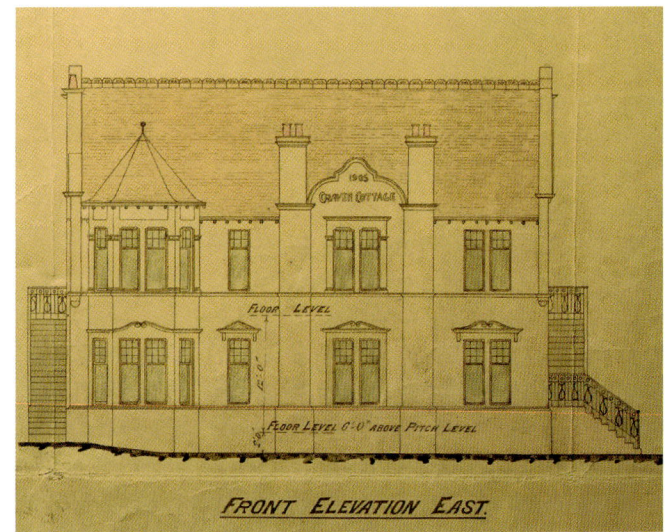

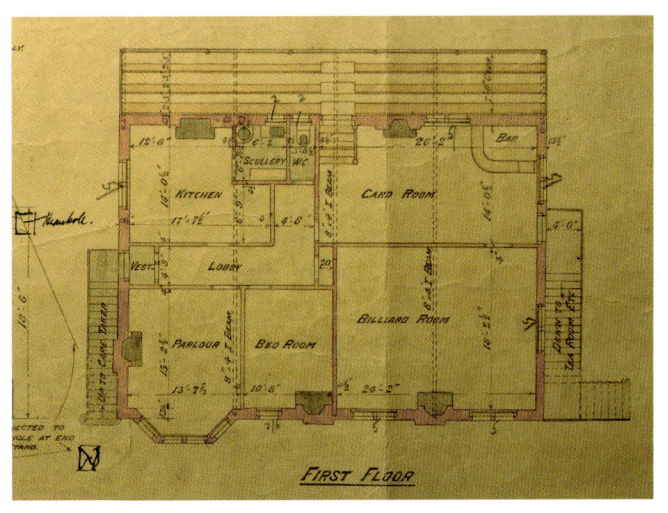

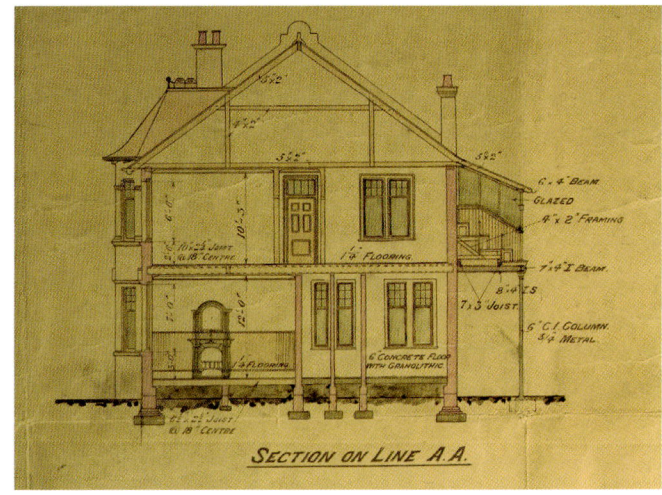

▲ Fulham's Grade II listed **Craven Cottage** (the building that is, rather than the ground as a whole) is the only surviving detached pavilion at a senior football ground in Britain.

Even at the time of its erection in 1905 the fashion for separate pavilions was dying out, as facilities for players, directors and club officials were integrated into grandstands – although they remained the fashion in Scotland until well into the 20th century. Leitch himself designed a fine one at Ibrox in 1899 (*see page 17*).

But there were two good reasons to provide a pavilion at Fulham.

Firstly, there was insufficient space between Stevenage Road and the near touchline – barely 90 feet at the narrowest point – to provide a main stand deep enough to incorporate the full range of facilities needed, at least not without building higher than would have been desirable given the low rise streetscape in the vicinity.

Secondly, the site's historical connections made the idea of a separate pavilion an obvious one. The original 18th century Craven Cottage, once a royal hunting lodge, had been destroyed by fire

74 Engineering Archie

in 1888 (which is why the site had become available in the first place), so why not build a new Craven Cottage in its place?

As Leitch's original drawings show, the building housed not only offices, dressing rooms, a billiard room and card room, but also a compact, one bedroom caretaker's flat. Club captain Alec Chaplin occupied this during the 1920s with his wife and four children.

Some back garden!

And some advantages too. On one occasion in 1926 Chaplin overheard the directors in the room below voting to sack the club's manager, Andy Ducat.

On the other hand, as is indicated by the web of wiring seen above, no electricity was supplied to the building until 1933.

That apart, there was nothing remotely rural or cottage-like about the building. And yet its very presence and not least its homely vernacular style – a deliberate echo of the district's Edwardian red brick terraced villas and mansion flats (those on Stevenage Road facing Bishop's Park, for example) – make Craven Cottage a ground quite unlike any other.

Engineering Archie **75**

Fulham

▲ August 1933 – and Port Vale are the visitors for the opening home match of the season.

The year before, Fulham had come within a few points of promotion to the First Division.

But expectations down at the Cottage are seldom inflated – it must be the river air – and it would take another 16 years before they finally made it to the top flight.

Fulham were among several of Leitch's clients to feature images of their ground on the club stationery.

Naturally the Cottage appeared on theirs, together with a note of their telegraphic address.

Leitch's telegraphic address was, for many years, 'Terracing'.

Fulham's, memorably, was 'Fulhamish'.

As is this view from the Cottage.

It could be nowhere else in the football universe.

So please, spare a moment to take in the sun-bathed scene.

Scan the faces. Enjoy the hats. The odd bonnet too. Is that a chauffeur in the white mac? Is that young lady out with her pa? The young cove with a cocked hat, is he having a laugh?

Whatever, it's all very Fulhamish.

▲ Years of under-investment and uncertainty over the ground's future left Fulham struggling to meet the demands of the Taylor Report during the 1990s, particularly the all-seater requirement. On one occasion fans even had to be led out of the Stevenage Road Stand (*above*) as a safety precaution.

From 2002-04 the club then played their matches at nearby Loftus Road, home of Queen's Park Rangers, while they planned the ground's complete redevelopment.

Had this scheme gone ahead, the Cottage would have been demolished and only the Stevenage Road frontage left intact.

In the end, however, the projected costs rose too high, and not for the first time, Leitch's buildings won a popular reprieve.

In 2004 both end terraces were converted to seating, with new roofs addded. Nearly 1,500 seats were also installed in the Stevenage Road Stand's enclosure, roughly half its former capacity as a terrace.

The fabric of the stand has also been overhauled, except in one respect. The original Bennet seats as specified by Leitch in 1905 – now numbering 3,571 – remain as robust as ever, and apparently are still deemed more comfortable than their plastic counterparts.

▲ Until a stand was built on the Riverside, the Cottage balcony was the preserve of the directors. Now it is used by players and their guests.

For many years Fulham's chairman was the comedian Tommy Trinder. Later it was a bluff Yorkshireman, Ernie Clay. Following him, the bearded Jimmy Hill.

Currently it is the owner of Harrods, Mohamed Al Fayed.

Never a dull moment.

But success under Al Fayed has put a strain on the facilities. Now that Fulham are mingling with the mighty, they find that their dressing rooms – on the Cottage's ground floor – are smaller than the specified Premier League minimum.

So to avoid a fuss the visitors are put in the home dressing room which is marginally roomier.

Engineering Archie 77

Fulham

Thanks to a £750,000 clean up and refurbishment in 1998, Craven Cottage's Stevenage Road frontage looks smarter now than it did for a long time. One of the tasks was to reinstate two of the gables that had been taken down as a safety precaution. The costs of the façade's restoration were met partly by a supporters' group called Fulham 2000. Other campaign groups to have been involved in the long running saga over the ground's future have included the Fulham Alliance, formed by local residents, and both Back to the Cottage and Fulham United, formed by fans, anxious for the club to stay put.

▲ In an area such as football ground architecture, where so few interesting buildings present themselves for detailed scrutiny, it may be tempting to seize upon anything remotely competent and laud it beyond its worth.

But the Grade II listed **Stevenage Road Stand** is a genuine delight, by any standards, and surely proof positive that Archibald Leitch possessed a keen eye for scale and context. The shame is that there were never enough clients within the football world willing to let him exhibit his full range of skills.

For that reason we must therefore be grateful that not only has the Fulham stand survived, but that is now clearly valued and appreciated.

It is of course an unashamed exercise in window dressing, both literally and metaphorically. Leitch was, after all, a factory architect.

So, as handsome as the street façade undoubtedly is – with its procession of arched and mullioned windows, cartouches and Dutch gables – behind this outer screen, within the stand's shadowy undercrofts, good old honest engineering takes over. Nothing is hidden. Every expense is spared.

Archie knew his business alright. And on this occasion he excelled.

▲ No-one in their right mind would build a football ground in a location like Craven Cottage; accessed from only one narrow road; hemmed in between quiet side streets, a river and a public park, with no room to expand, and a fair walk from the nearest tube.

At least in Henry Norris's day all those villas around the ground – many of which his company erected – were occupied by blue collar workers. There also existed a number of factories in and around the Hammersmith district.

Whereas now, since the gentrification of the area, the majority of the club's supporters come from far beyond the immediate catchment area.

And yet on match days there is not a single car parking space within the club's boundaries, while the site's capacity limit of 25-28,000 (22,000 currently) is hardly enough to compete with the likes of Arsenal or Chelsea.

Two factors render all these objections absolutely redundant.

Firstly, Craven Cottage offers a context totally outside the norm. In a one club town fans will follow wherever the stadium is located.

But in a crowded football market such as London's – with more clubs than any city other than Buenos Aires – Craven Cottage is an asset not to be dismissed lightly.

Secondly, the Cottage and the Stevenage Road Stand.

Had Leitch slapped up one of his routine stands (of which he built many); had there been no corner pavilion; whether in a pleasant riverside spot or not, the ground would have succumbed to developers years ago.

Such is the power of place. Such is the aura of architecture.

There are countless football grounds bereft of character. But there is only one Craven Cottage.

And for much of that, the credit lies with Archibald Leitch.

Leitch advised Fulham for many years after 1905. When he lived across the river in Barnes from 1915-22 they were also his local club. His son, Archibald Kent Leitch, carried on this role by designing a 6,000 seat stand for the riverside of the ground in 1935. But the £11,000 price tag proved beyond the club, and by the time the scheme was dusted down again, in 1950, it had risen to £40,000, and was shelved for good. The designs, which do not survive, were very probably the last stand designs drawn up by the Leitch company before it ceased trading in 1955. The current Riverside Stand dates from 1972.

Engineering Archie 79

Chelsea

Grounds
Stamford Bridge, London 1905–46

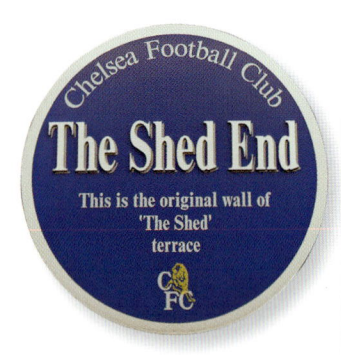

No trace of any of the Leitch structures described in this section survive, apart from one 5m tall wall, rendered in rough cement and topped by ivy. Snaking some 150m around the back of the new Chelsea Village stadium complex, and casting a deep shadow over a walkway leading to the football club's retail store, ticket office and the hotel entrance, this curious survival used to act as the retaining wall of the South Bank terrace, better known as the Shed End. Even odder, on the wall's other side lies a completely different world; a 1930s Italianate village of studios, apartments, courtyards and gardens.

There now follows a tale which, although perhaps familiar to a number of readers, tells us much about the world in which Archibald Leitch operated.

It is the story of Gus Mears and his dog.

Without this dog Archibald Leitch would never have designed the new Stamford Bridge, and there would have been no Chelsea Football Club.

Had there been no Chelsea, Henry Norris, the Fulham chairman, might well have been content to remain at Craven Cottage and, as a result, Woolwich Arsenal would have stayed in Plumstead, which in turn means that there would have been no Highbury (and therefore probably no Charlton Athletic either).

So in the history of football, this was one very important dog.

The story revolves around Stamford Bridge, which, as recounted in Colin Benson's history of the ground (see Links), had been the home of the London Athletic Club since 1877.

Two regulars at the LAC ground were Gus and Joe Mears, the sons of one of London's largest building contractors, based on Crabtree Wharf, Hammersmith, a few streets away from Craven Cottage. (The Mears company, coincidentally, had been responsible for laying out Craven Cottage, in 1896, nine years before Leitch arrived on the scene.)

As we learnt in the previous section, in 1904 Gus Mears took possession of Stamford Bridge with the intention of developing it into London's first purpose-built stadium for football and athletics.

Mears was a genuine sports lover, no question, but like Norris, he sensed that whoever built such a stadium would stand a very good chance of winning the right to stage Cup Finals and internationals, especially given the widespread dissatisfaction with the existing *de facto* national stadium, Crystal Palace, which, though huge – it held nearly 115,000 for the 1901 Cup Final – was inconveniently located and appallingly designed.

Stamford Bridge, on the other hand, was centrally situated and served by Walham Green Underground Station (later renamed Fulham Broadway).

Mears' original assumption was that once his plans were revealed, Fulham would jump at the chance to become his tenants.

After all, they were only renting Craven Cottage and it was hardly as well placed. It also occupied a six acre site, compared with some eleven acres at the Bridge.

They would be crazy to turn him down.

But of course they did, or rather Norris did, and when he struggled as a result to find any other investors willing to share the risk, Mears reluctantly decided to abandon the whole stadium idea and sell the site.

One Sunday in late 1904 he arranged to meet up at the Bridge with an LAC member who had been one of the leading advocates of the stadium proposal, a man called Fred Parker.

League Champions Manchester United play Southern League Champions Queen's Park Rangers in the first ever Charity Shield Cup, at Stamford Bridge in 1908. Note that, as at Craven Cottage, Leitch inserted voids under the pediment of the gable, to allow for a press box to be fitted at a later date.

80 engineering Archie

Mears wanted to tell him personally of his decision.

As the two men strolled in the grounds, mulling over their shared disappointment, Mears' dog suddenly leapt up and bit Parker on the leg, drawing blood.

Instead of showing concern, Mears merely shook his head.

'Scotch terrier,' he muttered. 'Always bites before he speaks.'

Despite his pain Parker could not help but laugh.

He told Mears that he was the 'coolest fish' he had ever met.

Mears thought about this remark for a moment and then, out of the blue, told Parker that he had changed his mind about selling the ground.

He said that Parker had reacted so well to the dog bite, and made so little a fuss, that perhaps his judgment on the stadium scheme was to be trusted after all.

In the words of Alexander Pope, 'What mighty contests rise from trivial things!'

The following day Mears made contact with Archibald Leitch.

It is of course possible that Archie had been their choice all along to oversee the scheme and were already in contact with him.

But however the contact came about, within a matter of days Mears and Parker travelled up to Glasgow to be treated by Leitch to a guided tour of the city's three immense stadiums, namely Ibrox Park (Archie's own design), Celtic Park, and the newest wonder of them all, Hampden Park, opened in 1903 and already able to accommodate 80,000 spectators.

The two visitors' sense of excitement and wonder can easily be imagined. London had nothing like any of these three vast bowls, and yet could draw on a much larger populace, and indeed much wider affluence.

From that visit onwards, events advanced with extraordinary rapidity. No planning inquiries. No environmental impact studies. No drawn out negotiations with local residents or businesses.

From conception to inauguration, the new Stamford Bridge would be ready for use within just eight months.

Being in the construction business himself meant that Mears was able to start his own men on site almost immediately, building up the embankments using clay from excavations then being carried out to create the Kingsway tram tunnel and London's expanding tube system.

There could hardly have been a better time to undertake such work. Not only were there vast amounts of soil and clay to be had, but the contractors responsible for the excavations were paying Mears to take it off their hands, at a shilling or more per load.

Leitch, meanwhile, submitted his first plans to the London County Council – the same body with whom a few weeks earlier he had joshed in court over Fulham's temporary stand (*see page 40*) – on February 23 1905.

Whether Archie had not been that busy at the time, or he simply dropped everything to get the job started – Stamford Bridge was, after all, a fabulous opportunity to make his name in the capital – we cannot say.

Whichever, the plans Leitch submitted for Stamford Bridge accorded to what would become his standard lay out for all new grounds; that is, a single main stand, and three sides of terracing.

His proposed stand for Stamford Bridge (*see above right*) also established a model he would return to on a number of occasions, namely a seating deck of 4-6,000 seats, depending on the footprint available, covered by a steel-framed roof with a pedimented gable, and fronted by a terraced enclosure.

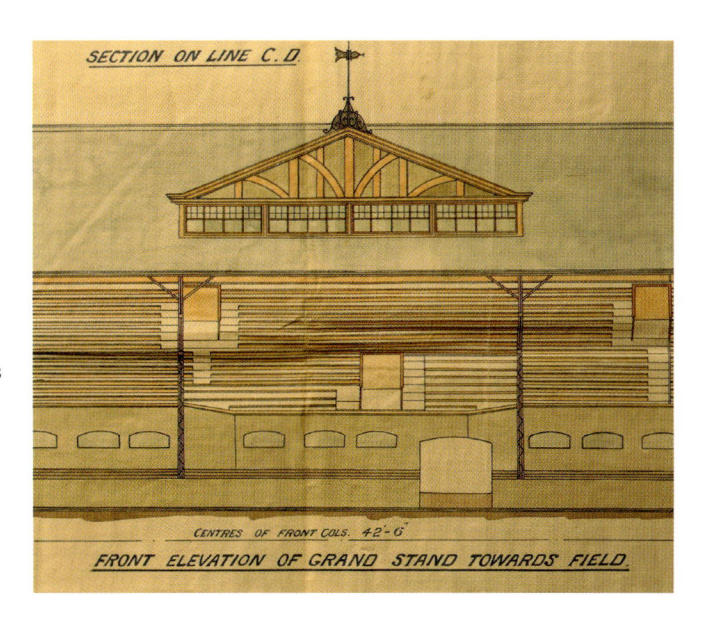

The other three sides of Stamford Bridge's terracing, it was reported in the local press, were to be large enough to accommodate 50,000 spectators.

Leitch also proposed a double barrel-roofed cover over the central section of the west terrace, opposite the main stand, featuring another central gable, this time an arched one.

It is an indication of where his clients' priorities lay that although Leitch specified similar terrace covers at virtually all his grounds, none were ever built.

The man on the terrace, it would seem, would just have to get wet.

Leitch's arched gable design for Stamford Bridge did materialise elsewhere however; an exact copy was attached to the roof »

Football fans today often complain that modern stadiums all look the same. But in the case of Chelsea and Fulham's new stands in 1905, they were the same. 'Exactly the same dimensions' according to Leitch's own letter to the London County Council, seeking their speedy approval. The main difference between the final versions was that whereas Fulham's stand had a brick façade, Chelsea's was clad entirely in corrugated sheeting. But then it did only back onto a railway line, so there was not quite the same need to impress.

Engineering Archie 81

Chelsea

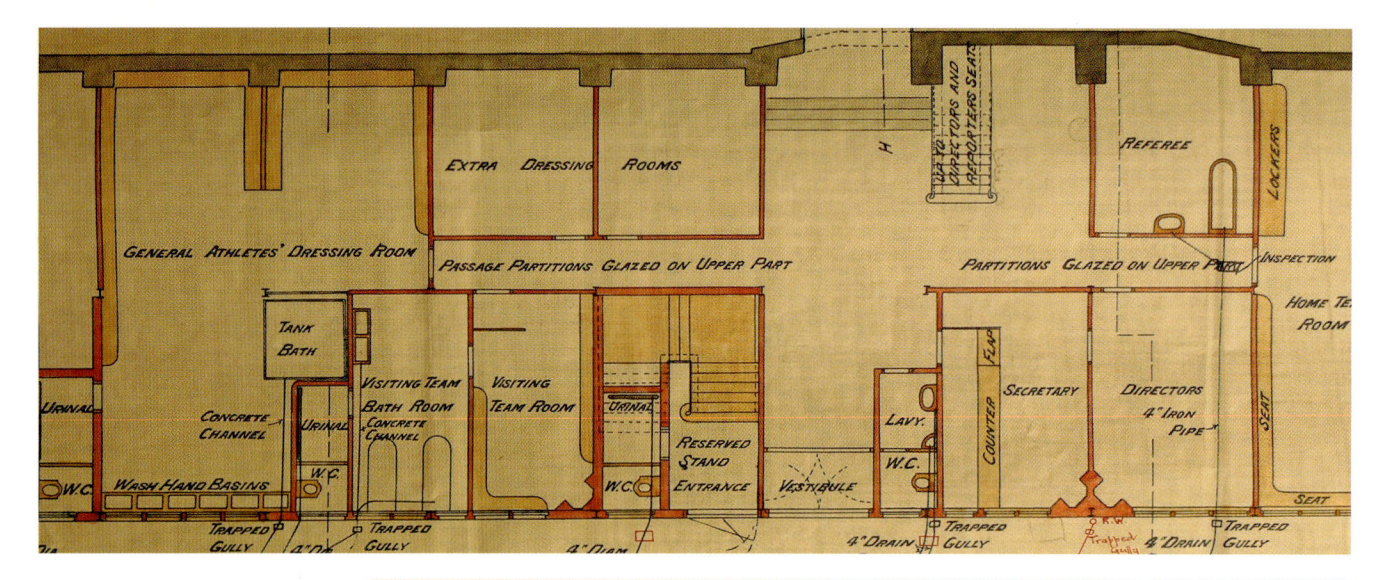

▲ As **Stamford Bridge** was designed for both football and athletics, Leitch had to provide extra dressing rooms in the main stand. His original plans also include the provision of bench seats on each wing of the enclosure, although these were never fitted.

In both section and elevation, the stand shown here established a model that Leitch would repeat in various scales and finishes at a number of his later grounds; including White Hart Lane, The Den, Tynecastle, Dens Park and Selhurst Park.

The rooftop gable was, however, an optional extra.

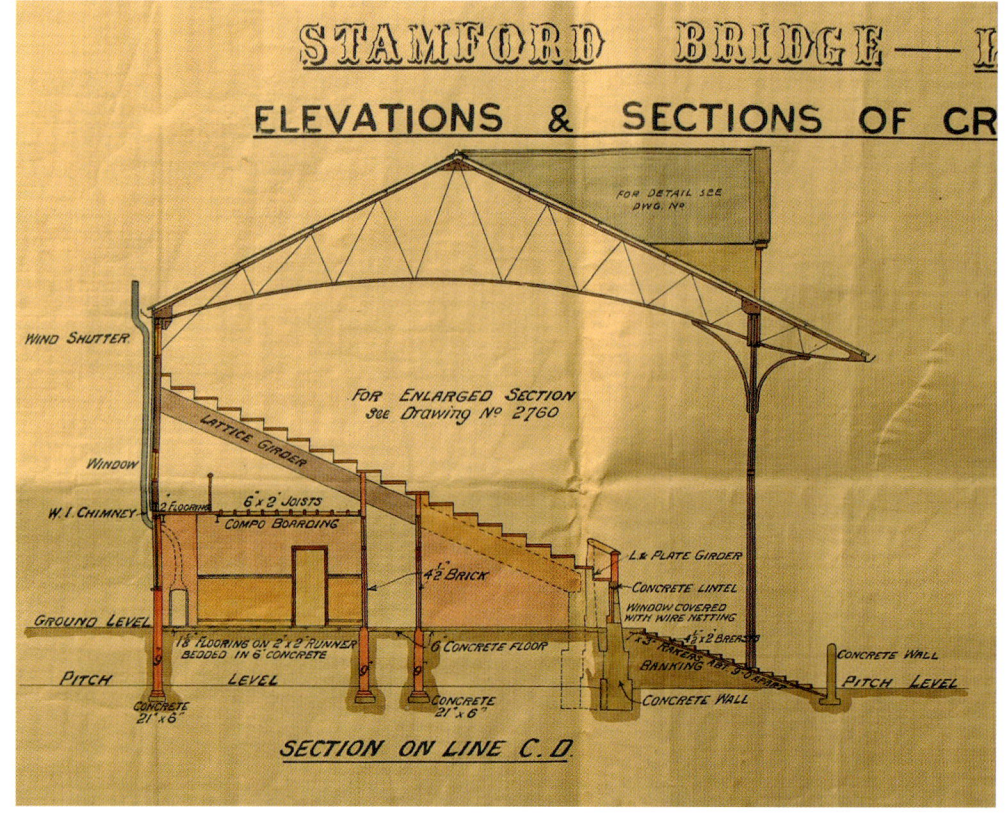

82 Engineering Archie

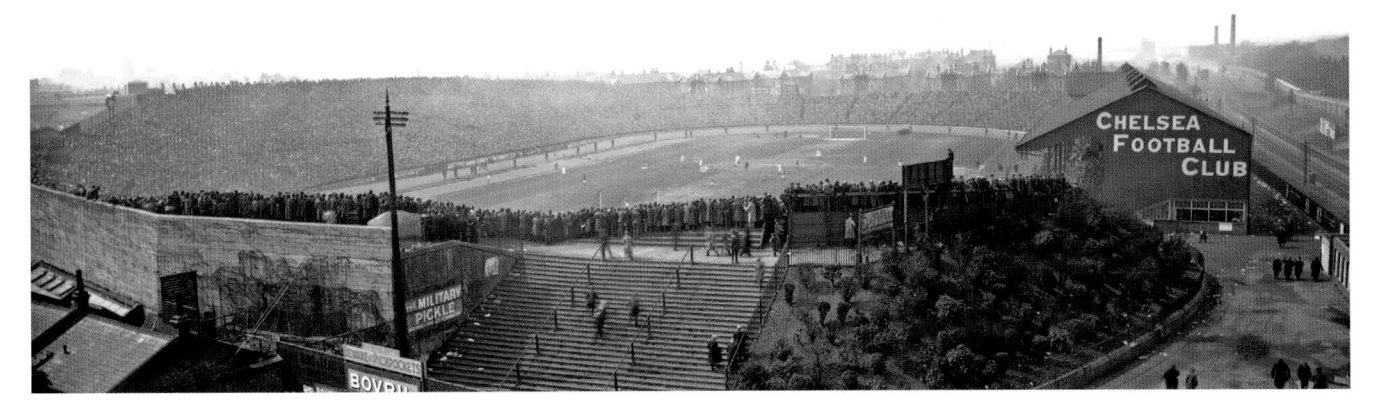

of his main stand at Anfield, Liverpool, the following year (see page 87).

So if his clients were intent upon economy, so, in his own way, was Archie.

Now that Mears was busy redeveloping Stamford Bridge, and the newspapers were starting to report on his intention of setting up a new club – Kensington FC was the putative title – over at Craven Cottage, Henry Norris was in a panic.

Apparently unconcerned that Archie was now working for his rival, he quickly re-engaged Leitch, who, in April 1905 submitted plans for a new stand at Craven Cottage that were virtually identical to those he had drawn up for Stamford Bridge.

Not only did this save him drawing time, but it also made it easier for the London County Council. Leitch asked them to approve the Craven Cottage stand plans on the basis that they 'were exactly the same dimensions' as the ones they had already approved for Stamford Bridge.

(In fact there were differences, as the photographs show.)

Leitch now had his hands well and truly full.

In March it was announced that the new club at Stamford Bridge was to be called Chelsea. Three thousands shares in the new company were snapped up almost immediately – in stark contrast to the poor response to Fulham's own issue.

And in May Chelsea managed to gain admission to the Football League, despite the fact that they did not yet have a full team and had never kicked a ball in earnest.

(Fulham were at the time still in the Southern League.)

Now it was up to the men from Mears to get the ground ready in time for the forthcoming season, while Leitch flitted between Craven Cottage and Stamford Bridge, trying to satisfy both clients.

There was no doubting who was the easier. Norris was a brusque, domineering fellow, Mears an easy going chap whose catch phrase was apparently, 'Don't worry.'

Stamford Bridge in particular must have seemed like a home from home for Archie. The steelwork contract was being carried out by the Clyde Structural Iron Company, who were also engaged on Fulham's stand. The pitch was being laid by a team of Scottish workers. And the Chelsea manager, and several of the newly recruited players were Scots too.

Craven Cottage opened its doors on September 2 1905.

Stamford Bridge followed two days later with a friendly match against Liverpool.

Early responses to the ground were breathless. Stamford Bridge 'will stagger humanity' was one.

Ernest Edwards from the *Liverpool Echo* reported, 'When I told the Chelsea half that his Kop did him well he said, "They're only just starting on it really. It won't be finished until the end of the season."

'Good, goodness, gracious! It'll hold a mighty crowd when it is finished.'

As indeed it did. Building up as the first season progressed, from crowds of 6,000 to 20,000, to 30,000, in April 1906 the visit of Manchester United drew an astonishing 67,000 spectators; the largest crowd yet to have seen a League match in London.

For Archie, Stamford Bridge »

▲ April 1920 and **Stamford Bridge** stages the FA Cup Final.

This was its golden opportunity to replace Crystal Palace as the leading football venue in London.

But overpriced tickets kept the gate down to only 50,000, and once Wembley opened in 1923, its chance was gone forever.

For all the Bridge's scale – its capacity between the wars was 82,000, larger than any other club venue in England – it still had only 7,000 seats, and no terrace cover. It also suffered from having access only from the southern approach to the ground.

The South Bank's retaining wall, the only structure from the ground as it existed above to survive today, is seen in the left foreground.

Engineering Archie **83**

Chelsea

▲ This view of **Stamford Bridge** from the south, in 1960, shows the full assortment of Leitch structures added over the years. None did the company's reputation any favours.

The fact that the **Main Stand** was located on the east side was a particular drawback, forcing spectators in the stand to look into the sun on a Saturday afternoon.

Nor was the stand finished to a high standard, so that with various extensions added to the rear during the 1930s, it formed an unappealing jumble.

Leitch also added the tote booths at the rear of the large west terrace.

But again they were cheap, utilitarian buildings.

Similarly, the **South Bank** cover sat at an odd angle at the rear of the terrace, having been designed primarily to shelter bookmakers at greyhound meetings.

But the most telling sign that Leitch as a company had run out of steam was the **North Stand**, flanking the end of the West Stand.

Designed by Archibald Kent Leitch, in 1939, it was poorly conceived and cheaply executed. Admittedly its construction was interrupted by the war, so that it lay half finished for five years. But with a capacity of only 2,483 seats, it was never more than a half measure and was demolished after only 30 years' use in 1976.

Stamford Bridge today is one of the most advanced stadium complexes in Europe, the result of a ten year redevelopment programme carried out under the former Chelsea chairman Ken Bates.

In its form above it held around 83,000 spectators, of which under 10,000 were seated. Now, without the track, and with two hotels occupying the south east corner of the site, it holds 42,500 all seated.

It is as much an exemplar of modern thinking as was the original in 1905.

But it is also the most valuable piece of real estate in football, which means that its future can never be entirely assured.

» was a wonderful showcase. In its first 15 years the ground fulfilled all its promise. Chelsea were soon promoted to the First Division and became the country's best supported club. Increases to the banking raised the capacity to 85,000. The Bridge also became a regular host of summer athletics meetings, and in 1920 received the ultimate goal; the right to stage the FA Cup Final, after Crystal Palace became unavailable.

Compared with the capital's other modern multi-purpose stadium, at White City, opened for the 1908 Olympics, Stamford Bridge was in effect a stadium for all London.

But it did not last.

The premature death of Gus Mears in 1912 was the first blow, and a serious one.

His brother Joe, who later bought the freehold, started to treat the stadium as a milch cow. Instead of being part of the Chelsea team, he set himself apart as landlord, entering into a series of disputes with the club over catering rights and lease arrangements.

In 1921 he also embroiled Leitch, who was by then living in London, in a bitter argument with the directors over repairs to the ground carried out by Mears' building company; an affair which led to an investigation by the FA and accusations that Mears was overcharging the club for work in cahoots with Leitch.

On this occasion, working in the interests of two masters – the landlord and the football club – proved to be a thankless task.

Certainly one aspect of the repair work was revealing.

The Bridge's embankments had been raised and terraced so hurriedly that the material had not

84 Engineering Archie

been allowed to settle, causing the rakers on which the barriers were bolted to shift. This meant that a programme of continual running repairs was necessary.

The pitch suffered too. So many events were staged during the close season – 65 alone in 1922 – that the Football League had to issue Mears with a warning.

Yet he continued to add more events to the Bridge's schedule. Speedway arrived in 1928. This forced the Amateur Athletics Association to switch their annual championships to White City.

Then in 1932 greyhound racing arrived, and for the next few years its interests were placed before those of the football club, whose finances were now, in any case, in a perilous state.

The advent of greyhound racing created a good deal of work for Leitch's company, in the form of Tote booths, kennels, and so on.

But it turned Stamford Bridge into an unwholesome mess.

From this point on Archie's son, Archibald Kent Leitch, appears to have taken on the responsibilities for design work at the Bridge.

The results, shown on these pages, were hardly impressive.

And so the promise of Stamford Bridge faded, its deterioration and lack of facilities becoming ever more acute until the 1960s.

There can therefore be no regret that none of the original structures have survived.

Stamford Bridge could have evolved into one of Leitch's best efforts. Instead, it is his work for Henry Norris, not Gus Mears, for which he will be best remembered.

The explanation is simple. Speculative stadiums built for profit seldom prosper.

Stadiums built with heart endure.

◀ Susan Benson was one of several artists who chose Stamford Bridge, and the **North Stand** in particular, as their subject when entering a Football and Fine Arts competition organised by the Football Association in 1953.

In pen and ink the North Stand certainly had an imposing presence. The stand also offered an excellent view from the front rows.

Spectators in the nearside corner, however, had their view of the far goal blocked by the glazed screen, while a section of the roof had to be cut away for the benefit of those sitting at the rear.

The Shed cover (*left*) was hardly better, and was therefore aptly named by its regulars.

Engineering Archie 85

Liverpool

Grounds
Anfield, Liverpool 1906–07

On Saturday August 25 1906, readers of the Liverpool Echo were offered a bird's eye view of Liverpool's new football ground.

'From the sketch herewith (for which we are indebted to Mr Archibald Leitch, MIME, the engineer who has laid out the ground) it will be seen that the aspect of the old football enclosure at Anfield has been entirely changed.

The ground has been completely walled in with fancy brick setting, with large exit gates on the four sides, as well as numerous entrances. Therefore there will be no difficulty in either entering or leaving the enclosure. The directors' aim has been to provide as compact and comfortable a ground as possible, in which every person, no matter what portion he may visit, will have a full view of the game.

The playing pitch has been raised about five feet, with a paddock all round. Roofed-in stand accommodation will be plentiful, and at one end, as seen in the sketch, will be an elevated terrace consisting of 132 tiers of steps, which will afford space for something like 20,000 spectators.

The entire scheme is modelled on a new departure from what football grounds are generally supposed to be, and when completed, will provide ample space for about 60,000 visitors.

The stands, of which two only are erected at present, are built on massive brick foundations, and are as safe as skill and good workmanship can make them, and ample provision for the comfort of players in way of bath and recreation rooms has been attended to.

The ground has been in the hands of a gang of workmen for the past three months, but another season at least must elapse before it is perfected and the full ambition of the directors becomes reality. The main features of those connected with the new erection have been compactness, comfort, and an uninterrupted vision of the field of play.

The constructional steelwork for the grand stand has been supplied and erected by Messrs. EF Blakely and Co., of Vauxhall Ironworks, Liverpool, who also erected the big grand stand for the Everton Football Club, at Goodison Park.'

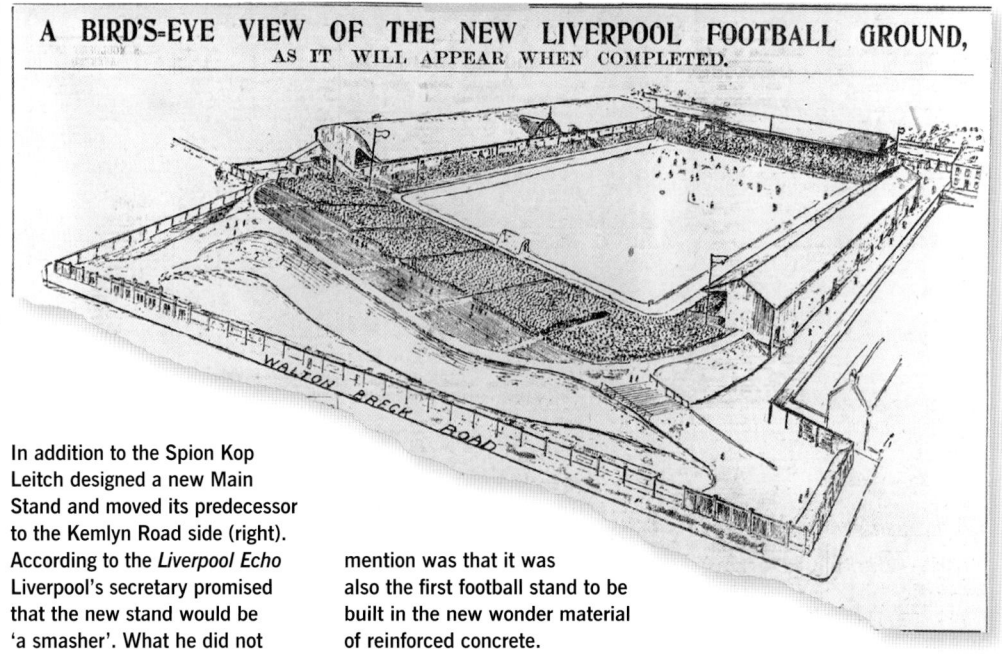

Leaning on a Leitch barrier on the famous Spion Kop, the Scottish centre half Ron Yeats looks out over Anfield at the end of his distinguished Liverpool career in 1970. Although the Kop was largely characterised by its roof – designed in 1928 by Joseph Watston Cabré – the banking itself was built to Leitch's design in 1906. At its peak it held 28,000 spectators.

In addition to the Spion Kop Leitch designed a new Main Stand and moved its predecessor to the Kemlyn Road side (right). According to the *Liverpool Echo* Liverpool's secretary promised that the new stand would be 'a smasher'. What he did not mention was that it was also the first football stand to be built in the new wonder material of reinforced concrete.

A BIRD'S-EYE VIEW OF THE NEW LIVERPOOL FOOTBALL GROUND, AS IT WILL APPEAR WHEN COMPLETED.

86 Engineering Archie

As is firmly entrenched in football lore, Anfield was first the home of Liverpool's rivals, Everton.

It was Everton who first laid out Anfield in 1884, and it was as a result of Everton's success – they won their first League championship in 1891 – that Anfield developed into a tidy ground holding 16,000 spectators.

But this high point in the Blues' career was followed within a few months by a fearsome, and now famous row with the club's landlord, John Houlding, which ended in Everton vacating the ground in mid 1892 and relocating to the opposite side of Stanley Park, to Goodison Park.

In a fit of pique, Houlding then formed his own club to take over the tenancy of Anfield.

Thus was born Liverpool FC, and the great Merseyside rivalry which has dominated the sporting character of the city ever since.

(Liverpool's birth also put paid to the city's original second club, Bootle, who were, at the time, members of the Second Division.)

By the time Leitch was called in by Liverpool's Irish-born chairman, John McKenna, in early 1906, Anfield was able to accommodate around 25,000, and, in certain respects, was the equal of Goodison (although Goodison won the honour of staging the 1894 Cup Final).

Its main stand, opened also in 1894, was described by one paper as 'probably the most imposing football erection in existence.'

That was debatable, but the stand was certainly serviceable enough for Leitch to be asked to oversee its removal from the west side of the ground – where his new stand would be built – to the east side, backing onto Kemlyn Road.

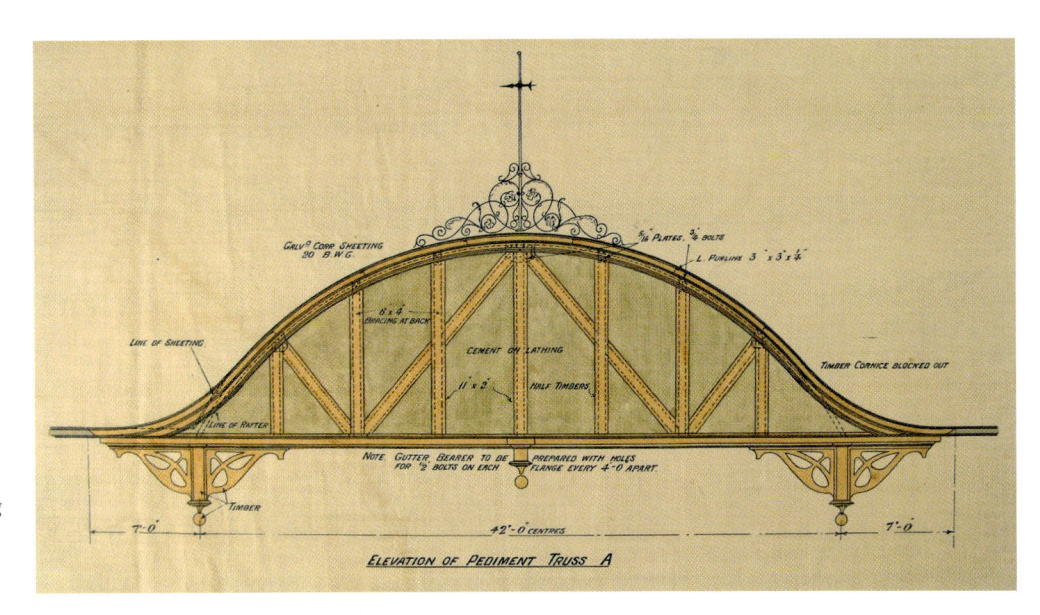

Another existing structure, the Anfield Road cover, dating from 1903, was also retained.

In every other respect, however, the revamped Anfield was a new ground; another example of a Victorian enclosure brought into the 20th century by Leitch's rigorous engineering approach.

The tall embankment, which soon became known as the Spion Kop, would in particular emerge as a symbol of the game's growing importance within urban working class culture.

Anfield re-opened its doors a week after the *Liverpool Echo*'s glowing report, on September 1, when a crowd of 32,000 attended Liverpool's game v. Stoke.

Over at Goodison, meanwhile, Everton were planning their own redevelopments to keep pace with their upstart neighbours and, after problems with their first architect, they too called for Leitch, in 1908.

From then on, the city of Liverpool would loom large in Archie's life.

As recounted in Chapter Four, in around 1909 he moved his family from Glasgow to a large house in Blundellsands, just north of Liverpool, and set up his main office in Dale Street, where he would remain until 1915.

But although Leitch would end up designing three stands for Everton, when Liverpool finally decided to build a roof over the Kop, in 1928, they turned not to Archie but to a local architect called Joseph Cabré Watson, whose other work was principally housing, a war memorial and sundry church halls.

Cabré designed a fine roof nevertheless, even if he did remodel the terracing in a way that rendered it more difficult to manage.

But at least Archie's Main Stand maintained its presence for many more years to come.

Indeed, although few visitors to Anfield realise, it is still there today, forming the core of the Main Stand currently on view.

Until a much larger and plainer roof replaced it in 1970, Anfield was instantly identifiable by the curvaceous gable of Leitch's 1906 Main Stand. Measuring 56 feet wide and 18 feet high – excluding its wrought iron flourish, a standard feature of Leitch gables, if one that rarely survived – this style was unique to Anfield. (In fact Leitch designed an identical one for a terrace cover at Stamford Bridge, also in 1906, but it was never built.) The Liverpool signboard on its front (see back cover and page 51) was added shortly after World War Two.

Engineering Archie 87

Liverpool

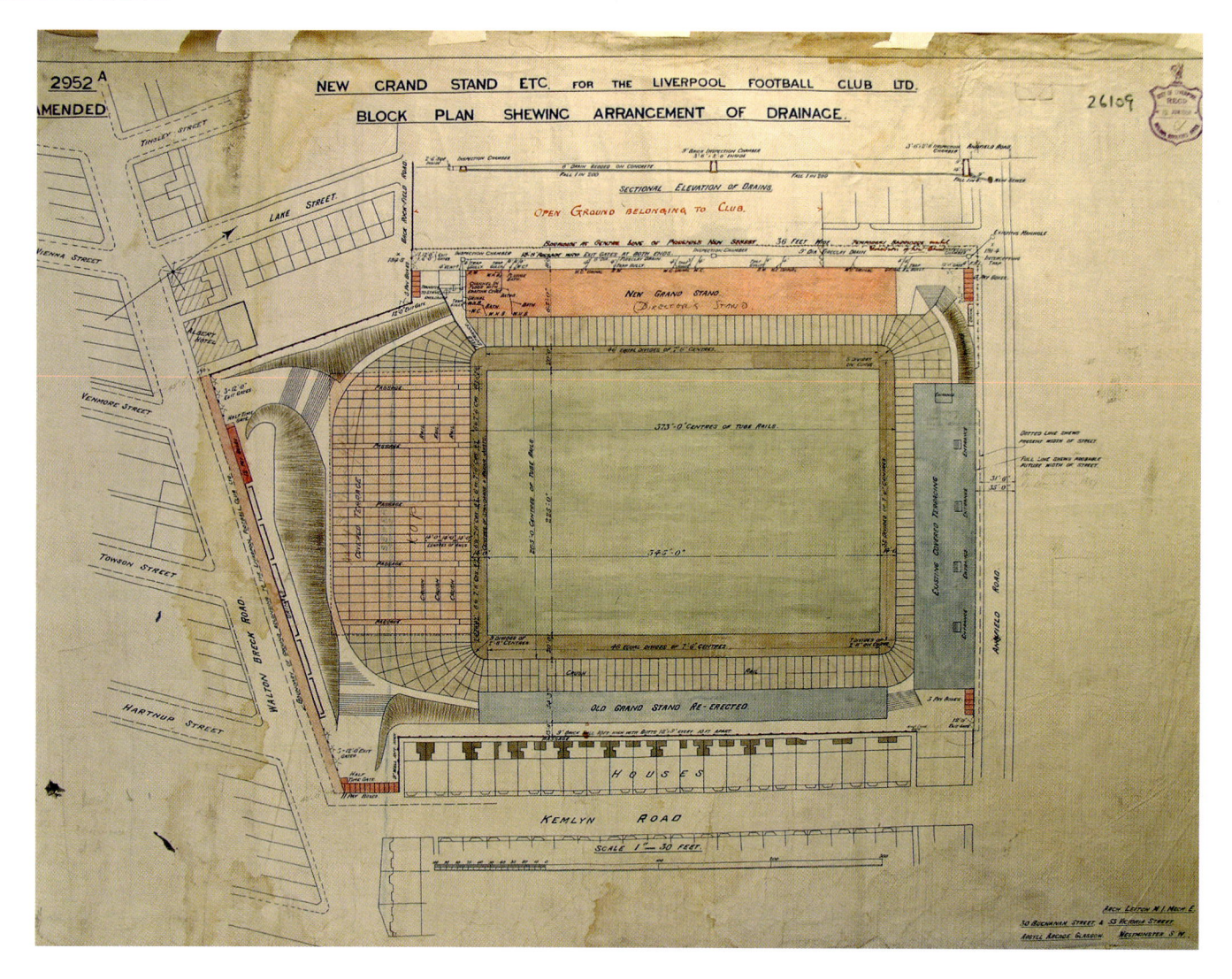

▲ Dated June 20 1906, Leitch's plan of **Anfield** shows that two elements of the original ground, shaded blue, were to be retained: the Anfield Road cover (*right*), and the old grandstand, which was moved to the Kemlyn Road side.

Note, however, that this is an amended plan. An earlier one, dated April 24, differed in two important respects.

Firstly, the area shown behind Leitch's grandstand, marked 'open ground belonging to club,' was earmarked on the earlier plan for a new street. Had the club not prevented this going ahead, their access, and future options, would have been severely limited. As it is, the space was half taken up with an extension to the rear of Leitch's stand, between 1970 and 1973.

Secondly, on Leitch's original plan the Kop end was only half the depth shown here, even though Liverpool owned the site up to Walton Breck Road.

Among other surviving plans from June 1906 is one for a roof over the Kop. Until Cabré's design was built in 1928, the upper reaches of the Kop were notoriously exposed to cold winds.

88 Engineering Archie

Football Grand Stand, Liverpool.
Built for THE LIVERPOOL FOOTBALL CLUB.
Engineer: ARCHIBALD LEITCH, M.I.Mech.E.

▲ Anfield's **Main Stand** was Leitch's first in reinforced concrete, and probably the first in Britain.

According to *The Builder* of April 14 1906, 'the great elastic strength, homogeneity, and durability' of the concrete used in its construction made it 'distinctly worthy of imitation'.

Designed 'on the Hennebique system' (named after the French engineer François Hennebique, who patented his technique in 1892), the stand was built three years after Leitch's first known use of ferro-concrete at the Sentinel Works in Glasgow (see page 35). Although vacant, the Works still stand, as does the Main Stand at Anfield.

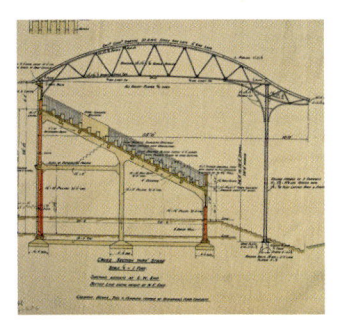

But only if one looks closely can its presence be discerned.

Between 1970-73 its roof was removed, the paddock was reprofiled for seating, and an upper tier was added at its rear, so that now, under a new roof, the original core (*below left*) forms the central section of the enlarged stand.

But the brick rear wall of the paddock is still visible, and the upper tier's original 18 rows of wooden seats, on a four inch thick slab of concrete, remain in use.

(Hillsborough's South Stand, built on the same system, has been similarly revamped, see page 135.)

Leitch's Anfield stand may yet celebrate its century, but only just.

By 2006 Liverpool are hoping to move into a new stadium, a short distance away in Stanley Park.

Even using the best in modern concrete technology, it will do well to last as long as Archie's effort.

▲ Anfield's **Spion Kop** pictured from the corner of Walton Breck Road and Kemlyn Road c. 1910.

The name Spion Kop – applied to numerous terraces elsewhere in later years – was still fresh in the collective memory at the time Anfield was redeveloped by Leitch.

In January 1900, during the Boer War, 322 troops, many from Liverpool, had been killed in the battle for a lookout hill, or 'Spion Kop', 20 miles from Ladysmith.

Woolwich Arsenal – a club with a large support amongst soldiers – were the first to adopt the name, in 1904, when a terraced embankment was raised at their ground in Plumstead.

Anfield's new terrace seems to have attracted the same tag within three weeks of its opening.

'This huge wall of earth,' reported Ernest Edwards, or BEE, in the *Liverpool Echo*, 'has been termed "Spion Kop", and no doubt this apt name will always be used in future in referring to this spot'.

Seen above is another symbol of Anfield, the topmast of the SS Great Eastern, one of the world's first iron ships, launched in 1860.

18m tall above ground (plus another two below), the mast was salvaged when the ship was broken up, floated across the Mersey and then hauled by horses to Anfield, where it was raised shortly after the Kop opened in 1906.

The Kop was undoubtedly one of the great football terraces of the 20th century. But its final years were beset by problems.

An awkward barrier lay-out, different from the one originally specified by Leitch (see *opposite*) contributed to a high rate of routine injuries. In 1987 part of it collapsed into a sewer.

The banking was finally cleared in 1994 in the wake of the Hillsborough disaster (in which 96 Liverpool fans died), to make way for a new 12,000 seat Kop Stand.

Only the Great Eastern's topmast remains.

Engineering Archie

Ewood Park, Blackburn 1906–13

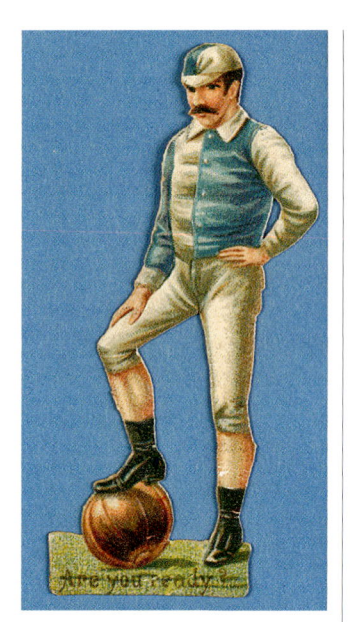

Grounds

Five time winners of the FA Cup from 1884-91, Blackburn Rovers were prestige clients for Leitch. Before adopting their familiar blue and white halved shirts, Rovers' founders in 1875 agreed that the colours be 'white jersey' with a 'blue-and-white skull cap', and that trousers were 'optional'.

After a year or more of working for the two footballing property barons of west London, Messrs Norris and Mears, Archibald Leitch next found himself in the heartland of English professional football.

Blackburn Rovers were 'old school' in every sense. One of six Lancashire clubs to form the original Football League in 1888, they were established in 1875 by former pupils from Shrewsbury School and Blackburn Grammar, one of whom, John Lewis, was a vocal campaigner for the Temperance movement and later became England's leading referee.

In 1882 they emerged as the first northern club to challenge the southern, amateur monopoly of the FA Cup, by reaching the final, where they lost to Old Etonians. The following year a rival team of artisans, Blackburn Olympic, went one further, by managing to beat Old Etonians in the final.

Olympic's travelling supporters, descending noisily on the Kennington Oval in their Sunday clogs with brass rivets, their neckties and scarves in club colours, provided bemused Londoners with a first glimpse of football fanaticism, northern style.

The players were a shock to the system too. Olympic were pioneers of a professional approach to tactics and training that soon would become universal.

But they could not sustain their run, and were soon overhauled by the more middle-class, better connected Rovers, who signed several of Olympic's best players and went on to win the FA Cup five times in eight seasons.

In short, by 1906, when Leitch arrived, Blackburn was already widely respected as a football town of the strongest traditions.

So too was Ewood Park well established. Laid out originally in 1882 as a commercial sportsground by 'four enterprising Blackburn tradesmen' and taken over by Rovers in 1890, it had already staged an England international, in 1891.

Five years later Rovers became the first football club to be found guilty of negligence when a stand collapsed in a crowd of 20,000 spectators, leading one of the injured to win £25 in compensation. It is highly likely that Leitch would have known of the case, in light of his experiences at Ibrox in 1902.

Leitch's brief at Blackburn – one he would face repeatedly throughout the period – was thus to turn an overstretched Victorian ground with wooden stands, cinder banking and wooden barriers, into a robustly enclosed, 20th century arena formed in brick, concrete and steel.

The extent of his work is illustrated on the following pages. But what characterised the redevelopment most of all was, once again, the character of the club's chairman.

Blackburn was of course a mill town, built up and enriched by the profits from spinning and weaving; a time when, it was said, Britain's bread hung by a Lancashire thread. By 1907, at the industry's peak, there were nearly 80,000 looms in Blackburn alone.

A fair number of them belonged to the Rovers' chairman, whose name, appropriately enough, was Lawrence Cotton.

Between 1905-14, Cotton lavished a fortune on his beloved Rovers. On players he spent around £12,000, including a record £2,000 on Danny O'Shea from West Ham in 1912 (twice the previous transfer record, paid by Middlesbrough in 1905).

On Ewood Park the outlay reached £33,000. This was more than Norris had spent on Craven Cottage or Mears laid out on Stamford Bridge, and was all the more remarkable given that Cotton was no new convert to the game. He had been to Blackburn Grammar School with several of the club's founders and had joined the Rovers committee in 1891.

But if Cotton was cut from different cloth from the likes of Leitch's London clients, he certainly shared their relentless ambition, and unlike them, his investment did yield honours. Rovers were League champions in both 1912 and 1914.

Inevitably the club could not sustain this success. After the First World War the cotton industry went into the early stages of a terminal decline. Half the mills were closed by 1922. Lawrence Cotton himself died in 1921, fondly remembered as a devout philanthropist, a popular Lord Mayor and a generous benefactor.

But he was by no means the last of his kind. During the 1990s, by which time Rovers had fallen on very hard times indeed, another Blackburn potentate, the steel millionaire Jack Walker, gifted at least £25 million to turn Ewood Park into the modern stadium it is today and, in the process, eradicate everything that Leitch had built for Cotton 90 years earlier.

Or rather, almost everything.

The ornate, panelled boardroom which adorned Leitch's main stand at Ewood Park (*illustrated on page 54*) and was, for many years, one of the most welcoming hospitality lounges in football – famed for its tea urns and heaving plates of baps and butties – was in 1994 lovingly re-assembled inside one of the club's new stands, where it remains in use today.

Similarly, a slab of masonry bearing the name 'Rovers FC' – taken from a turnstile block built during Leitch's stint at the ground – now forms part of a memorial to the late Jack Walker (*see page 200*) outside the same stand which houses the old boardroom.

Thus by rebuilding the ground, the team and people's dreams, both Cotton and Walker left their mark. But so, thanks to these two acts of conservation, has Leitch.

▲ King Cotton's domain – **Ewood Park** in 1928. Nearest to the camera is Leitch's cranked **Nuttall Street Stand**. Running off Nuttall Street were Tweed Street, Velvet Street and Plush Street. Behind the opposite **Riverside Stand**, also by Leitch, flowed the River Darwen. To the right, Fernhurst Mill borders the Darwen End. Behind the Blackburn End, to the left, lay Kidder Street, cobbled and with tram lines until the 1980s. Once, this corner of Lancashire formed a favourite backdrop for Hovis adverts. Now, other than the houses in the foreground, all else, the mill included, has succumbed to time and the expanding girth of Ewood Park. Now, King Football rules.

Engineering Archie 91

Blackburn Rovers

▶ Funded by a mill owner, designed by a factory architect, Blackburn's **Nuttall Street Stand** shows the unadorned face of northern football in the Edwardian era – in blunt contrast to the decorated façade commissioned by the house builder Henry Norris for Fulham, twelve months earlier.

But there were riches within. Behind those groundfloor windows lay a sumptuous boardroom, the court of King Cotton (*see page 56*).

Opened in January 1907 and built by Booth & Son of Bolton, the stand had seats for 4,112 on its upper tier (*below right*) with standing for 9,320 in front.

After Leitch had completed his work at the ground six years later, someone calculated rather generously that Ewood Park would hold 70,866. In fact, its record was 62,522, in March 1929.

But if, in later years, there was plenty of room for Rovers' diminishing support – the average when Jack Walker became involved in 1988 was under 10,000 – the club eventually outgrew the Nuttall Street Stand and converted two terraced houses on the other side of the street into offices and a reception, where managers could be interviewed after the game. On one occasion a reporter knocked on the wrong door but was ushered in by the householders nevertheless and served tea while he waited, non-plussed, wondering where all his colleagues were.

Neither the stand nor the houses exist today. The stand was demolished in 1994, as were over 60 homes, and Fernhurst Mill, to make way for the new stadium, which seats 31,000. By 1996 it was reckoned Walker had spent £71 million on the ground, on the team, and on buying up properties in the surrounding streets.

BLACKBURN ROVERS NEW GRAND STAND.
400 FEET LONG, 36 FEET WIDE, WITH OVERHANGING EAVES 15 FEET WIDE.
SEATING ACCOMMODATION 5000. STANDING ACCOMMODATION 4000 (IN FRONT).
STEELWORK BY JOHN BOOTH & SONS, BOLTON.

◀ Blackburn's **Riverside Stand**, completed in 1913 and seating 2,944 on its upper tier, was one of several Leitch built from 1906-14 in reinforced concrete, a material chosen because its foundations were rooted on the banks of the adjacent River Darwen.

However the stand's exposure to wind from the open scrubland behind – undeveloped still today – put paid to its first roof within 15 years of its opening, while the more stringent safety requirements introduced after the 1985 Bradford fire led to the closure of the upper tier when defects were found in the now corroded concrete. And yet, as shown here in 1987, a year before its demolition, like the rest of Ewood Park, from a distance it looked admirably pristine.

The chimney seen behind the Darwen End terrace was part of the Fernhurst Mill, now cleared to make room for a car park. The floodlight pylon, a standard issue GEC design, was erected in 1958, and replaced by a tubular mast in the 1990s. Indeed the only part of old Ewood Park to survive is the Riverside Stand terrace, which forms the base of the reprofiled, single-tiered Walkersteel Stand.

Also shown here in 1987 (*left*) is the **Nuttall Street Stand**. Note its saw-tooth fascia boards; a feature typical of grandstands from the pre-1914 period.

Engineering Archie **93**

Bradford

Grounds
Park Avenue, Bradford 1907

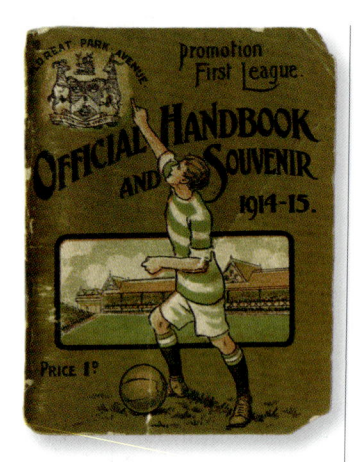

Leitch's distinctive grandstand and pavilion often featured on the covers of Bradford Park Avenue publications. Although demolished in 1980 the buildings remain emblematic of the club to this day. Another Scottish influence was Tom Maley. Appointed manager in 1911, Maley changed Bradford's colours to green and white hoops – those of Celtic – and with a predominantly Scottish team led Park Avenue into the First Division in 1914, seven years after the club's formation.

Extracts from the *Yorkshire Daily Observer*, August 20 1907:

"Those who were present at the cricket match at Park Avenue, Bradford, yesterday, could not fail to notice that the ground adjoining to that one which the counties of Yorkshire and Worcestershire were trying conclusions was a scene of great activity.

The Bradford Football Committee are, indeed, relying implicitly upon the public support in their adoption of Association football, and are giving heavy hostages to fortune. A sum of over £6,000 is at present being expended in order to make Park Avenue one of the most convenient and commodious grounds for Association in the country.

In order to do the very best that was possible with their site the committee secured the advice of Mr. Alexander Leitch (sic) of Glasgow, an architect who has earned for himself a high reputation in this special class of work, and who has been responsible for the planning and arrangement of several of the finest athletic grounds in the country, including those at Fulham, Chelsea, and Hampden Park (Glasgow).

(On this last point the paper was mistaken. Leitch did not work at Hampden until at least 1927.)

Under his direction far-reaching changes are taking place…

The accommodation for spectators has been completely overhauled. The old grand-stand – grand only in name – has been swept away, and in its place is being erected a huge steel pavilion no less than 360 feet long. This rises to a considerable height, with sixteen tiers of seats, so that it will accommodate no fewer than 4,000 persons.

By an ingenious utilisation of the space under the football seats, a considerable amount of seating will be rendered available for cricket requirements, while other parts of the basement of the stand will house the refreshment department.

New dressing-rooms are being erected in a villa-like pavilion adjoining Canterbury road. This building… will have a separate entrance and a passage way to the playing field, quite clear of the public parts of the ground, so that there can be no crowding upon players or referees on their entering or leaving the field. In the basement of the building are a good set of baths.

The large dressing-room is capable of division into two, for the home and visiting teams, when a match is in progress, while at other times it can be used for training purposes as one apartment. A room is provided for referees, and on the floor above a large room which commands a splendid view over the ground will at match-time be the committee-room, and at other times will be available as a reading-room for the players.

An immense amount of space is rendered available as standing-room…

Very careful consideration has evidently been devoted to this part of the ground by the architect, who, it may be suspected by the antiquary, has not been above accepting a few hints from the arrangements of the Coliseum in Rome.

The principal feature in the connection is the skilful arrangement of distributing passages, so that it shall be possible for every part of the terracing to be reached with the greatest facility.

At the same time the crowding pf the passages by spectators who decline to move on to their proper place is discouraged by sinking the passages somewhat, with the effect that they command less a advantageous views than the terraces…

At the Horton Park end of the ground the increase is very considerable, several thousands of loads of earth having been tipped here.

94 Engineering Archie

A novel feature, so far as Bradford is concerned, is in the provision for boys, which is in front of the ordinary terraces on the Canterbury Avenue side, and is sunk 2ft. 6in. below the level of the playing-field. This place, which commands good views without obstructing the sight of those on the terraces, is reached by a sub-way.

The accommodation provided is consequently as follows: - Grand pavilion, 4,000 persons seated and 3,000 standing under cover; under cover on the Park Avenue side of the ground, 5,000; terraces at Canterbury Road end, 9,000; terraces at Horton Park end, 14,000; standing room in front of pavilion, 2,000 – a total of no less than 37,000. To deal with this enormous crowd new entrances from Park Avenue, with new pay-offices, have been constructed.

The alterations are being carried out by Messrs. Henry Barrett & Sons, Bradford (steel works) and Messrs Roberts & Cottam, of Bradford, who are pressing on with the work so that the arrangements may be as forward as possibly by the opening of the season in September."

And ready they were. The ground re-opened on September 2, 1907, to widespread acclaim. A year later Leitch was back in town, designing a new stand for Park Avenue's neighbours, Bradford City (see page 98).

But though good for Archie's business, the existence of two professional football clubs, barely two miles apart, in a city the size of Bradford – only Stoke with two clubs was smaller – was always a risk-laden proposition.

That it came about at all says much about the business in which Leitch was operating.

Here was a branch of the burgeoning leisure industry, ripe for exploitation by entrepreneurs with egos to match their resources.

In the late 19th century west Yorkshire was regarded primarily as a rugby area. Then in 1903 Manningham became the first of several rugby clubs to switch to what was now viewed as the more lucrative code, football.

Manningham adopted the name Bradford City and were rewarded for their gamble by immediate election to the Football League (itself anxious to colonise new areas of the country).

Leeds, Huddersfield and Halifax would follow suit soon after. »

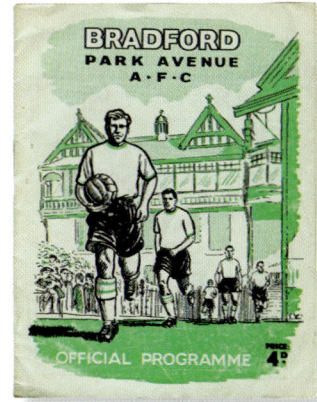

The provision for cricket, football (or rugby) and bowls on one site was common in the latter half of the 19th century. But only in Yorkshire did three such senior grounds survive into the modern era; at Headingley (see page 41), Sheffield (page 63) and Park Avenue (left) where the grounds were first laid out in 1880, opposite the recently opened Horton Park station. Although after Leitch's makeover in 1907 the football capacity was estimated at 37,000, the largest recorded gate was 32,429 for a Christmas Day derby v. Leeds in 1931. The cricket ground's capacity was approximately 20,000. This aerial view shows both pitches in use in May 1966. The football team were losing to Port Vale in front of 4,978 diehards.

Engineering Archie 95

Bradford

Bradford Park Avenue was the first ground to feature a Leitch double decker stand – with the balcony detailing that would become his trademark – albeit at a lower level than any of his later designs. At the rear, a narrow spectator gallery faced the cricket pitch. Three gables were repeated on both sides of the roof, which, unusually, was covered with Welsh slate. The clock on the central gable was regularly targeted by batsmen.

» Across Bradford at Park Avenue, meanwhile, the resident rugby club, formed in 1863 and called simply Bradford FC, appeared content as they were, sharing with the Bradford Cricket Club (formed 1836). They became Northern Union champions in 1904, and Challenge Cup winners in 1906.

But for the club's benefactor, Harry Briggs, the owner of the Brigella Mills at nearby Little Horton and much else in the wool business besides (with interests in Russia and Poland as well as Yorkshire), honours in the parochial world of northern rugby were not enough.

First Briggs tried to persuade Bradford City to merge with his club and make Park Avenue the new base for football. This made some sense. Park Avenue offered more potential than Valley Parade, while Briggs was wealthier and better-connected than any of the City directors.

But City's members voted against the deal – rather as Fulham rejected Joe Mears' offer to move to Stamford Bridge two years earlier – leaving Briggs more determined than ever to bring professional football to Park Avenue. Funding this seemingly reckless move, plus the implementation of Leitch's plans, cost Briggs at least £10,000 in 1907 alone. But then he spent as much on shares in another newly formed company three years later. Its name? Rolls Royce.

For a short period, both investments appeared sound.

After only one year's action, bizarrely in the Southern League – Briggs picking up the considerable travel expenses – Park Avenue somehow managed to secure election to the Football League alongside Bradford

City. The ground even staged an England international, v. Ireland, in February 1909.

Season 1919-20 saw the club finish 11th in the First Division. But just as they hit these heights, Briggs died. The following year, Park Avenue were relegated.

And there, more or less, the dream ended.

In 1938 one of Briggs' successors, Stanley Waddilove – another indulgent benefactor from the textile industry – again suggested a merger with City. He also advocated the development of a single municipal stadium for football and rugby.

But there were no takers, and matters went from bad to worse from the 1950s onwards. Park Avenue were finally voted out of the League in 1970. Four years later they disbanded.

Bradford Corporation bought the site in 1974, hoping that Bradford Northern RLFC (now Bulls) would rent it, thereby allowing their own Odsal Stadium site to be sold.

Northern, ironically, were formed by rugby players forced out of Park Avenue in 1907. But like City before them, Northern stayed put, and Park Avenue was left to rot.

Leitch's structures were demolished in 1980. The cricket pavilion followed in 1986, and although the cricket pitch survives, half the football pitch is now taken up by a fitness centre (originally built as a cricket school in 1988).

Otherwise, only the perimeter walls and stretches of Leitch's terracing, overgrown and crumbling, survive.

All professional sport is a gamble. But rarely are its failures so exposed to the lingering gaze as they are still, at Park Avenue.

The inexorable decline of Bradford Park Avenue's ground in Horton during the period 1973-80 is poignantly illustrated by these snapshots taken by a number of the club's bereft supporters. But if the ground now lies neglected and seemingly unwanted, the Park Avenue club itself reformed in 1988, and now plays non-league football at the Horsfall athletics stadium.

Engineering Archie 97

Grounds
Valley Parade, Bradford 1908

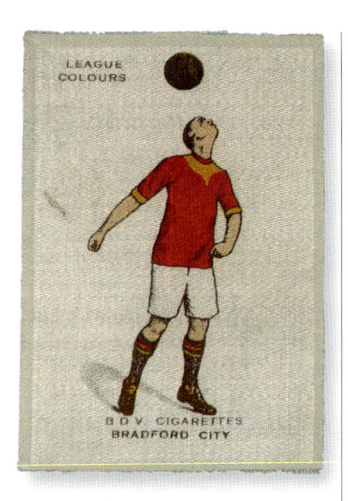

Throughout his working life Archibald Leitch was adept at finding pragmatic solutions for constricted or irregular sites.

Few were as idiosyncratic as Valley Parade.

Squeezed into just four acres, the ground had originally been laid out in 1886 by Manningham rugby club. Earlier still it was the site of a holy well.

Valley Parade's chief characteristic, however, was that it was dug into the side of a hill. From the western, or Manningham Lane side of the ground, down to the eastern, Midland Road side, there was (and still is) a fall of some 40-50 feet.

When Manningham dropped rugby and joined the Football League in 1903, the League were clearly so delighted to have secured a foothold in west Yorkshire that they appeared to overlook the ground's deficiencies. The home team had to change in a shed; the away team in an adjacent pub. Lorries provided extra vantage points on the unterraced ash banks. There were only three entry points.

The ground had also claimed its first fatality; a boy crushed when a wooden barrier on the Midland Road side collapsed in 1888.

Yet for all its faults, Valley Parade, and Manningham as a district, still exerted a powerful hold on City's members. As we learnt on page 96, they rejected a move to Park Avenue in 1907, and would repeatedly baulk at other suggested moves in later years.

Leitch arrived at Valley Parade in 1908. City had just won promotion to the First Division and, like most clients, demanded as much extra capacity as the site would yield.

Funded by the transformation of the club into a limited liability company, a programme of works costing £9,958 began immediately.

The existing iron and timber main stand was extended. The Manningham End was doubled in extent and transformed into a standard Leitch terrace, with barriers, sunken gangways and concrete footings. It was named Nunn's Kop, after a City director.

Two terraced houses adjoining the Kop were converted into club offices and changing rooms, and their cellars linked to the pitch by a tunnel under the terracing.

But Leitch's toughest challenge was the construction of a new stand on the Midland Road side, where the ground fell steeply by 20-30 feet to the road below.

Bridging this slope was further complicated by the fact that Midland Road was itself on a gradient, and did not run parallel to the touchline. Leitch thus had to span uneven ground at varying heights along the stand's 330 feet length, and to create a seating deck whose width had to taper from 27 feet to 13 feet from south to north.

Here, it would seem, was the ideal location for ferro-concrete, a relatively new wonder material Leitch had recently used at Anfield.

Concrete took longer than steel to erect, so only the foundations were in place when City made their First Division debut in September 1908. Some of the 30,000 crowd actually perched on the foundations to follow the game.

Within a few days of this sell-out occasion Leitch agreed to drop plans to put seats in the new stand, on the basis 'that two can stand

Long before their adoption by JK Rowling's fictional Hogwarts School, claret and amber were the unique colour combination of Manningham FC, the rugby club from which Bradford City emerged in 1903. One theory suggests that the colours were selected to signify blood and mustard, or blood and strength. Certainly their use in City's modern plastic seating creates at Valley Parade a vivid glow that can be seen for miles around.

Bradford City's first team lines up in 1921 in front of Leitch's Kop and Midland Road Stand (*right*). For another view of this unusual stand see page 50.

whereas one can sit' (a calculation which still holds true today).

Now holding 8,000, the Midland Road Stand opened on Christmas Day, 1908. Overall, Leitch's work had almost doubled the ground's capacity, so that Valley Parade was now able to accommodate a record 39,146 crowd in March 1911.

That same year City finished fifth in Division One and won the FA Cup for the first and only time in their history (at Old Trafford, another of Leitch's commissions).

Like many an early concrete structure the Midland Road Stand did not endure, partly owing to the inadequacies of the mix, partly because the stand was regularly wafted by noxious, acidic fumes from the nearby works.

The stand was demolished in 1951-52 and its steel upper framework re-erected as a stand for Berwick Rangers, where it is still in use (albeit in a quite different form.)

Valley Parade, meanwhile, has been completely transformed since the creaking iron and timber Main Stand – not a Leitch design – was destroyed by fire in 1985.

Fifty six fans died, yet still City and their fans clung to their home. Valley Parade now holds 25,136, including 4,500 in a new concrete and steel Midland Road Stand, opened by the Queen in 1997.

◀ Leitch's **Midland Road Stand** had two quite distinct elevations. To the rear its exposed concrete supports towered above the road; their clean, modern lines contrasting with the soot encrusted Victorian mills and chimneys of Valley Parade's industrial neighbours (until pollution took its toll on the concrete, at least).

But seen from the pitch, instead of emphasising the stand's concrete roots, its steel-framed upper section was finished with three traditional mock-Tudor gables, topped by decorative ironwork – yet another example of how British sporting interests preferred their buildings to be cloaked in familiar, vernacular guises.

After the Burnden Park disaster in 1946 safety checks on the Midland Road Stand led to the closure of its rear half, as shown (*left*) in this action shot from a match against Accrington Stanley in April 1949.

The stand was eventually cleared in 1952, and for the next 14 years Valley Parade operated on three sides only. The pitch was also moved closer to the Main Stand when it was feared the whole east side of the ground might subside.

These concerns, and the design faults which exacerbated the effects of the 1985 fire, were all consequences of the ground's hillside location.

Engineering Archie

Everton

Grounds

Goodison Park, Liverpool 1908–1938

Long before the Blues, the district of Everton was made famous by the toffees produced by one Molly Bushell. Thus Everton are known as the Toffees, Goodison is sometimes called Toffeeopolis, and before every home match a modern day Molly parades around the pitch before kick-off, distributing samples to the crowd. The toffees now of course come in a familiar striped mint coating.

In March 1907 one of Everton's directors, the cheery Dr Jimmy Baxter – medical practitioner, local councillor, community activist and football devotee – set off for London in the company of the club's architect, Henry Hartley.

Their aim was to visit the new grounds of Fulham and Chelsea, to learn how best they might plan the redevelopment of Goodison Park. Another director visited a new stand at Celtic, but was not impressed. It had windows along the front that kept steaming up.

Everton had, by that time, been at Goodison Park for 15 years, and were one of Britain's best supported and wealthiest clubs. A month after Baxter and Hartley's visit they were back in the capital to see Everton's second Cup Final appearance in succession.

Since the split with their patron John Houlding in 1892 – the famous row that led to Everton leaving Anfield and laying out their own new ground on the other side of Stanley Park – some £27,000 had been spent on Goodison Park, a considerable sum for the period, to attain a capacity of 55,000.

Goodison was indeed, until Villa Park opened in 1897, the best ground outside Glasgow. The 1894 Cup Final was staged there, as was the prestigious England v. Scotland international, a year later.

But modern methods were now catching up with Everton, while across the park their upstart rivals were gathering in strength. In 1901 Liverpool won their first League title. By 1907 their gates were matching those of the Blues.

And of course in 1906 Anfield had been given a complete makeover by Archibald Leitch.

Stage one of Goodison's revamp, starting soon after the 1907 Cup Final, was the erection of a new stand at the Park End, designed by Henry Hartley.

It was not an easy site: a line of terraced houses abutted the centre, requiring a wedge-shaped alcove to be cut into the stand's rear. But then, in the opposite corner of the ground there was another impediment to development, the church of St Lukes (b. 1901), and its adjoining church hall (1908), overshadowing the corner flag.

Only in England!

Hartley's stand may have looked the part, but the club minutes record a catalogue of quibbles with the Corporation's Building Surveyor and Health Committee over barriers, handrails, staircases and toilets. The stand's sightlines were also suspect, requiring the goal to be shifted seven feet northwards.

By January 1908 Hartley was complaining that his fees had not been paid, while the bill for the stand approached £13,000. For 2,657 seats on its upper tier with a terrace below, this did not appear to represent good value.

But before we leave poor Hartley – whose stand did, after all, remain in use for 87 years – we should credit him with contributing in one respect to Archie's own career as a designer.

While he was still engaged at Bradford City, in mid 1908 Everton hired Leitch to design a new main stand on the Goodison Road side, plus a cover at the North End.

They also requested Leitch-style terracing all round.

(The Bullens Road Stand, built 1895, would be left as it was.)

100 Engineering Archie

By November 1908 Leitch had prepared a model of 'the new Goodison Park'.

But the directors demanded one significant change.

Until Hartley's Park End Stand, the standard pattern for stand design was to place seats on a raised, covered tier, with a terrace directly in front. Hartley, however, had raised his seating deck higher, allowing the terrace to continue underneath, right up to the back wall, thereby offering a significant increase in capacity.

In effect, the Park End Stand was football's first large scale double decker.

In fact Leitch had already built his own first double decker, for Bradford Park Avenue (see page 94ff), in 1907. But it was a rather more tentative design, geared towards creating space at the rear for cricket spectators.

Now, at Everton, he was handed the opportunity to develop the form to a hitherto unprecedented scale.

Thus, in January 1909 began a 30 year relationship that would see Leitch build three double deckers, and in the process turn Goodison Park into the first ground in Britain to have standing and seating on all four sides.

Reprinted from a 1929 history of the club Leitch's scheme for Goodison shows the towering, cranked Main Stand on Goodison Road, built 1909 (with the roof of St Luke's Church in the foreground) and his proposed Bullens Road Stand opposite. Hartley's stand is at the far end. The Gwladys Street end had yet to be developed, awaiting the puchase of the houses behind.

Everton

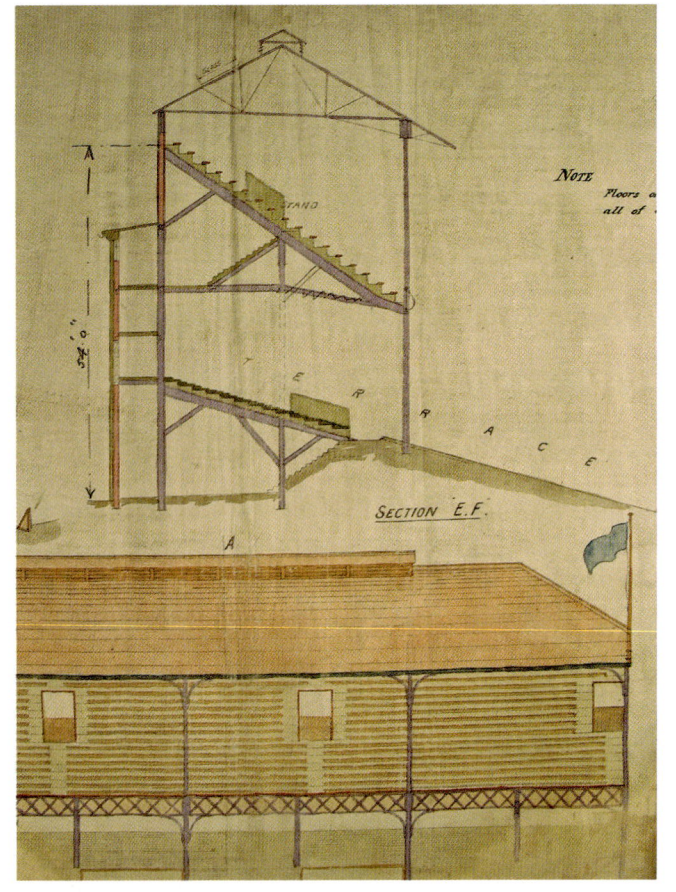

◀ 'Visitors to Goodison Park will be astonished at the immensity of the new double-decker stand,' gushed the *Athletic News* in September 1909. And so they were.

Leitch's first stand for Everton, the **Main Stand** on Goodison Road, was a colossal edifice.

Seating 3,500 on its upper tier, with a tapering terrace underneath holding 11,000, it towered 80 feet above the houses opposite – which did not seem to perturb local planners – and was his first large scale double-decker. It was also only the second to feature the criss-cross balcony detailing that became his trademark (the aforementioned stand at Bradford Park Avenue being the first, in 1907).

As we read earlier (*see page 44*), the steelwork contract was won by Francis Morton & Co., with their tender of £5,928, plus the offer of an extra two coats of paint.

By the end of 1908, however, Leitch had gone £3,500 over the original £12,000 budget. Everton's income for the entire 1908-09 season was just under £16,000.

Yet the club did not stop there.

Leitch was instructed to carry out a further £12,000 worth of improvements to the terracing in other parts of the ground.

Of this, £558 was spent on machinery tools and 'moulding boxes' to speed up the laying of concrete footings. Once the work was completed, Leitch then sold the boxes on to his next major clients, Manchester United.

Leitch clearly liked Everton, and the city of Liverpool. Everton's secretary, Will Cuff, a solicitor and fellow freemason, took over his legal affairs. The docks also offered scope for more industrial work, which may well have been drying up in his native Glasgow.

But whatever his reasons, by the time Everton's new stand opened, Leitch and his family had moved to Blundellsands, on the Crosby seafront, where they would remain for the next six years.

Ernest Edwards of the *Liverpool Echo*, the man credited with first giving Leitch's Anfield terrace the name of 'Spion Kop', wrote of Goodison's new stand in September 1909, 'It is of great height, of great length, and when Mr Leitch, the architect, told me that the winds blew when one mounted the top of the structure, there was not a suggestion of denial.

'The building, as one looks at it, suggests the side of the Mauretania at once.'

(The Mauretania, which had recently docked in Liverpool, was the world's largest ship.)

But though Edwards repeated the reference on several further occasions, unlike the Kop, the name 'Mauretania Stand' appears not have caught on. A shame.

Goodison Park staged a number of internationals until Wembley's monopoly started in the 1950s. In this one, v. Portugal, played as part of the Festival of Britain celebrations, Harold Hassall of Huddersfield is seen scoring England's fifth goal in a 5-2 win. Leitch's 'Mauretania Stand' forms a stirring backdrop.

▲ **Goodison Park** and its environs in 1938, showing all three of Leitch's stands, plus Henry Hartley's **Park End Stand** (*left*), with its oddly scooped rear, designed to accommodate the last house on Goodison Avenue.

Everton ended up buying these houses and renting them out to players, including the legendary Dixie Dean, whose statue now stands just a few yards away from where the houses once stood.

Leitch's second major work for Everton was the **Bullens Road Stand** (*foreground*), completed in 1926 at a cost of £30,000 and almost identical to one designed for Twickenham the year before.

This was joined in 1938 by Leitch's third stand at the **Gwladys Street End** (*right*).

Its construction, which totalled £50,000, had required the purchase and demolition of an entire row of houses (*seen on the artist's impression on page 101*).

Leitch was 73 when George VI and Queen Elizabeth came to inspect the structure that year.

It made Goodison Britain's first ground to have double-decker stands on all four sides.

Everton

▲ Snapshots of Goodison taken by a member of the groundstaff in 1963 show that, apart from the addition of floodlights and a newly constructed roof for the **Bullens Road Stand** (*above*), little had changed since 1938.

From this image and the action photo (*right*) we can see how, in between each of the upper tier's supporting columns, a sequence of four cross braced panels in the centre of the balcony is flanked by two with single inclined stays.

Designed to ensure optimal structural efficiency, this pattern, in varying numbers depending on the length of spans between columns, was echoed on all his other double decker stands, for example at Roker Park (*page 126*), Fratton Park (*157*), the Baseball Ground (*168*) and Ibrox Park (*183*).

▲ July 1966 and Leitch's **Bullens Road Stand**, with its new upturned roof, added three years earlier, is packed for North Korea's epic World Cup Quarter Final against Portugal, whose star striker Eusebio lies floored in front of goal.

No fewer than six of the eight World Cup venues used that summer had either been laid out by Leitch or still featured his stands.

To the left can be seen the **Gwladys Street End**; its simplified balcony detailing showing it to be a later construction. Tottenham's 1934 East Stand (*see page 112*) was similar.

Compared with World Cup stadiums today Goodison Park appears a humble setting. And yet in 1966 it was ranked highly, its capacity then being 52,000, compared with its highest ever attendance of 78,299, recorded v. Liverpool (naturally) in 1948.

Anfield's record, by comparison, was 61,905, four years later.

Yet when international football next came to Liverpool, for the 1996 European Championships, Goodison lost out to Anfield as a host venue. Leitch's legacy, it was now all too clear, was fading fast.

104 Engineering Archie

▲ Worries over hooliganism during the 1960s prompted Everton to experiment by cutting away a section of terracing behind each goal, to deter fans from throwing objects at the players. Within a few years the idea was abandoned.

On many other occasions the police had to contend with dozens of fans climbing on top of the roof of St Luke's Church.

Three years after this view was taken and 60 years after its opening, Leitch's Main Stand was demolished. In its place arose an even larger stand – a triple-decker no less – almost twice its height and therefore tall enough for the floodlight pylons (erected in 1957) to be taken down and the lights installed along the roof's leading edge (a practice now common).

Another change from this time onwards concerned the colouring of the ground. Until the 1960s the steelwork on Leitch's balconies was painted not in the club colours but in matt green. That, the absence of advertising, of coloured seating, and the dull grey-brown shade of the stands' corrugated sheeting lent grounds like Goodison a rather sombre air.

Engineering Archie **105**

Everton

▲ And so to the colourful Goodison of today; the reclad gable end of the **Bullens Road Stand** (*above*) providing a contrast to the scene in 1946 (*top*). A car park now occupies the training area. To the left is the single tier stand which replaced the Park End in 1994.

Goodison Park today provides an excellent opportunity to see the inner workings of a Leitch stand. Although modernised, the basic layouts of both the Bullens Road and Gwladys Street stands remain much as he designed them. One can even see original Kleine terracotta brick linings on the underside of each stand's upper tiers, while on the Bullens Road lower tier (*above*), the original wooden seats also survive on their timber treads. Less visible, alas, is Leitch's balcony (*top*), now virtually concealed behind advertisements.

106 Engineering Archie

▲ **Goodison Park** – shown here from the upper tier of the Gwladys Street Stand in 2004 – is a ground living on borrowed time. Since its capacity was reduced to 40,565 by the all-seater rule in 1994, and with up to 10 per cent of its seats suffering from restricted views in the Leitch stands' lower tiers, Everton have been desperately searching for an alternative.

Liverpool are planning a new 60,000 capacity stadium for 2006 on a corner of Stanley Park, no more than 600 metres from the scoreboard visible in the far corner.

In that sense the situation is similar to how it was a century earlier, when Everton again had to catch up with their neighbours.

For this reason Goodison's two Leitch stands – two of the eleven that remain in Britain today – may not be around much longer.

Tottenham Hotspur

Grounds
White Hart Lane, London 1908–34

It is assumed that the choice of a cockerel to represent Tottenham Hotspur – who were formed by members of the Hotspur Cricket Club in 1882 – alluded to the fact that fighting cocks wore spurs. The name itself reflected the ownership of large tracts of north London by the Duke of Northumberland, one of whose scions was the legendary 14th century warrior, Henry Percy, better known as 'Harry Hotspur'.

The year 1908 was a momentous one both for Tottenham Hotspur and Archibald Leitch.

That summer, Spurs resigned from the Southern League, fed up with its parochial attitudes and narrow fare, only to find, much to their horror, that their application to join the Football League failed for lack of support.

Then, just as it looked as if they might face a season with no competitive action at all, Stoke dropped out of the League and Spurs were in, courtesy of a ballot amongst members of the Management Committee.

To celebrate their good fortune, a souvenir booklet was issued.

'The Spurs...' waxed an excited John Cameron, their Scottish secretary-manager, 'there is magic in the name, and what a halo surrounds it... That they are the most popular club in the South there is no denying.'

Cameron had joined the club shortly before its move to White Hart Lane in 1899 and led them to become the first, and only, Southern League club ever to win the FA Cup, in 1901.

That same year Spurs bought the ground for £8,900 from the brewers Charringtons, who owned the adjacent White Hart Inn on Tottenham High Road (still extant). Once again, the prospect of all those thirsty fans had helped to shape the football map.

Over the following few years White Hart Lane, as the ground became informally known – that being the nearest railway station – would develop into a 40,000 capacity enclosure, with timber and iron stands, cinder banks and wooden barriers. Just about adequate for the Southern League, but not for a League club in the new century.

Hence, a few pages after John Cameron's piece, there appeared a portrait of Archibald Leitch, M.I.Mech.E., 'the well known Football Ground Expert' and 'Engineer for the reconstruction of the Spurs' Ground.'

Reproduced on page 34, the portrait is the earliest published photograph of Archie so far discovered in a football context.

And most telling its inclusion was too, for Leitch, aged 43 at the time, was to establish a bond with Tottenham that would endure for the rest of his life, and perhaps even match his relationship with Rangers – his first club – and Everton, with whom he also started work in 1908.

Of course this may simply have been owing to the fact that Spurs gave him so much work. Between 1908 and 1934 his company designed stands and redeveloped the terracing on all four sides of White Hart Lane.

Added to that, for two spells in his later life Tottenham were his local club; when he lived in Southgate during the mid 1920s and in Cockfosters from 1935 until his death.

But there may have been a further reason for Archie's attachment to Spurs, and that was the character of the club.

If it possible to characterise a football club by the composition of its board, then over the years Leitch worked for Spurs they were what may be considered a true footballing outfit. Unlike some of his other clients, such as Fulham, Arsenal, Chelsea, Bradford Park

750 Tottenham High Road was actually the address of the White Hart Inn, by the ground's main entrance. However in 1921 Spurs set up their offices in the property directly across the driveway, at number 748. This was a former Coffee Palace known as the Red House. The clock (*above left*) was mounted on its wall in 1934.

THE SPURS GROUND is situated at 750, High Road, Tottenham, within three minutes of White Hart Lane and Park Stations.

TRAMS PASS THE GROUND.

108 Engineering Archie

Avenue and Manchester United, there was no wealthy patron at the helm. One of the longest serving directors was Morton Cadman, a founder member and former player, who worked for Edmonton Borough Council.

Another director in 1908, Vivian Woodward, was actually the Spurs and England centre forward, despite his amateur status.

The chairman from 1898-1943, moreover, Charlie Roberts – once described as 'an enthusiastic member of the Herts Yeomanry' – was a great promoter of military tournaments, boxing and also of baseball. Apparently he had once been a pitcher for the Brooklyn Dodgers in New York. Roberts dominated the club, and yet also made sure that life was never dull.

The Spurs directors obviously valued Archie too.

Writing in a history of the club published in 1946, another director, G Wagstaffe Simmons, a journalist for *Sporting Life*, wrote of the late Mr Archie Leitch, 'It was due to his fertile brain, allied with an almost uncanny perception of the possibilities of sites, that the Spurs may now claim to have one of the best and most completely equipped football grounds in the world.'

'The Lane' was a Leitch ground through and through, as shown by this 1934 sketch by the company artist of the time, 'MacDonald'. All four stands were by Leitch, culminating in the grandest of them all, the East Stand, in the foreground. Just behind the West Stand gable can be seen the Red House and White Hart Inn, facing each other across the drive that led from Tottenham High Road.

Engineering Archie 109

Tottenham Hotspur

▶ Tottenham face Oldham Athletic in October 1932, with Leitch's **West Stand** and its distinctive Tudoresque gable looking down on the action.

Mounted on top of the gable can been seen a distinctive cockerel and ball. Crafted by WJ Scott, a former Spurs amateur, at Braby's coppersmiths in Euston Road, it was 9' 6" tall, cost £35, and is still on display elsewhere at the Lane (see page 113).

The stand itself, which held 5,300 seats on its upper tier with an enclosure for 6,000 in front, was opened on September 11 1909, when Spurs made their First Division debut with a visit from Manchester United, another of Leitch's clients at the time.

Two years after the photograph on the right, the West Stand's roof was re-erected under the direction of Leitch's son, Archibald Kent Leitch (who became a partner in the firm in 1927), with a new main truss and five solid columns instead of the original ten lattice supports.

As can be seen from the exterior (right), the stand was not one of Leitch's more elaborate efforts, being clad entirely in corrugated sheeting. The poet Alan Ross was not impressed. In 1950 he wrote, 'Huge grey walls surround the ground, a barrier to revolution. They might have enclosed a prison or a mental home.'

110 Engineering Archie

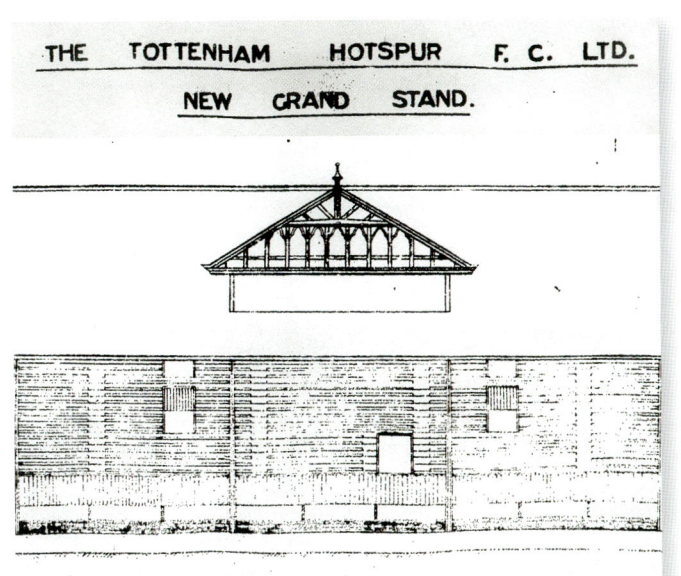

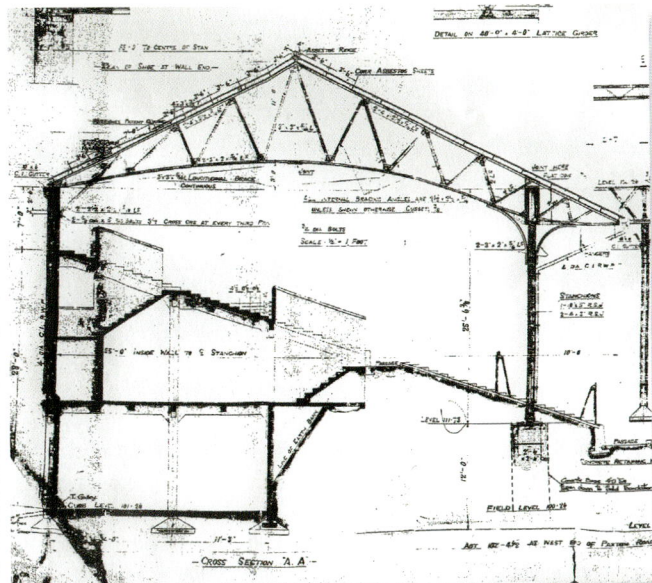

▲ Tottenham were the first club to build substantial covered terraces at both ends of the ground.

After the completion of the **West Stand** in 1909 (*top left*) Leitch continued expanding and converting the other three sides of banking into concrete terracing with his usual patented crush barriers, taking the overall capacity up to 50,000 by 1911.

Ten years later the profits from a second FA Cup Final win were used to build a roof over the **Paxton Road End** terrace (*top right*), followed in 1923 by an almost identical roof over the **Park Lane End**. Each cost around £3,000.

As can be seen from the 1920s aerial view (*above right*), this left the narrow east side, hemmed in by a row of terraced houses.

Spurs eventually bought these properties with the intention of clearing them. But a housing shortage stayed their hand, and it was only after they managed to rehouse some tenants, and compensate others – bringing the total cost of the exercise to £5,000 – that demolition could proceed in 1934 (*above left*), thereby creating the space for Leitch's last stand.

Engineering Archie **111**

Tottenham Hotspur

▶ 'There is no need for me to dwell upon the majestic lines of the new Stand. They are a credit to Mr Archie Leitch, the designer.'

Thus wrote G Wagstaffe Simmons in his 1946 history, in which he put the total costs of the **East Stand**, the clearance of the houses, and the re-roofing of the West Stand, at £60,000, a sum that was, much to Spurs' relief, underwritten by Barclays Bank.

And – as seen in these views from 1959 and 1985 – majestic the stand was too, if somewhat conservative compared with the two Art Deco stands built for Arsenal during the same period (albeit at a much higher cost).

Two features which made the stand a cut above the standard Leitch double-decker were the provision of a mid-level terrace, which became known as 'the Shelf,' and a 'crows-nest' press box (which in 1958 became the new home for the cockerel and ball).

But although similar to one Leitch designed for the South Stand at Ibrox in 1928 (see page 183), the 109-seat box was never used by the press.

Otherwise the stand had seats for 4,983 on its upper tier, and standing for 13,349, bringing the Lane's total capacity to 75,000.

The East Stand opened in September 1934. The following May, Spurs were relegated.

▶ Tottenham's **East Stand** is one of eleven Leitch stands still in use. But apart from its brick façade (*below right*) one needs a keen eye to detect its original form.

The first major alterations to Leitch's work elsewhere in the Lane saw the installation of seats in the rear sections of both end stands in 1962-63, resulting in a reduced capacity of 60,000.

The replacement of Leitch's West Stand, between 1980-82, reduced it still further to 48,200, as the board deliberately aimed at a more upmarket audience by providing 72 executive boxes, more than any other ground in Britain at the time.

A Spurs manager famously walked away from the Lane during this period, lamenting 'There used to be a football club over there.'

The East Stand received its first makeover in 1989. By then the press box was so rickety that Paul Gascoigne – 'Gazza' – then a Spurs player, fell through the floor while up there shooting pigeons.

The initial refurbishment resulted in a new roof (*top right*) and, much to the chagrin of regular fans, the installation of yet more executive boxes, and seats, on the Shelf.

Finally, during the 1990s, both of Leitch's end stands were replaced, and the East Stand's lower terrace seated (*centre*).

White Hart Lane is thus now an all-seated and more or less joined up bowl holding 36,237; effectively half the level Leitch attained (thereby proving his rule that 'two may stand where one can sit').

But it is not enough, which means that either the East Stand must be replaced, or Spurs must move on. Archie, of all people, would understand this.

After all, it was this same drive for modern facilities that brought him to the Lane in the first place.

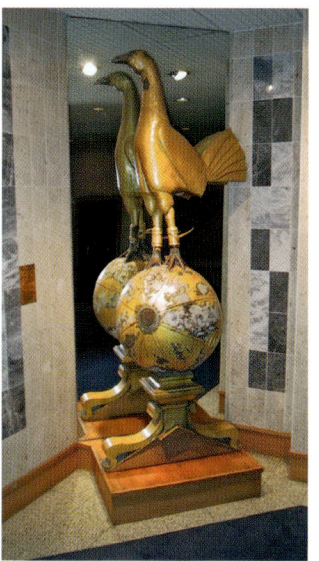

The cockerel which once topped the West Stand, and later the East, is now retired to the lobby of the East Stand (*top*), while a modern replica now takes its place on the roof. For years it was rumoured the original ball contained secret documents, but when it was finally opened up for restoration in 1989 only a very soggy 1909 handbook was found.

Engineering Archie 113

Grounds
Old Trafford, Manchester 1908–10

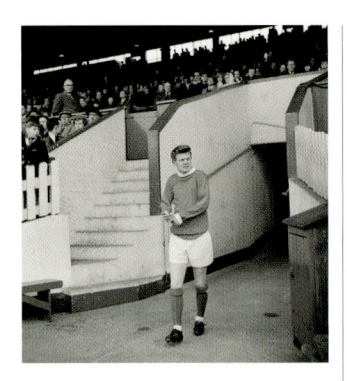

'The directors, players and officials will obtain access to the field of play from a tunnel which will debouche from the centre of the stand.' (*Athletic News, March 1909*) That same South Stand tunnel, shown above in the mid 1960s – and now used only as an access route – is all that remains of Archibald Leitch's work at Old Trafford. The stand itself was destroyed during an air raid in March 1941, while Leitch's terracing was swept away in a series of redevelopments between 1965-93. Making his debouche above was a United youth called Bobby Noble.

At the tail end of the 20th century there was considerable debate in football circles as to whether the national stadium should be in London, at a rebuilt Wembley, or in either Birmingham or Manchester.

There was also continued friction between the Football Association and leading clubs in the professional game.

Ninety years earlier Archibald Leitch was caught up in almost exactly the same tensions.

One encounter neatly sums up the two factions. Charlie Sutcliffe, the Rawtenstall solicitor and League official, was in a motor-coach after an international match, when a suave gent in an FA blazer boarded. Someone asked who this man represented. 'The public schools,' came the response, to which the questioner added, 'And so who do we represent?'

Said Sutcliffe, 'The public houses.'

Manchester United were one of a new breed of football clubs. Before being rescued from bankruptcy and renamed in 1902 they had been called Newton Heath. Their base was a ramshackle ground in Clayton, a district dominated by the belching chimneys of local factories.

The man who saved them was a wealthy brewer, John Henry Davies. He knew little of football, but a good deal about business.

Edwardian Manchester had many such characters. Enriched by the profits generated by the recently opened Manchester Ship Canal and keen to embrace the burgeoning leisure industry, the city's entrepreneurs poured investment into billiard halls, amusement parks, an ultra-modern racecourse and Britain's most advanced ice rink. The city fathers, meanwhile, pumped money into the most palatial municipal swimming baths ever known, the Victoria Baths.

But as yet, the city had no stadium to match the likes of London or Glasgow, and no footballing honours either.

This was about to change. In 1907 the local press revealed that United were eyeing a move to Old Trafford, a good three miles from Clayton on the other side of the city, close to the borders with Salford, and in a part of the old Trafford Park estate where sport and leisure had been concentrated since the 1860s. Trams from the city and trains from the new suburbs passed close by. The roads were wide, the nearest houses were distant enough not to matter, and there were 16 acres of level, unused land available.

The site, it transpired, had been bought for use by one of the two companies Davies chaired, the Manchester Brewery.

Here was the perfect opportunity for Leitch to use all the experience he had gained since the 1902 disaster to build a large scale stadium from scratch, with virtually no site constraints, for a client with deep pockets.

Except at Ibrox in 1899, when he was still new to the business, and Ayresome Park in 1903, where money had been tight, before United came along all his work had been at grounds that already existed (even Stamford Bridge, which had been an athletics venue and occupied an eleven acre site with limited access).

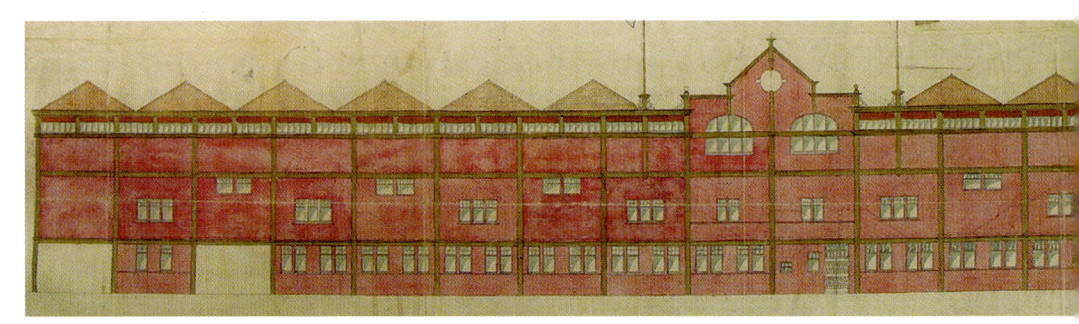

114 Engineering Archie

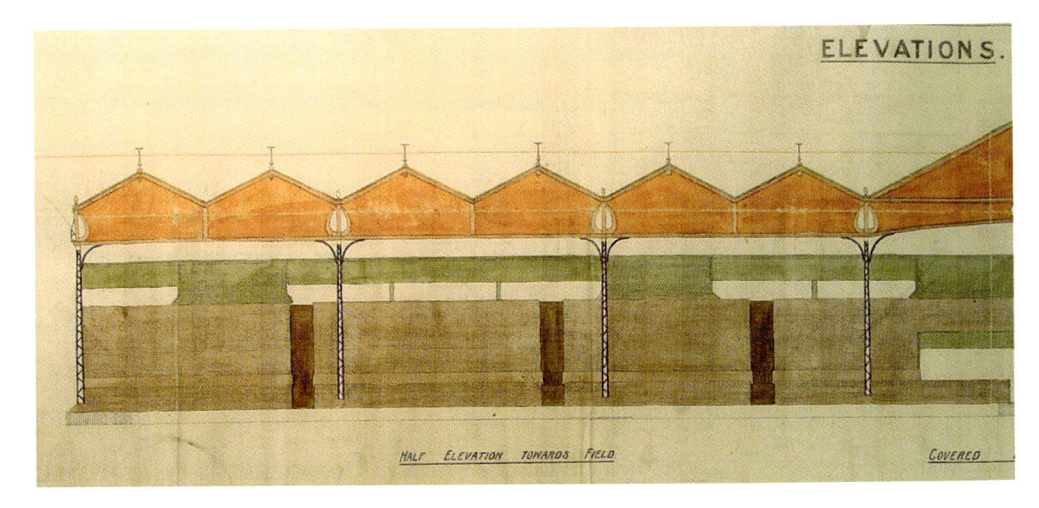

But there were other issues at play by the time Leitch arrived.

The early 1900s saw a string of clubs punished by the FA for financial irregularities. United themselves were continually targeted for investigation, though they also benefited from this crackdown by signing four top players from neighbours Manchester City, who were hit by a particularly stiff suspension in 1906. Bolstered by these signings, just as Leitch was starting on his scheme, United won their first League title in April 1908. Their winning combination of business nous and footballing guile made the amateur enforcers at the FA appear like helpless onlookers.

Then, two months after United's League triumph, the Olympic Games opened in London. They were staged at the hurriedly completed White City Stadium in Shepherd's Bush. (Rome, the original hosts, had dropped out following the eruption of Mount Vesuvius in 1906.)

Although it was no great work of architecture, and was upstaged by the surrounding pavilions and halls of the Franco-British Exhibition, also held in 1908, White City was nevertheless the world's first purpose built Olympic Stadium of the modern era. With a capacity variously stated at 60-130,000 it had cost a staggering £85,000.

With better planning White City might have replaced Crystal Palace as the *de facto* national stadium. Instead, it proved ill-suited for viewing field sports – the curse of many an Olympic venue – and after the Games survived only on a diet of occasional athletics and, after 1927, greyhound racing.

Leitch played no part in the White City design. But he must surely have scrutinised it closely, and shared with United's directors, and the Manchester press, a desire for Old Trafford to upstage the capital and wrest from Crystal Palace the right to stage Cup Finals and internationals and perhaps, in the process, transfer power from the FA in London to the powerbase of the professional game in the north.

Manchester's ally in this was John Bentley, president of the Football League, an FA Councillor, a director of United and a former editor of the best selling football weekly, *Athletic News* (itself based in Manchester). It was Bentley who had helped persuade the FA to stage two Cup Finals in the north in 1893 and 1894 (the former, embarrassingly, a fiasco at a poorly equipped athletics stadium in Fallowfield, Manchester).

Such was the loaded stage onto which Archibald Leitch stepped in 1908. »

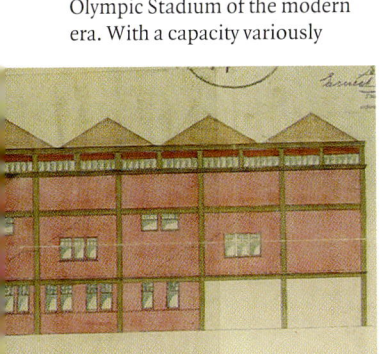

Old Trafford was designed by Leitch in collaboration with the Manchester architects Brameld and Smith, although the level of their input is hard to discern from the drawings that survive, such as these two elevations emanating from the temporary office Leitch set up during the ground's development, in King Street. The contractors were, as so often, Humphreys of Knightsbridge. Note the similarities of the multi-spanned roof design with that of another Leitch-Humphreys collaboration, the East Stand at Highbury (see *page 130*), built three years later.

Manchester United

THE NEW HOME OF MANCHESTER UNITED.
A GREAT GROUND FOR THE NORTH.

THE ARENA WHEN COMPLETED.
(FROM COPYRIGHT DRAWINGS BY MR. A. E. LEITCH, M.I.M.E.)

Reproduced here are edited extracts from an article in *Athletic News*, March 8 1909, written by 'Tityrus' (JAH Catton, John Bentley's successor as editor). Several of the design elements cited would become enshrined in basic stadium design for the next 80 years. Note that Old Trafford's opening took place in February 1910 rather than September 1909, as anticipated. By then certain cuts had been ordered by John Bentley to reduce costs. The capacity was limited to 80,000, and the north terrace cover omitted. Even so the final cost was double the figure of £30,000 reported here, crippling the club and delaying further developments until the 1930s, by which time United's star had well and truly waned.

"The West of Manchester is destined to be the Mecca of the sportsmen of that great commercial city. "To the West, To the West" will be the cry of our football folks when leaves are falling next autumn. Already we have the Lancashire County Cricket Ground, the Northern Lawn Tennis Club, the Manchester Gun Club, the Polo ground, the curling pond, the Manchester Golf Club, and numerous other organisations of a similar character devoted to pastime and recreation to the West of the city.

In September the Manchester United Football Club will fling open its portals and bid all welcome in the same locality. The contrast between Clayton and the new headquarters of this great football club need not be insisted upon. Clayton is situated in the very heart of a working class community, and dominated on every hand by about forty huge stacks of chimneys, belching forth Cimmerian smoke and malodorous fumes. No doubt there are those who feel thankful for a football ground in the vicinity, as it does tend to remind the immediate residents that there is some space left where the toiling people can be amused in a healthy and vigorous manner that pleases them.

But an ambitious and a vast club like Manchester United appeals to the 800,000 folks of Manchester and Salford – and an arena of larger dimension, with better accommodation for seeing and housing the spectators, and situated in a more attractive locality, became essential.

The club have resolved to lay out and equip a huge ground wholly and solely devoted to football. There will not be any running or cycling track round the grass, and for football alone there will not be a better enclosure in England. It is to accommodate 100,000 people, and if some of the greatest matches of the day are not in turn decided in Manchester we shall be surprised, especially as the club is not frightened to expend £30,000 on their undertaking.

The ground will be rectangular in shape, with the corners rounded, and it is designed so that everybody will be able to see. The pitch will be excavated to a depth of nine feet from ground level, so that the boundary or containing wall which is to surround the whole place will only be 30 feet high. There are numerous entrances and spacious exits and it is estimated that a full ground can be emptied in five minutes.

Now let us assume that the ordinary spectator has passed through the turnstile. He will find himself in a passage twenty feet broad which girdles the whole arena. From this access can be obtained to any portion of the popular terracing, which is virtually divided into three sections. There will be 100 steps of terracing – constructed on a special plan, and a nicely judged gradient – with, of course, Leitch's patent crush barriers. The lower portion of this terracing is solid ground, the next higher is formed by the excavated earth, and the last and highest is built entirely of ferro-concrete – which is as hard as rock and non-inflammable.

The difficulty of club managers hitherto has been to get the spectators properly distributed. Gangways and finger-posts, and other devices, have been brought into use to avoid people bunching themselves into solid masses and preventing the later arrival from getting to portions which are not, so to speak, thickly populated. With his practical experience of all the best grounds in these islands, Mr Archibald Leitch, M.I.M.E., of Manchester, who has been the only designer, has endeavoured to cope with this problem. There seems every reason to believe that he has solved it.

Now, from this 20 feet passage, which will, of course, afford protection from rain until it is absolutely necessary to go into the open, the horde of human beings can melt away at will. Right in front of the visitors, whichever entrance they take, will be a flight of very broad but easy stairs, which end in a wide opening or mouth, 60 feet wide, and split into three sections. The stream of sightseers mounting these stairs and reaching the opening find themselves rather above the middle of the terracing, over which they can spread themselves at will. We can picture these great mouths vomiting thousands upon thousands of human beings on to this glorious amphitheatre. The advantage of each mouth is its central position.

But if the spectator wishes to go right on top of the terracing, any tier above the sixtieth, he will take another wide staircase which lands him on the top of the forty tiers of ferro-concrete, resting on foundations of the same material, the space underneath being utilised for refreshment rooms and other conveniences.

The accommodation will, as said, provide for 100,000 people. Of these 12,000 will be seated in the grand stand, and 24,000 standing under steel and slated roofs, so that altogether there will be room for 36,000 folks under cover and 64,000 in the open, divided between the two arcs of a circle – the mammoth terraces behind the goal. The roofed part for the populace will be on the northern side, and will have open ends with overhanging eaves, so that no portion of this erection will obstruct the view of those who are not

116 Engineering Archie

fortunate enough to secure its shelter on an inclement day.

The special feature of the grand stand compared with similar erections is that there will not be a paddock in front of it. The spectators will be seated from the barricade round the pitch, direct to the back of the stand, in 50 tiers. These 50 tiers are again divided into three sections, the lower, the middle, and the highest. Spectators desiring to be comfortable in the grand stand will enter from turnstiles facing the south, or Chester-road. They are specially reserved for grand stand spectators only, and there they can obtain tickets for any part of the stand.

Entering there, the spectators will find themselves in a corridor, along which run tea-rooms, referees' apartments, the players' quarters, a gymnasium, billiard-room, and laundry, all of which are to be fitted up in the most modern manner. From this central corridor there are means of access to the three sections of the grand stand. The lowest or front portion will be approached by a number of passages on the ground floor. To the middle or central portion there are stairs which run practically the whole length of the stand. The highest part is to be gained by means of a distributing passage, which is as long as the stand, and 20 feet broad. Stairs lead from this to the loftiest section. Thus the structure is designed in such a manner that each person will be able to get to his seat with the least discomfort to himself and the minimum of inconvenience to his neighbours, because there is a separate means of ingress to each section.

The man who wishes to go to the top of the stand has not to disturb those sitting on the lower rungs, and this applies to each portion – for every detail has been carefully thought out both by Mr Leitch, the master-mind, and Messrs Brameld and Smith, of Manchester, who were responsible for the extensions and improvements at the Clayton ground, the present home of the Manchester United F.C. The directors, players, and officials will obtain access to the field from a tunnel, which will debouche from the centre of the stand. The offices for the secretary and clerks will be constructed in a portion of the ferro-concrete terracing, almost facing the bridge over the Cheshire Lines. Thus they will be well placed for intending visitors and the home officials. Between the grand stand and the railway there will be an enclosed street 45 feet broad – entirely reserved for private motors – not public vehicles.

Altogether, the entire area of the new home of Manchester United will be 16 acres. The outward circumference of the ground will be about 2,000 feet. The ground will be 630 feet long and 510 feet broad, the width of all the terracing being 120 feet. This is a palatial ground which will challenge comparison with any arena in Great Britain. The executive of Manchester United are to be congratulated on their spirited policy, which, no doubt, will meet with reward from the football public."

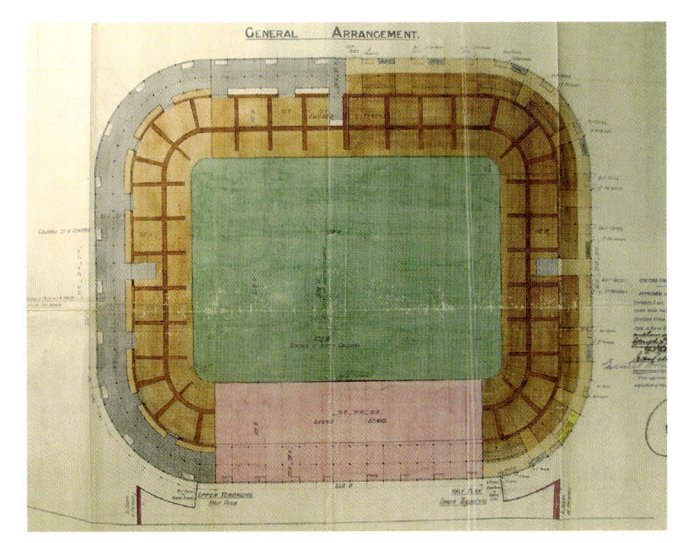

Old Trafford's only drawback was its east-west axis, so that goalkeepers defending the Warwick Road end must face the sun. Also, only in 1934 would terrace cover be provided, with two wing stands being added to the south stand in 1938.

Engineering Archie 117

Manchester United

▲ Opening day at **Old Trafford** on February 19 1910, and members of 'Rocca's Brigade' assemble with their accordions to usher in the new era. Louis Rocca, who set up United's scouting system (which extended even to a network of Catholic priests), came from an ice-cream making family in the Little Italy district of Ancoats. He joined Newton Heath as a tea boy and was said to be the one who suggested the name Manchester United, in 1902.

Old Trafford's opening packed the streets with 'trams, buses, cabs, taxis, costers' carts, coal lorries, and all manner of strange things on wheels,' reported the *Manchester Guardian* (whose editor CP Scott had been a vocal champion of the club in its formative years).

Officially the crowd numbered 45,000, but a further 5,000 were said to have sneaked in, many through an unfinished window.

'The grandstand,' continued the *Guardian* '...was a new luxury unknown till then, with stewards to direct VIPs to "plush tip-up seats" as though in a theatre or cinema. The pitch itself – after the years of mud and glue at Newton Heath and Clayton – resembled the surface of a bowling green.'

Liverpool, United's opponents on the day, adapted better to the unfamiliar surroundings, winning the game 4-3.

As the *Guardian* concluded, 'These swell grounds need some living up to.'

» Documents from the period before and after Old Trafford's construction reveal much about the process of ground development at this time.

For example, we know that Leitch played an active role in trying to secure funding. In one letter he requested a £10,000 loan from the Cheshire Lines Railway, whose line ran immediately alongside the site, and who, it was presumed, would be eager to build a station close by. They declined.

For their part, Humphreys, the builders, yet again found themselves in the position of having to chase a football club for payment; a process they went through so often and with so many clubs that one can only marvel at their commitment to the sport.

Meanwhile, United continued to be plagued by Football Association officials, who were clearly concerned at the blurring of John Davies's private business and that of the club.

United's minutes suggest a catalogue of crises. While the team won the FA Cup for the first time in 1909, shortly before they moved into Old Trafford, and a second League title in 1911, the directors seemed overwhelmed by expense.

Ellison's, the Salford turnstile manufacturers who supplied most of the leading clubs, were not paid until seven months after the ground's opening. By October 1910 solicitors acting for Humphreys had to intervene, beginning a process of debenture payments that continued for decades. At times United were paying up to a third or more of their gate receipts to Humphreys, the sums often outstripping the wage bill.

Davies had frequently to loan the club substantial sums

therefore; £1,000 in November 1910 (the equivalent of £57,000 today), £2,500 the following May, lesser sums almost weekly.

And yet the ground was a real success. A crowd of 65,000 attended a United match in February 1911. Two months later Old Trafford staged the Cup Final replay, and in April 1915 it was the venue for the so-called Khaki Cup Final, when Crystal Palace was unavailable due to military use.

Old Trafford also hosted an England v. Scotland international in 1926, three years after Wembley had opened. But it never quite managed to accommodate the 80,000 Leitch had intended. Its record was 76,962, for a Cup semi-final in 1939.

As for United, the cost of the ground seems to have worn them down. John Bentley resigned in 1916, exhausted by the financial juggling act he had been forced to perform since he took over as secretary in 1912.

On the pitch, after their brilliant manager Ernest Mangnall decamped to rivals Manchester City in 1912, United not only sank into the Second Division but one year only just avoided relegation to the Third. During the 1930s crowds of under 10,000 would often echo in the vast arena.

As for John Davies, ever generous, always charitable, he died in 1927, shortly after the club finally agreed the purchase of the ground from his company, the Manchester Brewery (a deal handled, incidentally, by Charlie Sutcliffe). It needed the emergence of another tough magnate, James Gibson, a clothing manufacturer, in 1932, to provide the stability on which the post war revival under Matt Busby could eventually be founded.

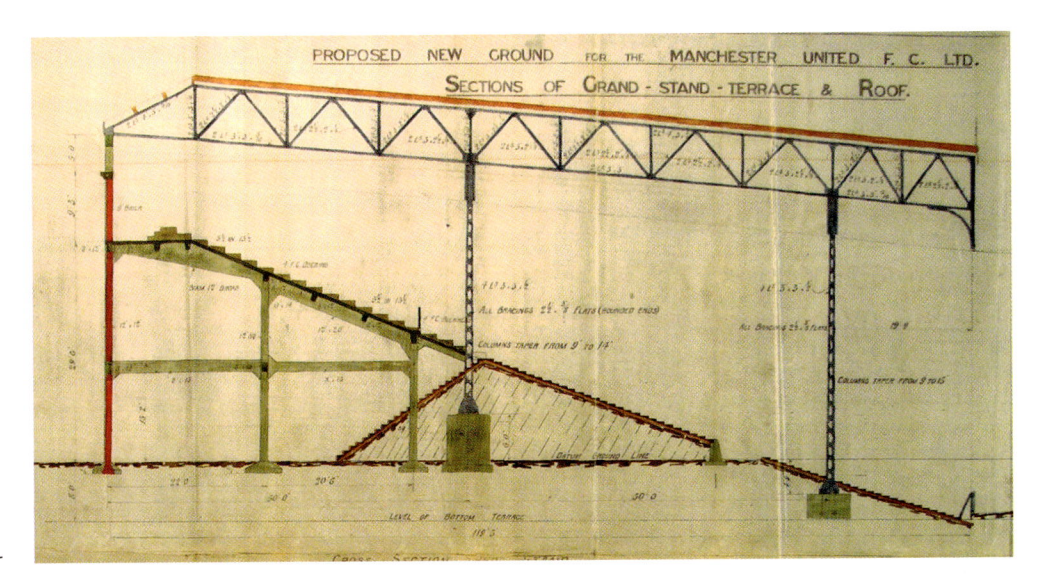

Yet in two major respects United's original decision to invest in Old Trafford has paid off.

Firstly, the site itself has stood the test of time, in terms of access and space. When needed United have also been able to gain the room needed for expansion.

Secondly, by investing from the start in a rationally planned stadium, a platform was laid upon which two subsequent major redevelopments, from 1965-93, and from 1995 to the present day, were able to follow in a relatively seamless progression. No other British club venue has advanced in such a planned, orderly fashion throughout its history.

In that sense alone, Leitch's Old Trafford truly was the first modern stadium of the 20th century.

The destruction of Leitch's South Stand during an air raid in March 1941 left only the two wing stands (added in 1938 by E. Wood & Sons) intact, forcing United to share with Manchester City until repair work was finally sanctioned by the Ministry for Works in 1949. Yet the club's post war revival under manager Matt Busby proved so lucrative that having faced debts of £75,000 in 1940 they were finally able to clear what they owed on the ground in 1951, 41 years after its inauguration. Leitch's section (*above*) shows how the pitch was sunk nine feet below ground level.

Engineering Archie 119

Millwall

Grounds
The Den, London 1910–1949

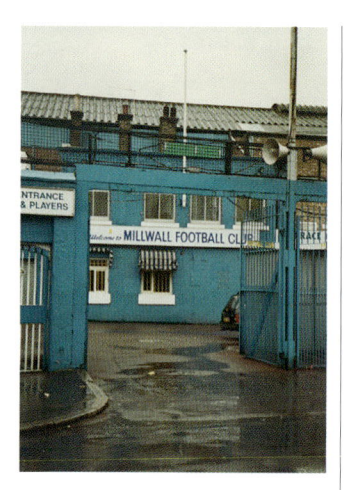

After the unabashed ambition of Old Trafford, Leitch's next commission called for a rather more pragmatic approach.

Millwall Athletic – the Lions – were, in 1909, an insecure Southern League club with a proud tradition. They were the dockers' team, based on the Isle of Dogs, where they had been formed in 1885 by mainly Scottish workers at a jam factory. But the lease on their North Greenwich ground was about to expire and so, like Manchester United, they decided to build a larger ground in a more advantageous location, using Leitch as their masterplanner.

Millwall moved barely two miles. But the distance seemed greater for their new home lay on the other side of the Thames.

Fans on the island felt betrayed by this departure. But there were never enough of them in North Greenwich, while the antiquated docklands railway serving their old ground was notoriously unreliable. New Cross, by contrast, had a dense population and three suburban railway stations close at hand.

At Old Trafford Leitch had a generous budget and 16 acres at his disposal. At New Cross the Millwall directors struggled to raise £10,000 to develop a rhubarb and cabbage patch barely covering four acres. More challengingly, Leitch and his regular building partners, Humphreys of Knightsbridge (his collaborators also at Old Trafford), had to fit the ground into an awkward, almost triangular site, its boundaries formed by three railway lines, with only one side accessed by road, at the Coldblow Lane End. Just carting in the rubble needed to form the embankments took months of arduous manual labour.

Yet the ground's limitations were also its strengths.

The Den – as this new home of the Lions was suitably titled – soon earned its place in the demonology of football.

One of the first to experience its rough-house atmosphere was Lord Kinnaird, the portly Old Etonian and President of the FA, who was only able to perform the opening ceremony – in October 1910 – after being manhandled over a wall as crowds blocked the ground's narrow approaches.

Still, Kinnaird put on a brave face as he posed for cameras shortly after this ordeal. To his left stood Leitch; bowler-hatted, apparently smoking, just as he had appeared before the opening of Old Trafford eight months earlier (*see front cover*).

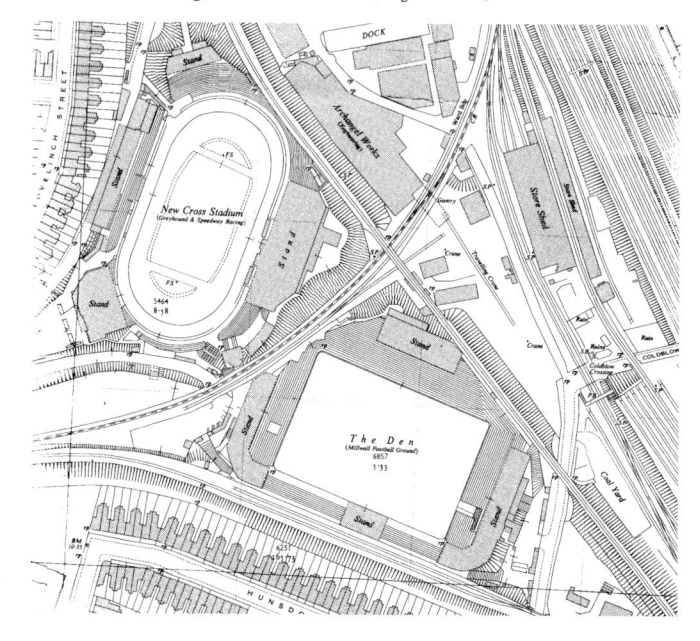

Aptly named and oft referred to by visiting reporters, Millwall's address from 1910-93 was 'The Den, Coldblow Lane'. Secreted in a web of narrow streets and railway lines between the Old Kent Road and Rotherhithe, if Arthur Conan Doyle or Jack London had ever woven football into one of their murkier plots, this is where they would have come for inspiration. The offices above, added by Leitch in 1929, offered a suitably downbeat welcome.

Three lines skirt the Den, while from 1934-75 the New Cross greyhound and speedway stadium loomed large above the west, or Ilderton Road terrace. This 1950 Ordnance Survey map shows how embankments, cuttings, bridges, yards and industrial sheds enveloped The Den in a tight grip.

120 ENGINEERING ARCHIE

There was never enough money, nor any demand, for much architectural expression at The Den. Millwall did turn out to be regular clients, however.

After they joined the Football League in 1920, Leitch expanded, concreted and partially covered the three other sides of terracing at the ground, and built offices and a club area behind the Coldblow Lane end.

This work culminated in a record crowd of 48,672 for a Cup tie v. Derby in 1937, when Millwall, still in Division Three, reached the semi-final of the competition.

Millwall were also one of only two clubs who we know for sure hired the Leitch company after the war.

Archie having died in 1939, it was his son, Archibald Kent Leitch in charge at the time. Most of the work, between 1947-49, was restitution required after extensive damage caused by bombing in 1943, followed a week later by a fire in the main stand (a discarded cigarette rather than enemy action being the culprit this time). Apart from other minor projects at Craven Cottage this may well have been the company's last meaningful work in football before it ceased trading in 1955.

As for The Den, it was finally replaced in 1993 by the New Den, built a short distance away and designed, like its predecessor, by Scottish architects, the Miller Partnership. The New Den was England's first purpose-built all-seated football stadium.

Few would have imagined Millwall being such trendsetters. And yet their new home was in a quite familiar setting; an almost triangular site, bound by industry and two railway lines, with only one road leading to its door.

◀ As lions' dens go, Millwall's was no place for the timid. No other British ground was closed more often than The Den as a result of crowd trouble. Small wonder that from 1964-67 Millwall remained unbeaten there for a record 59 successive games.

Before it was levelled by fire in 1943, Leitch's main stand featured a standard gable (*shown left in the 1930s*). Behind the far Ilderton Road terrace the taller structure visible was the Tote Board of the New Cross Stadium. After this was demolished in 1975 a turfed rise (*just visible in the 1985 image, left*) offered a free spot from which to view matches inside The Den. Indeed the view from there was better than from the corner of the Ilderton Road terrace itself. So hemmed in behind the floodlight pylon was it that in 1991 three fans successfully sued Millwall for recompense. Thereafter, clubs were ordered to warn spectators of restricted views before entry.

Also shown is The Den's North Terrace, or 'The Halfway' as it was known (*seen left in 1967*), and the unprepossessing approach to the Ilderton Road End (*below left in 1992*), after the railway lines had been cleared. The brick exterior was typical of Leitch's work at the lower end of the football market.

The site of The Den is now occupied by housing.

Engineering Archie **121**

Huddersfield Town

Grounds
Leeds Road, Huddersfield 1910–11

Football has always been a fickle business, as Archibald Leitch's next clients, Huddersfield Town, were about to discover.

As outlined in the earlier sections relating to Bradford, the association game was a late starter in west Yorkshire, and even later in Huddersfield, where the Northern Union had famously formed at the George Hotel in 1895, signalling the birth of what would later be called rugby league. Six years after Bradford City and four years after Leeds City, Huddersfield Town were not born until 1908.

Leitch was called in towards the end of their second season in regional football; his task, to draw up improvement plans that would back up Town's application to join the Football League.

Up to that point Leeds Road had been laid out on a shoestring, with a wooden stand, no turnstiles and a disused tramcar serving as a ticket office. But the five acre site was at least level, easily accessed and with houses bordering only the Leeds Road boundary.

A crowd of 8,000 had attended an amateur international there in February 1910, on the same day Leitch had been in Manchester for the opening of his greatest work to date, Old Trafford. Now he was busy preparing another new ground in London, for Millwall.

Leeds Road should have been a routine commission. Apparently one of its drawbacks was its exposure to strong winds, gusting in from the surrounding moors. Leitch's first suggestion was therefore that the pitch be turned by 90 degrees. This would also ensure that the new main stand was on the west side (the most favourable orientation for viewing on winter afternoons).

He also recommended that a cover be erected over the Leeds Road End terrace, presumably because the other two sides had more space to expand and could be built up steadily by inviting local people to tip their rubbish (a common practice at the time).

Although Town had wealthy backers – the Crowther family, well established woollen manufacturers in the Colne Valley – Leitch's budget was modest, at just £6,000 (compared with £10,000 at Millwall and £60,000 at Manchester United).

Nevertheless, armed with Leitch's plans, Town's representative won over the League delegates in June 1910, and two days later he was back in Huddersfield to start planning.

The realigned Leeds Road hosted its first League match the following September, watched by a modest crowd of 7,000.

Meanwhile, the new Main Stand, built in reinforced concrete and steel by Humphreys of Knightsbridge for an extremely reasonable £3,047, took longer to complete, being finally opened in September 1911.

For all the optimism generated by Town's new facilities, League football did not capture the public's imagination. Another concern was the pitch. New drains and turf had been laid under Leitch's supervision during the summer of 1911 (*see page 43*), but by the end of the season there was barely any grass.

Equally threadbare was the club's bank account, and after only two years in the League, Town

Nicknamed the 'Babes' when they entered the League relatively late in 1910, Huddersfield Town changed their colours to blue and white striped shirts in 1913, as shown on this 'silk' produced at the time by the BDV tobacco company. Another indication of commercial interest was a request for filming rights at the ground from the Pathé Animated Gazette newsreel company.

122 Engineering Archie

went into liquidation. In stark contrast, barely a mile to the west, at Fartown, Huddersfield's rugby club were entering what would prove to be their most successful decade ever, drawing regular crowds of up to 30,000 spectators.

Town reformed for the following season, but still the debts mounted. Nor did the pitch improve. In February 1913 Leitch was summoned by the board, and by May the club minutes hint that legal action was in the offing.

Judging by the problems he would experience at Hearts the following year, after war had broken out, these were not the easiest of times for Leitch in the football business.

But for the football club the real drama had yet to unfold.

By 1919 Town owed £25,000 to the Crowthers, who suddenly announced that they were moving the club, lock, stock and barrel to Leeds (where Leeds City had just been disbanded by the Football Association for financial malpractice).

Yet not only did local fans rally round, raising £8,000 in donations, but by the end of the season the reconstituted club reached the FA Cup Final and won promotion to the First Division.

In a quite unprecedented turnaround, from gates of 3,000 before the crisis, within five months the Leeds Road terracing needed expanding to cope with crowds now approaching 50,000.

But there was more. Town emerged in the 1920s as the most powerful team in the land, winning three league titles in a row and recording a record gate of 67,037 for a Cup tie in 1932. On two occasions it was a miracle that no-one was killed in serious incidences of overcrowding.

'Only four people taken to the infirmary,' the club's programme noted breezily after the second occurrence, in which a barrier collapsed. Whether it was a Leitch patented barrier is not recorded.

Leeds Road is one of seven Leitch grounds no longer in use, having been redeveloped in 1994. But it is hardly missed, for Huddersfield now play a few hundred metres to the east, at the ultra-modern Galpharm Stadium, which in 1995 became the first stadium to win the coveted Stirling Prize for architecture.

Radical in design the stadium is also radical in concept, for it is the home not only of Huddersfield Town, but of the local rugby league club too. After a century at loggerheads, co-existence at last.

Not a car in sight at Leeds Road, in the late 1930s (*above*). The concrete structure of Leitch's Main Stand is evident, as is the roof gable, shown left during a Manchester United v. Charlton Cup replay in February 1948. Fire destroyed the stand roof two years later and the gable was never restored. Leeds Road was last used in 1994. A DIY warehouse now occupies the site, with a plaque on the car park marking the site of the former centre spot.

Engineering Archie **123**

Sunderland

Grounds
Roker Park, Sunderland 1913–36

When Sunderland left Roker Park in 1997 they changed their nickname from the Rokerites to the Black Cats. Yet far from being a contrived piece of marketing, the name has a long tradition. During the Napoleonic Wars, as local legend has it, an inebriated volunteer fled from a gun battery positioned in the town, convinced he had heard the devil howling. It turned out, of course, to have been a black cat, and the tale endured.

Roker Park was one of a number of grounds laid out in the 1890s whose rudimentary wooden stands and terraces proved hopelessly ill-equipped to cope with football's rising popularity during the Edwardian period. Sites that had seemed ideal in the early years of professionalism were now being tested to the limits.

Sunderland's emergence in the 1890s as the 'Team of All Talents' (the majority of whom were Scots recruited with backing from local shipbuilding and brewing interests), culminated in the laying out of Roker Park on farmland in 1898. Terraced houses were already starting to overshadow its boundaries. A few streets to the east lay the harbour front.

Roker Park soon developed a reputation. One visiting team was pelted with stones. A referee had to be smuggled out disguised as a policeman. During one of several pitch invasions – mostly caused by overcrowding – a police horse was stabbed. Twenty fans were hospitalised in 1912 after the roof of a coal depot gave way under the weight of onlookers.

Crowds rose further when in 1913 Sunderland won the League for the fifth time, and only missed out on the Double by losing to Aston Villa in the FA Cup Final at Crystal Palace, watched by a world record attendance of 121,919.

Both for financial and safety reasons, the club had to act.

Flush with cash from the previous season, they started during the summer of 1913 at the south, or Roker End, where the site was too pinched in one corner to raise a sufficiently high embankment. (Typically, the rear slope of an embankment occupied as much room as the terraced part, yet was effectively wasted space.)

The solution was, for its time, a novel one. Instead of banking, the new Roker End terrace was built on a web of reinforced concrete pillars, raising the overall capacity to 55,000 and costing £6,000. It was, in effect, a concrete version of the ill-fated iron and wood terrace at Ibrox, eleven years earlier.

There is no written proof that Leitch designed this structure. But local newspapers referred to the construction as being the responsibility of a Liverpool firm, and Leitch was then based in Liverpool. The exposed nature of the structure – echoing that of Bradford City's Midland Road Stand built in 1908 – also pointed to his involvement.

Similarly, when the Fulwell End was expanded in 1925, this time on conventional banking, it bore all the hallmarks of a Leitch terrace.

Leitch was certainly responsible for the next major development at the ground, the construction of a new Main Stand. A typical no-frills Leitch design, the double-decker stand cost £25,000 and was opened in September 1929.

Four years later Roker recorded a record attendance of 75,118 for a Cup tie; remarkable given that the match kicked off on a Wednesday afternoon (this being 20 years before floodlighting allowed midweek Cup replays to start in the evening). Apparently the whole town came to a standstill.

Following Sunderland's sixth League title in 1936, Leitch's company completed the fourth side of the ground, building the Clock Stand for 15,500 standing

124 Engineering Archie

spectators, thereby, according to Leitch, raising the capacity by a further 6,000 (though this was never proven). The stand was opened by the wife of the local MP, Lady Raine, to whom Leitch presented 'a wristlet watch' as a memento.

Apart from the arrival of floodlights in 1952 there would be just one further addition; the Fulwell End was covered in 1964 in advance of Roker Park hosting the World Cup two years later.

Otherwise, the ground as it appeared on its final day of action in May 1997 was essentially a Leitch creation. Only one part of his work did not stand the test of time; the rear elevated section of the Roker End, demolished in 1982 as a safety measure.

Thus the capacity shrank to 22,657 by the mid 1990s, by which time the seven acre site was deemed too small for further development. By comparison, Sunderland's new stadium, on the nearby site of the former Wearmouth Colliery, holds 48,353 on a site three times as large.

A housing estate now occupies Roker Park, with Midfield Drive running through its centre.

Roker Park in 1966, showing the concrete elevated Roker End terrace, designed, it is thought, by Leitch, in 1913. The structure survived a 500kg bomb blast in 1943 (which destroyed a clubhouse on the site of the dark flat roofed building seen behind the terrace) but not the attention of safety inspectors in 1982.

Engineering Archie **125**

Sunderland

▲ Compared with other Leitch stands, Roker's **Main Stand** was a low budget affair, reportedly costing only £25,000 for 5,875 seats on the upper deck, plus standing for approximately 14,000 below. The stand had originally been planned for 1922 but a lack of funds delayed the project until 1929.

As shown here in 1982, the rear enclosure was converted to seating in 1950. Before the 1966 World Cup a hospitality and office block was added behind. Private boxes were then inserted into the enclosure's central section in 1973, and red plastic seats installed throughout, adding a brightness that would surely have shocked Leitch. In his day not even the balcony detailing would have been painted red, but the usual matt green instead.

As illustrated opposite, during its final years the stand's roof was reclad in grey sheeting and both end screens pierced by prominent exit stairways. The balcony's metalwork was almost entirely covered by advertisements.

But if it was, by then, hardly recognisable as a Leitch stand, inside lay proof of its provenance; a small sepia photograph of the architect, fixed onto the wood panelling of the former boardroom. No others like it were found at any of his other grounds.

Leitch's photograph disappeared when the ground was demolished in 1997. However, Sunderland found a better way to pay tribute.

They retained and restored two sections of the stand's distinctive balcony, and put them on display outside their new Stadium of Light (see page 200). For this act alone, the club is to be heartily thanked.

126 Engineering Archie

▲ On weekdays **Roker Park** appeared a modest venue, almost hidden – apart from its floodlight pylons – amidst the narrow, terraced streets which formed the district of Roker, between the Newcastle Road and the sea front.

And yet on matchdays, wide open skies stirred by bracing winds, whipping in from the North Sea, suggested a wild, hardier grandeur, from which any low rumble in the crowd might suddenly erupt and resonate, seemingly for miles around. The 'Roker Roar' this effect was aptly named.

The images here were taken shortly before the final curtain in 1997. They show (*top right*) the **Main Stand**, and (*top left*) the **Clock Stand**, built originally for standing spectators only, with wooden steppings on a steel framework at the rear. Seats were installed in the rear section for the 1966 World Cup. The stand took its name from a clock mounted on the roof, although in later years a television gantry was rather more prominent.

The rear of the Clock Stand (*above left*) backed onto the aptly named Association Road, where stood the **Black Cats Supporters' Club** shop, a typical example of how football clubs seep into the streetscape and lives of their neighbours.

Finally, the surviving rump of the **Roker End** terrace (*above right*) shows a little of the original concrete substructure erected in 1913, under which players would be sent for training in wet weather. By this stage stricter safety margins had reduced the terrace's capacity to just 3,400 spectators, a fraction of the original total.

Engineering Archie **127**

Arsenal

Grounds
Arsenal Stadium, London 1913

Woolwich Arsenal's transformation from a middling club in south east London to a leading force in English football constitutes one of the game's greatest ever rebranding exercises. Much of this process was due to Arsenal's manager from 1925-34, Herbert Chapman. One of his many ruses was, in 1933, to add white sleeves to Arsenal's kit, thus marking them out from all other clubs wearing red shirts. This 1930s tin badge is in the collection of the National Football Museum, Preston.

In 2006 Arsenal Football Club will bid a tearful farewell to their home in Highbury, Islington – its capacity limited to just 38,500 since the Taylor Report – for a new, 60,000 seat stadium, designed by HOK Sport and located half a mile away, in Ashburton Grove.

Thus will disappear one of the most prized arenas on the British sporting scene; a genuine London institution, famed in particular for its 1932 West Stand and 1936 East Stand (the latter of which houses the so-called Marble Hall entrance, and is listed Grade II).

These truly grand stands, to be converted into flats once Arsenal depart – the first such conversions ever in Britain – were by Claude Ferrier and William Binnie, architects with no previous experience of working in sport.

Art Deco in style, luxurious in concept, their designs reflected contemporary architecture in a way that Leitch, for all his technical skill, never quite managed. (And yet his Sentinel Works in Glasgow, built in 1903, clearly hinted that he was able to work in a modern idiom, if asked.)

That said, Leitch did play a major role in both finding and laying out the Highbury site some 15 years before Ferrier and Binnie's involvement. For as AG Kearney's account of the ground's chaotic opening in 1913 reminds us (*see pages 38-39*), the football map of London as we know it today is largely the construct of wealthy Edwardian speculators. They provided the bread. Leitch built the circuses.

Gus Mears at Chelsea was one. Henry Norris was another.

Norris, it will be recalled, was the pugnacious developer who, in 1904, hired Leitch to design a new home for Fulham (*see page 70ff*), only to conclude within a few years that the club would never be able to satisfy his wider ambitions.

In 1910 Norris thus took over Woolwich Arsenal, a club then based in Plumstead, close to its roots at the Royal Arsenal.

Arsenal were in the doldrums, but were hardly lame ducks. They had been the first London club to turn professional, and the first to gain admittance to the League. But access to Plumstead by public transport was notoriously erratic. Its audience was limited in scope.

Apparently Norris's original intention was to abandon Plumstead and merge Arsenal, then in the First Division, with Fulham, then in the Second, thereby bringing top flight football to Craven Cottage without the tiresome business of having to earn promotion. Unsurprisingly, the League turned him down flat.

Norris then re-hired Leitch to find his new charges a more propitious location, a search which ended with Norris agreeing a 20 year lease on six acres of playing fields attached to St John's College of Divinity in Highbury.

When Leitch supervised both Manchester United and Millwall's relocations to new grounds, three years earlier, the distances moved had been four miles and two miles respectively. Arsenal moved ten.

In London to cross the river was leap enough. In the football world ten miles was unprecedented.

But more than that, it landed Arsenal right on the doorstep of two other clubs in north London, Spurs and Clapton Orient.

128 Engineering Archie

Thus for both homeowners in the quiet residential streets of Highbury, and for Norris's fellow club chairmen – among them Charlie Roberts of Spurs, whom Leitch knew well – this was but 'a vulgar project', as one of the objectors put it.

Yet where Roberts was a football man, Norris was a businessman. Above all he understood that Highbury's great merit was its proximity to Gillespie Road tube station, recently opened in 1906.

And so the die was cast.

Highbury was, by any standards, a massive gamble, costing Norris £125,000 (double the outlay on Old Trafford). The outbreak of war in 1914 then totally ruined all his calculations, so that by the war's end, Arsenal were £60,000 in debt and still in the Second Division.

But Norris was not a man to be beaten. As soon as the League resumed business in 1919 he proceeded to bully (or bribe) other members into promoting Arsenal to the First Division, despite their finishing only fifth in Division Two at the end of the final wartime season in 1915.

Never before or since has there been a scandal to match this in British football. And Arsenal have never been relegated since.

As for Norris, having made too many enemies he was banned by the FA for some minor rule breaches in 1927. Thus he could only watch from afar as Herbert Chapman proceeded to turn the Gunners into *the* team of the 1930s, with a revamped ground to match their sparkling reputation.

Most of Leitch's terracing survived this process. But not his East Stand, and nor he did work for Arsenal again after 1914.

As we read overleaf, however, this was probably a blessed relief.

Highbury in the 1920s, occupying what had formerly been the playing fields of the St John's College of Divinity, itself hidden amongst the trees to the right of the aerial view. The ground's total lack of access from the west side (nearest the camera) meant that the main stand had to be positioned on the east side, facing into the sun. Note the terraced bays at each end of the stand (*left*). Though compensating for the lack of terrace cover elsewhere in the ground, this unusual arrangement would undoubtedly have resulted in poor sightlines.

Engineering Archie **129**

Arsenal

▶ As Alfred Kearney and the builders from Humphreys started work on preparing the Highbury site in early 1913 *(see pages 38-39)*, Leitch's Liverpool office submitted various plans to London County Council for the **East Stand** on Avenell Road, among them this elevation, and a section (not shown), dated May 1913. These depict a fairly standard two-tiered Leitch stand, not unlike those at Chelsea or Tottenham.

However, the stand actually built at Highbury was a lower structure with an entirely different layout and roof profile, presumably the result of late changes enforced on the club by objections from local residents in the houses opposite.

Note that the plans still refer to the club as Woolwich Arsenal. Once the club had moved, this was changed to 'The Arsenal' and then finally, in the 1930s, to plain 'Arsenal'. This last change was Herbert Chapman's idea. So too was the brilliant coup of persuading London Underground to change the name of the Gillespie Road tube station to Arsenal, in 1932, thus putting the club well and truly on the map.

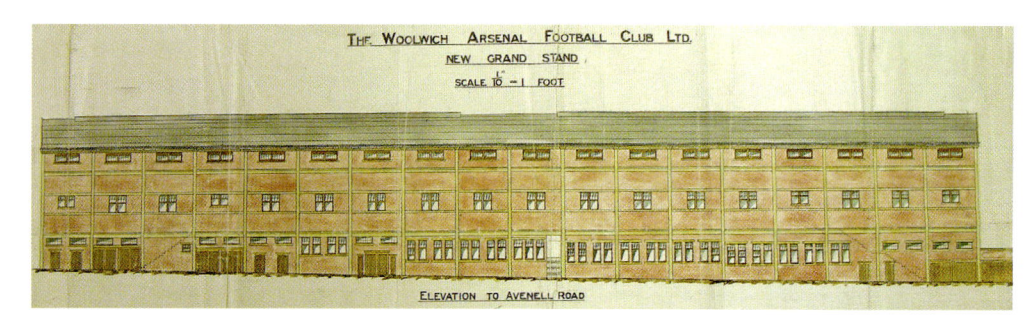

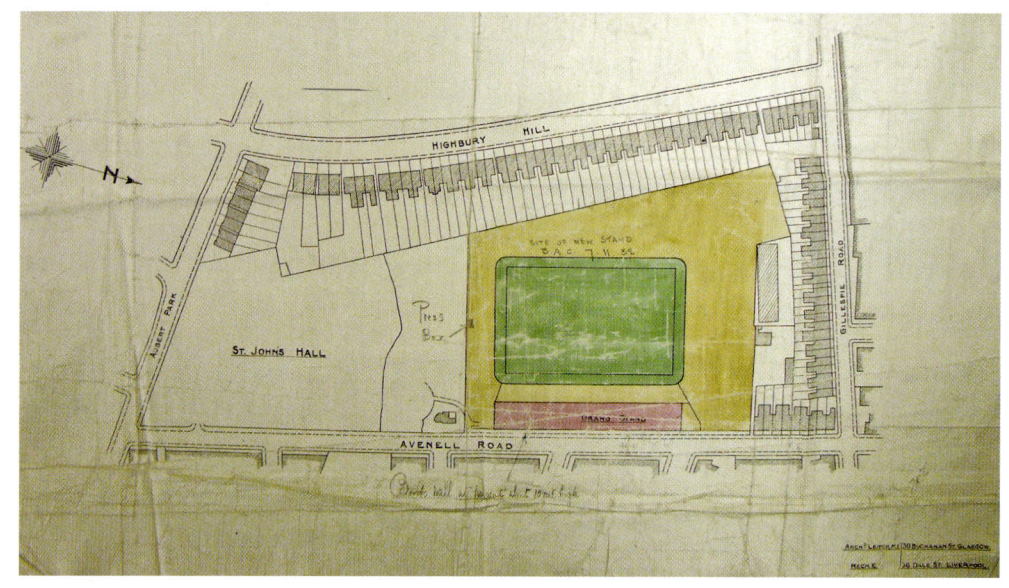

▲ It is not hard to see from this block plan why residents were so angered by Arsenal's arrival in their midst in 1913. Yet despite vociferous lobbying – much of it directed against the commercial ethos of the game – in the absence of any objections from district planners, it was the Church Commissioners, the owners of the site, who were chiefly responsible for leasing it to the football club.

Indeed one of the signatories to the deal was the Archbishop of Canterbury.

Nor would it have been of much comfort to Arsenal's new neighbours that no games were to be allowed on Christmas Day or Good Friday, or that gambling and alcohol were to be prohibited.

Highbury's early years were beset by problems. Hardly a week went by without LCC surveyors demanding Leitch's attention.

In March 1914 the boundary wall between the west terrace and the rear gardens of the houses on Highbury Hill – a wall 609 feet long and 12-17 feet high – started to list so badly that a match had to be postponed.

But when the club tried to blame a waterlogged pitch for the postponement, Orion of the *Daily Express* was having none of it. 'The postponement was due as much to the state of the playing pitch,' he wrote, 'as it was due to the revision of the voting lists in Honolulu.'

Highbury was a bodged job, and everyone knew it. Norris had tried to do too much, too quickly, and it cost him. The whole wall had to be rebuilt.

Note from the plan that Highbury's terracing initially had only three access points: two on Avenell Road and a single gate on Gillespie Road. And yet it could hold 60,000 in this state.

130 Engineering Archie

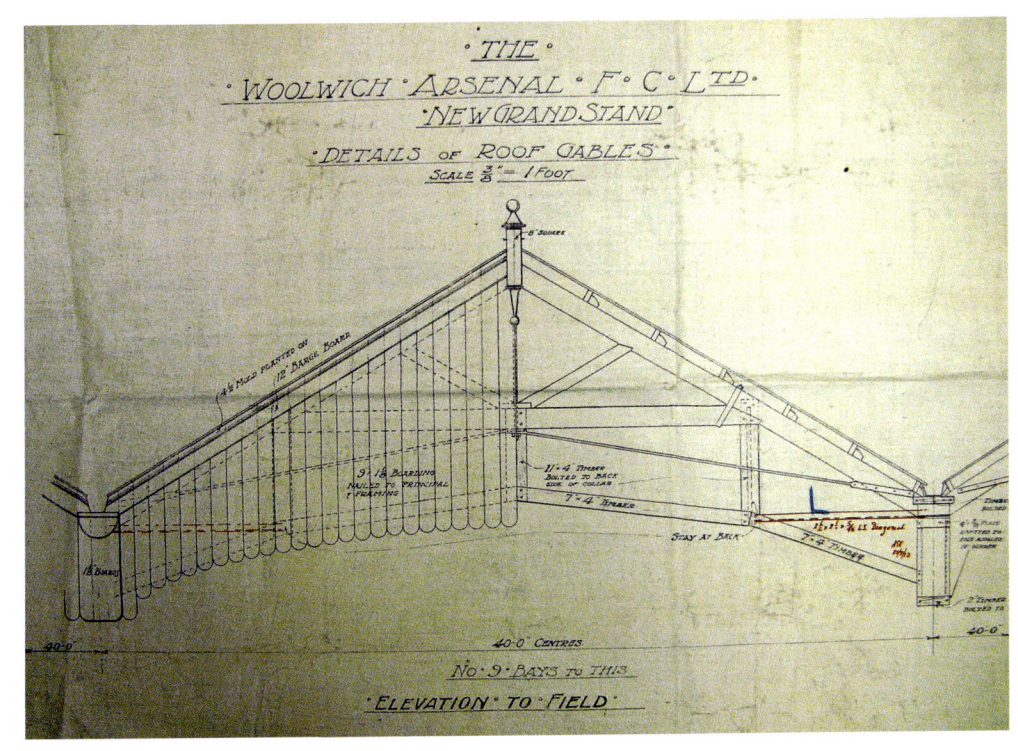

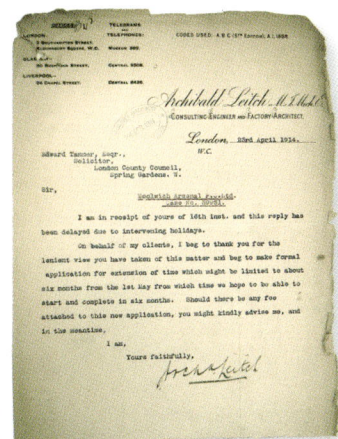

Leitch has to grovel once more to the LCC as Highbury's completion is delayed still further.

▲ Highbury's East Stand took over a year to complete, during which time Arsenal were repeatedly warned as to its unfinished state. In April 1914 the LCC told Leitch that 'the stand had been retained, and used by the public, without the Council's license,' that they took 'a very serious view of the matter' and would not 'overlook any similar breach of the law in the future.'

Each time they threatened, Leitch made assurances. For weeks he blamed poor steel supplies for some missing stays on the end of the stand. Somehow, he always managed to win more time.

The view on the right – taken during a match against Norris's old club, Fulham, in March 1914 – seven months after the opening, shows flapping tarpaulins strung across the rear.

The houses revealed on Avenell Road behind are still there today.

Leitch's stand, however, was replaced in 1936.

We have no idea what Archie thought of its stylish replacement, designed by William Binnie and costing a staggering £130,000, twice as much as Tottenham's own East Stand, completed by Leitch that same year.

When given the funds, it is true that Leitch had been able to deliver excellence, as at Villa Park and Ibrox in the 1920s. But as the heavy, wooden-framed roof of the old East Stand at Highbury made way for its light and airy successor, he must surely have sensed that the world had moved on.

Or maybe not. Only four years earlier, in 1932, Leitch's company designed for Wolves a stand almost identical to the original East Stand at Arsenal (see page 164). And for years it was much admired.

Indeed Leitch's order book remained full enough until his death in 1939, which was probably vindication enough.

Yet still, one wonders.

Engineering Archie **131**

Grounds
Hillsborough, Sheffield 1913–14

Although the club was officially known as The Wednesday FC when this Valentine card appeared in the early 1900s, the name Sheffield Wednesday had already crept into common usage, and was formally adopted in 1929. Wednesday's ground also underwent a name change, when Owlerton was absorbed into the new parliamentary constituency of Hillsborough, in 1914.

In earlier sections we read how, during the period 1910-13, three of Leitch's clients – Manchester United, Millwall and Arsenal – took a calculated gamble by relocating to districts away from their traditional roots.

All three surely gained comfort from the experience of Archie's next clients, The Wednesday FC.

Formed in 1867 by members of the Wednesday Cricket Club – which itself had been in existence since 1820 and was so-called because Sheffield workers enjoyed a half day holiday on Wednesday afternoons – the club had been forced to leave their ground at Olive Grove, south east of Bramall Lane, in 1899. After an anxious few months of searching for a new site Wednesday finally secured a ten acre plot on the banks of the River Don, in Owlerton, on the very north western edges of the city.

Costing nearly £5,000 to purchase, the land was part of the former estate of Hillsborough Hall (now Hillsborough Library), whose immediate grounds had been converted into a public park seven years earlier.

Moving there was a huge risk. Not only was Owlerton nearly four miles from Olive Grove, but it was thinly populated and poorly served by public transport. Also, Wednesday had just been relegated to Division Two, only a fortnight after neighbours Sheffield United had won the FA Cup.

And yet by 1913, when Leitch was hired, the move appeared to have paid off handsomely. Trams had arrived on the doorstep in 1901 as more streets in the area were developed, and in 1912 the ground staged the first of what would be numerous prestigious, and lucrative FA Cup semi-finals.

Best of all, Wednesday – now nicknamed the Owls – seemed reborn in their new surroundings, winning the League consecutively in 1903 and 1904, and the FA Cup in 1907. Their gates were even exceeding those at Bramall Lane.

What Wednesday needed now were facilities commensurate with their burgeoning reputation.

Leitch's first brief was therefore to design a new main stand on the south, riverside of the ground, to replace the modest wooden pavilion Wednesday had brought with them from Olive Grove.

Superficially, the stand Leitch proposed (see opposite) appeared to be a standard Leitch two-tiered design, holding 5,600 seats on the upper deck with an enclosure for 11,000 standing in front. As was now his norm, Leitch opted for reinforced concrete with infilled brick for the base, with a steel framed roof capped by a pedimented gable.

Structurally, however, Leitch repeated a form of construction he had experimented with at Anfield (see page 89), in which the seating deck was formed not by wooden boards on a steel or concrete frame, but by an angled slab of reinforced concrete, four inches thick, on top of which timber treads were then added to support the seats. Not only was this technically adventurous given the materials and knowledge available at the time, but it must also have added to the construction time.

Whether it added to the cost, we cannot be sure, but overall the stand cost £17,884, which suggested quality, though

Wednesday's long serving honorary secretary Arthur Dickinson, who worked in the cutlery business, played a key role in Wednesday's move to Owlerton. Eight days after he hosted this event in Leitch's new stand the Archduke Franz Ferdinand and his wife were assassinated in Sarajevo.

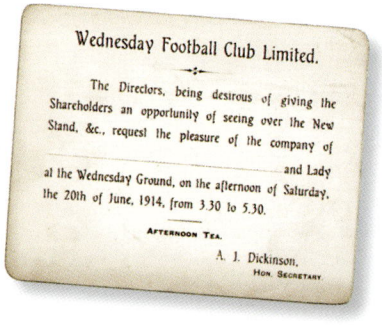

132 Engineering Archie

GROUND OF THE WEDNESDAY FOOTBALL CLUB LTD at SHEFFIELD

ARCH? LEITCH. M.INE.
36, DALE S? LIVERPOOL
30, BUCHANAN S? GLASGOW

hardly extravagance. Two sets of contractors, Freckingham & Sons and Hodkin & Jones, charged £10,819 between them. For the steel roof, the Clyde Structural Iron Company, with whom Leitch often dealt, received £1,395.

For his part Leitch's fees totalled £500, representing just under three per cent of the overall contract, and suggesting that Wednesday drove a hard bargain. (On other commissions his fees were usually five per cent.)

As seemed inevitable given Leitch's choice of concrete construction, work on the stand proceeded slowly (see page 43), so that when 3,000 spectators were first admitted onto the upper tier in September 1913 there was still no roof and they were all soaked.

Only the following January were the facilities complete.

But clearly it was worth the wait. Praise for the South Stand rang out in numerous reports, including from the directors of Hearts, who 'spoke in eulogistic terms' of Wednesday's new stand and immediately demanded 'practically a replica'.

In time the Hearts directors would come to regret their »

▲ Although the Owlerton district was starting to lose its rural feel by the time Leitch's artist penned this impression of **Hillsborough** for The Wednesday shareholders in 1913, for many fans it was still a welcome respite from the pollution of the city's industrial core.

For Wednesday chairman George Senior that had been one of its attractions when the club had considered moving there in 1899.

When asked by the club's honorary secretary, Arthur Dickinson, whether he might prefer an alternative site in Carbrook, Senior – a bluff, self-made man who was the proprietor of the immense Ponds Forge iron foundry in the city centre – reportedly replied, 'Do as tha' likes, lad. I breathe sulphur all the week and I'm sure not goin' to Carbrook to suck it in!'

Engineering Archie 133

Sheffield Wednesday

OFFICIAL SOUVENIR, SIXPENCE

DEREK DOOLEY TRUST FUND

Floodlight Match

WEDNESDAY, 9th MARCH, 1955, Kick-off 7.30 p.m.

SHEFFIELD XI.
v.
INTERNATIONAL XI.

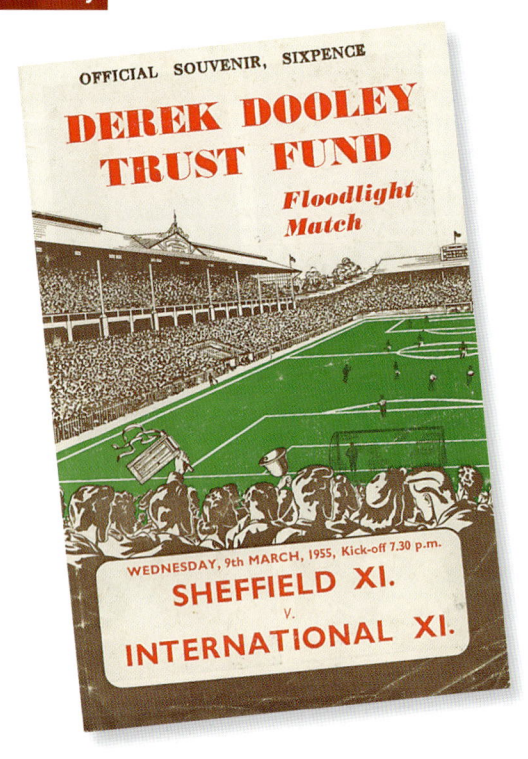

In common with many of Leitch's clients, Sheffield Wednesday often chose to portray his work on their programme covers and letterheads. This match programme recalls a particularly memorable occasion in football history. Wednesday striker Derek Dooley's career had ended tragically in 1953 when one of his legs had to be amputated following a serious injury. A crowd of 55,000 attended to support his benefit, a match which also marked the switching on of Hillsborough's new floodlights (yet to be added to this artist's impression of the ground). A galaxy of stars turned out to play on the night, including Stanley Matthews, Tom Finney, Nat Lofthouse, John Charles, Tommy Lawton and Jimmy Hagan.

involvement with Leitch, as we shall learn in the next section.

But Leitch would be in for a shock in Sheffield too.

As recalled earlier (*see page 27*), in January 1914, only weeks after the South Stand had been fully opened, at least 75 spectators were injured on the Penistone Road End terrace, three of them critically.

Such collapses were hardly unknown. But Hillsborough was one of the most modern grounds in Britain at the time.

Leitch's own responsibility, and his reaction, we can only guess. Work on upgrading the large terrace had started as the South Stand was being completed. There were Leitch patented barriers in place when the incident occurred, although it was the collapse of a recently completed wall, rather than a barrier, that had actually caused the accident.

What we do know is that only four weeks later a new record of over 57,000 packed Hillsborough – as the ground was now known – without incident, and that the following summer £800 was spent on concreting and completing the terrace in question, to the standard Leitch specifications.

Leitch himself appears not to have worked further for Wednesday as their ground was expanded and improved here and there during the 1920s, eventually managing to accommodate an all-time high of 72,841 for a Cup tie v. Manchester City in February 1934.

Post war, one other feature of Hillsborough deserves to be noted.

In 1961, a 10,000 seat stand designed by the Sheffield firm of Husband and Co., was built on the north side of the ground, as modern and as admired as Leitch's South Stand had been 47 years earlier.

Covered by a steel cantilevered roof of exceptional elegance, not only was it the largest column free stand yet built in Britain, but it was also the *only* piece of football architecture deemed worthy of mention by Nikolaus Pevsner in his entire *Buildings of England* series.

True, Leitch was more 'Our House' than 'Bauhaus' – to borrow a phrase from Tom Wolfe.

Yet not one of Archie's stands merited a single mention, even in passing, which at Hillsborough seemed particularly unjust given that for the 32 years the Leitch and Husband stands faced each other, both exemplified the best of grandstand design from their respective eras.

What is more, further improvements during the 1960s, including the installation of seats on the South Stand's enclosure, turned Hillsborough into one of Britain's most admired footballing arenas, a worthy host of the 1966 World Cup (one of six Leitch grounds to act as host venues).

And yet in modern times the name Hillsborough would become synonymous with tragedy.

The Hillsborough disaster of April 15 1989 – in which 96 fans attending an FA Cup semi-final died at the Leppings Lane End – was sparked by a catastrophic breakdown in crowd management at the ground, and exacerbated by the presence of perimeter fences along the front of the terrace, a terrace that was also fitted with Leitch patented barriers.

Thus was brought to an end the era of terracing that Leitch himself had helped to shape in the wake of the 1902 Ibrox disaster.

The tragedy also precipitated a complete remodelling of the South Stand, as shown opposite.

▲ Hillsborough's **South Stand**, as it appeared in the 1950s (*above*) and again in the early 1990s (*above right*) showed few external changes from its original appearance. Extensive checks in the 1990s also confirmed that its concrete structure, similar to that of the 1906 Main Stand at Anfield (*see page 89*), was in sound condition, with not a crack to be found in its seating deck, despite the apparent absence, remarkably, of any expansion or contraction joints. As the club's advisers, Eastwood and Partners, concluded, Leitch must clearly have had great confidence in the material, and in his own instincts as an engineer.

Assured by these checks, in 1993 Wednesday decided to retain the stand's core structure, build an upper tier and facilities block at its rear, and cover the whole in a new steel-framed roof. (Liverpool did much the same with their Leitch stand 20 years earlier.)

Since this work was completed in 1996, at a final cost of £6.8 million, few external elements of the original stand remain visible.

But the interior remains more or less intact, including the original boardroom, both dressing rooms and an unusually wide service corridor. One can see why so many visitors were impressed in 1914.

None of this is apparent when viewing the stand from the pitch (*right*). From here it may be seen that in order to span the extended seating tiers without intermediary columns, the original roof has made way for a goalpost structure, supporting a girder 125m in length.

But whereas all other stand structures of this type have their roofs suspended *under* the main horizontal truss, at Hillsborough the roof cladding is pitched *over* the truss, thus concealing it from view.

This, uniquely, has enabled Eastwoods to add a replica Leitch-style gable at the front, decorated with an exact copy of the old ironwork finial. In the centre of that finial is, however, the original ball.

For years this ball was so blackened by pollution that fans would joke that it was made of coal. In fact it is copper, and after restoration was found to have been inscribed with the date 1866. This was thought to have been the year of Wednesday's formation. In fact the actual date was 1867.

But no matter, for this single decorative feature is now the only one of its kind, and thus forms an apt token of Leitch's work, in a city where metalwork is as much an art as a business. Archie, no doubt, would heartily approve.

Engineering Archie

Hearts

Grounds
Tynecastle, Edinburgh 1913–14

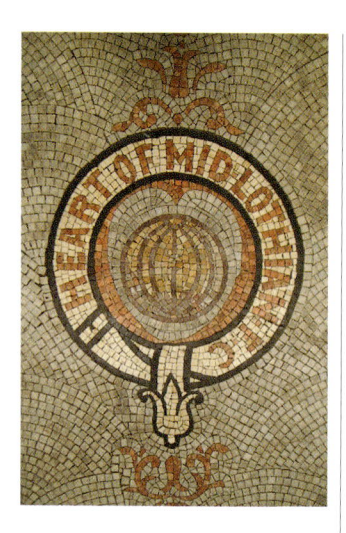

A typical mosaic welcome in the entrance hall of Leitch's McLeod Street Stand, Tynecastle, one of only two such examples known to survive. (The other is at Ibrox). Formed in 1874, the club took its evocative name from a popular dance club on Canongate, where the early players would meet, and which had itself been named after the original Heart of Midlothian, a 16th century tolbooth and prison close to St Giles Cathedral.

Archibald Leitch's next commission should have been plain sailing. Heart of Midlothian, his first major clients in Scotland after Rangers, wanted a low-cost main stand plus sundry works at their Tynecastle ground in the Gorgie district of Edinburgh.

What transpired instead is logged in the club's minutes.

'Discussions took place as to (the) advisability of securing particulars, plans, costs etc and to have plans perfected and pigeon-holed for use when required,' noted the minutes on February 10 1913. 'Secretary to get into communication with Mr Leitch, Stand and Ground specialist, 36, Dale Street, Liverpool.'

A week later Leitch met the board, and a week after that two members of his staff measured up Tynecastle (which Hearts had laid out in 1886 and which, for all its assorted array of cinder banks and small wooden stands was an orderly enclosure that had held 35,000 for one game in 1907).

In May Leitch reported that none of the firms he had approached to build a new stand 'would entertain the proposed scale of payments.' At this point the stand's cost was estimated at £6,000. To put this in perspective, Heart's gate receipts for that entire season, after match expenses, totalled £7,723.

Hearts' chairman, Elias Furst, a jeweller of Russian Jewish extraction, was deputed to oversee the negotiations. Another director, William Burns, reported favourably on Leitch's stand at Tottenham, which he visited in August 1913. To save costs, however, Hearts decided that unlike Tottenham they did not have the funds for one of Leitch's signature pedimented gables.

Early hints of the difficulties to come arose in the autumn of 1913. Leitch's plaster model of the proposed stand was, he claimed, smashed in transit. Then a replacement was delayed, so he promised a wooden model instead. Then he fell ill.

He was, at the time, already committed at Highbury, Hillsborough and Roker Park.

By February 1914 the stand's estimated costs had risen to £8,000, forcing Hearts to sell their star player, Percy Dawson, to Blackburn Rovers for the then British record fee of £2,500.

Still, as reported in the previous section, after visiting Leitch's new stand at Hillsborough, of which they spoke 'in eulogistic terms,' the Hearts directors seemed keener than ever.

Leitch was now awaiting tenders. He wrote to Hearts that 'if iron came in touch of concrete in price, to erect in iron, because of speed in completion.'

Iron won. Messrs Redpath & Brown were to supply and erect the framework at a cost of £3,298. J Millar & Sons were hired as contractors following their bid of £4,395. Two weeks later Millar added another £94, saying that materials and wages had risen in the interim. The Hearts secretary was told 'to break off' with them immediately. J Duncan & Sons were hired instead.

Edinburgh's planners now raised an objection to the stand's elevation. They would only pass the plans if the walls were 'rough-casted'. This would add £100 to the bill, forcing Furst to call twice upon Council officials to 'point out hardships on the club.'

Leitch was asked to argue the case further. He showed the City Architect, the Burgh Engineer and even the Town Clerk various brick samples. But adjacent to the ground there was a recently completed school, a police station and sandstone tenements behind one goal. The officials demanded quality. No mention was made of the soot-encrusted distillery hard against the ground's west flank.

In April Leitch appointed a Clerk of Works, J Nelson, on wages of £4 a week (the same, incidentally, as most of the Hearts players received). Leitch told the board that he hoped Mr Nelson's brickwork would, ultimately, prove acceptable to the Town Officials.

In June 1914 shareholders heard that 'the vexatious delay has been annoying to officials and public alike,' but were promised comfort 'not hitherto obtainable in most football grounds.'

Yet there was no respite. In early July Leitch was summoned to Tynecastle. Work was now 'practically at a standstill' and the board had just received a bill for £451 worth of Kleine flooring, which they insisted had not been part of the original tender.

(Kleine flooring was a form of lightweight fire-proof decking, consisting of hollow terracotta blocks. First introduced to Britain in 1906 Leitch used it in most of his stands. It can still be seen at Tynecastle, and lining the underside of the upper decks at Goodison Park, for example.)

From this point on, dealings between the client and architect took on a distinctly frosty note. Hearts noted that Leitch's fee of five per cent stood to rise as each extra bill came in, for the flooring, for some unbudgeted terracing and for £336 worth of seats from the Bennet seat company of Glasgow (another of Leitch's regular suppliers). The overall bill now stood at £8,750. Leitch meanwhile 'declared emphatically that the stand would be ready for occupation on August 15 next.'

On July 9 Hearts resolved that Mr Nelson should lay the terracing himself, reporting directly to the club, 'and that Mr Leitch shall not interfere… nor order any material' that was not part of the original tender documents.

On August 3 Leitch was back, admitting that only part of the stand would be ready for August 15. The following day Germany invaded Belgium. Britain was now at war.

And so, it would seem, were most of the parties involved in the stand construction. J Duncan & Sons, for one, were furious that »

Tynecastle in 1915 (*above*), shortly after Leitch's troublesome stand was finished, but still with wooden barriers and unterraced embankments. The Gorgie Road end terrace to the right of the stand (*shown below in 1955*) remained uncovered until it was replaced by an all-seated stand in 1997. When Hearts built a scoreboard at the back of the terrace some residents in the tenements behind applied for a rate rebate.

Engineering Archie **137**

Hearts

In the end it would seem that Mr Nelson's brickwork (*top*) did pass muster with the Edinburgh planners. Above is the plaque mounted on the same McLeod Street frontage, listing the Hearts directors at the time of the stand's construction. On plaques found at other football grounds the architect is often given an honourable mention. Not at Tynecastle.

Leitch had not been seen on the job for three weeks and had failed to respond to their last four letters seeking payment. 'The attitude of the architect' was now a matter for the club's solicitors.

Come August 15 part of the stand was ready for use. But much still remained to be done.

According to the minutes of September 10 1914, 'Leitch blamed everybody but himself.' He repudiated all liability. The board, in turn, noted his 'carelessness' in not replying to letters.

What caused these lapses from Archie we can only guess. We know he was just starting work for Aston Villa (*see page 140*), that he was in the process of moving his main office and his family home from Liverpool to London. It is further possible that he was suddenly in demand for war-related factory or shipyard construction. He may also have been embroiled in the ongoing disputes at Highbury.

But he was clearly *persona non grata* in Gorgie.

When the stand was finally completed in October 1914, Leitch sent Hearts a bill for £100 on account of professional services rendered, roughly a quarter of what he was owed. Furst responded, via the club's solicitors, that they refused to pay, owing to his 'want of supervision'.

Extra bills were now pouring in; £649 from J Duncan & Sons in lieu of Leitch's failure to measure up their work so far, followed by £820 from Kleine, who wrote, when asked why this was nearly double the original quote, that Leitch had made an error in his calculations. Bennet's final bill of £203 was also double Leitch's original estimate.

These were uncertain times. To show their support for the war effort the club sent 78 footballs to the front. Then in November 1914, as Hearts sat proudly at the top of the Scottish League, their entire first team signed up for military duty. Seven would not come home.

As for Archie, a showdown took place on January 8 1915.

Leitch began the encounter 'by expressing regret that mistakes in calculation had been made by one of his servants'. Several 'glaring discrepancies' were then brought to his notice and 'he gave, or attempted to give, explanation, in some cases not quite clear.' He also 'voluntarily stated (that) he only desired commission on (the) original figures supplied by him.'

Over the next nine months the mood grew uglier. Witholding payment from Kleine, Hearts wrote to Somerset House and heard back that several of their company directors had Germanic-sounding names.

Insisting that they were 'purely a British concern,' in March 1915 Kleine threatened to sue. 'We are doing our very utmost,' responded Hearts, sending a cheque for £200.

The following July Hearts tried to sell a corrugated iron terrace cover to raise cash. It had cost £453 in 1911. They were offered £150 by a man from Dundee.

Hit by a collapse in attendances, and then by the imposition of Entertainment Tax, they were still begging their creditors for more time when the war ended.

At the final reckoning the 4,000 seat stand – a fairly rudimentary one at that – cost Hearts £12,178, twice the original estimate.

Yet by 1925 Hearts had paid off their debts and expended a further £5,000 on buying the ground from Edinburgh Corporation.

But whether Leitch was ever paid in full is not clear.

◀ Here is the heart of the matter. Leitch's **McLeod Street Stand** at **Tynecastle** is close to the end of its useful life. Yet how to replace it? In 2004 Hearts were £17.6m in debt, largely as a result of the construction of three new stands, just visible here, in the 1990s.

Their pitch, moreover, does not meet the minimum dimensions set by European football's governing body. Hearts have thus had to stage UEFA Cup games at the 67,500 capacity Murrayfield Stadium, half a mile away.

As this book goes to press, the club directors are planning to rent Murrayfield on a permanent basis. Such a move, first suggested in the 1930s, has a powerful logic. Selling Tynecastle would virtually wipe out the debts.

But the move is hotly contested. Every club derives much of its identity from the character of its ground, Hearts more than most.

Tynecastle's neighbourhood setting, its maroon detailing, the intimacy of its approaches – the club offices are, for instance, located in that Victorian police station mentioned earlier – even the sickly odours from the nearby distillery, make it unique. And Hearts' average gates of 12,000 would surely be lost in Murrayfield.

And so Tynecastle's future hangs by a thread; the business of football as precarious as ever...

Engineering Archie **139**

Aston Villa

Grounds
Villa Park, Birmingham 1914–40

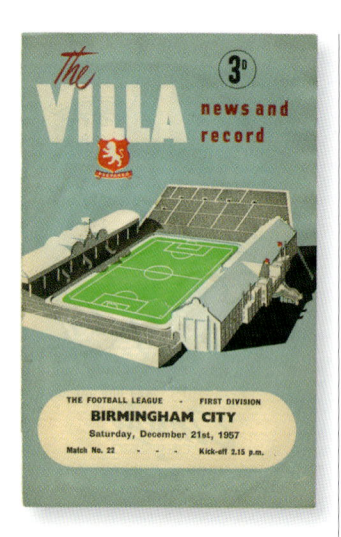

Aston Villa featured this graphic delight on its programme cover for most of the 1950s and early '60s, amending it faithfully each time the ground changed – such as when the 1897 Witton Lane Stand's original barrel roof (*left*) was replaced in 1963 – thereby providing a handy visual guide to Villa Park's development. Both the Trinity Road Stand (*right*) and the far Holte End terrace, were built to Leitch's design.

In Fred Rinder, Aston Villa's all-powerful chairman, Archibald Leitch would meet the best-informed client he was ever likely to find in the football world.

Rinder had no great personal wealth. But in his role as a senior surveyor for Birmingham Corporation, with responsibility for pubs, billiard halls and music halls, he knew a great deal both about how to manage a club and how to read a set of plans. He had also, following the introduction of the 1910 Cinematograph Act, become something of an expert on the new film industry.

But in his heart, Fred Rinder was a stadium builder.

For Leitch, working with such a client might well have turned into a nightmare, as with Henry Norris at Highbury in 1913. Instead, the relationship bore exceptional fruit.

For the Trinity Road Stand the two men planned together in 1914 – though the war delayed its construction until 1922 – was by far the most accomplished of Leitch's career up to that point, and at least the equal of his other great masterwork, the South Stand at Ibrox Park, completed in 1929. Until the redevelopment of Highbury in the 1930s the stand would also be the finest in England. But then, it was the costliest, as shall become all too painfully clear later.

Yet how could it have been otherwise? Villa Park's setting cried out for a grandiose architectural statement.

Overlooking the ground, from the heights of Aston Park, stood a handsome Jacobean mansion, Aston Hall. Close by was the 15th century church of St Peter and St Paul, some 17th century almshouses, and, immediately next to the ground, a superb late Victorian pub, the Holte Hotel, with 10 bedrooms, its own 400 capacity music hall, billiard rooms and two bowling greens.

The site of the ground itself had, until the 1880s, formed part of an extensive amusement park, the Aston Lower Grounds (not dissimilar to Manchester's Belle Vue). But as tastes changed the business collapsed and in 1897 Villa's new home was laid out on the site of the Lower Grounds' cycle and athletics track. Rinder later claimed to have laid down every 'level and line' of the ground before construction began.

A range of other buildings that had formed part of the amusement park (*see opposite*) were, meanwhile, turned into Aston Villa's palatial new headquarters.

The location and its new tenants were well suited. Football was the latest craze. Villa were the team of the day; five times League champions and twice winners of the FA Cup during the 1890s alone. Even so, no football club ever had offices or grounds like these. Villa soon took on an aura of solid, institutional respectability.

Within a few years, however, Villa realised they needed more seats and terracing, and so after the club raised the £11,250 needed to buy the freehold, in 1911, Rinder started planning afresh.

Three years later he was ready.

In June 1914, shareholders at the AGM were told 'that Mr Archibald Leitch, who had considerable experience in this class of work was the man to carry out their scheme.' »

140 Engineering Archie

PLANS AND PARTICULARS OF PROPOSED ALTERATIONS TO ASTON VILLA FOOTBALL GROUNDS.

▲ Before Leitch, **Villa Park** was an oval-shaped ground with a cycle track and a single stand. At one match in 1913 it managed to accommodate 59,740. But it had been an uncomfortable crush.

The Leitch perspective above, presented to shareholders in June 1914, proposed removing the track – a move bitterly opposed by the city's cycle enthusiasts – and creating a rectangular ground.

Many a Victorian ground underwent a similar remodelling to cater for the football boom.

The structures Villa chose to retain were the barrel-roofed Witton Lane Stand, designed by EB Holmes in 1897, and, on the left, the fanciful brick buildings left over from the Aston Lower Grounds Company. Designed by Thomas Naden in 1878 in a Byzantine style, before Villa turned them into the club offices and a gymnasium they housed an aquarium, menagerie, café and mineral water manufactory. For many years their faded majesty pervaded Aston Villa's culture and identity, until finally they were demolished in the late 1970s. The adjacent bowling green was lost too, in 1966.

Note that Leitch's original design for Trinity Road did not feature a roof gable or a central stairway, both of which appeared when the stand was finally built in 1922.

Of the two end terraces, only the Holte End (*right*) was built, raising Villa Park's capacity to 76,000. But neither Rinder nor Leitch lived to see it finished. Work did not begin until 1939, some 25 years after the drawing above first appeared.

Aston Villa

▲ Stairway to heaven – local photographer Albert Wilkes steps in front of his camera to explore the full splendour of the **Trinity Road Stand** in 1923.

Hardly typical of a Leitch stand, the level of detail reveals much about Fred Rinder and his sense of Aston Villa as both a club and a national institution. Other than the electric lamps on the steps and the use of metal framed windows, there is not the slightest concession to modernism. Rather, the openings of the balustrades echoed the style of the old Aston Lower Grounds buildings where Villa's offices were now based, while the Dutch gable was absolutely characteristic of earlier civic buildings in the Aston area, such as the **Holte Hotel** (b.1897), the **Albert Hall** assembly rooms on Witton Road (1899), and the **Aston Manor Tramway Depot** (1903) on Witton Lane (all extant in 2004). The stand's round windows also appear to have been copied from the Albert Hall.

Wilkes himself was a former Villa and England footballer, who played in the ill-fated international at Ibrox in April 1902. He took up the camera in 1906, and was then transferred to Fulham, where he would have become familiar with Leitch's earlier brickwork, at Craven Cottage. He eventually became a Villa director in the 1930s.

Rinder added that he was 'perfectly confident' Leitch's proposals would create 'ample provision' for no fewer than 104,000 spectators.

But shareholders were also warned that the first stage, digging up the track, squaring off the end terraces and building a new Trinity Road Stand, would cost £7,000 over their budget of £20,000.

Villa were wealthy, but they had no indulgent backers, and their dominance of the English game was already fading.

Still, understandably seduced by Rinder and Leitch's vision, the shareholders gave their loud approval, and ten days later work started. Unfortunately, days after that, so too did the Great War.

Work ground to a halt in September 1914 as attention turned to the war effort, and although the crowds flocked back once peace was declared, with the imposition of Entertainment Tax and a rise in the price of building materials and labour, all Leitch's pre-war estimates were found to be hopelessly out of date.

By 1919 the total had risen to a crippling £66,000. So Rinder had to wait still longer and try to work in some savings. In 1921 he reported that he could bring the cost down to £54,000. Finally, a year later, Leitch was instructed to advertise for tenders.

Given the shortage of work at the time the offers flooded in.

Ten companies bid for the building contract, E Garfield Ltd of Birmingham coming in with the lowest at £25,225. No fewer than 25 firms bid for the steelwork, which went to Francis Morton & Co, for £9,650. This was not the lowest, but Villa insisted on the use of British steel, even though this added £2,000 to the bill.

Once all the other extras were added – for example for Kleine Floors and Bennet Seats, two of Leitch's regular suppliers – the final estimate came to £41,775.

By now Rinder, aged 64, had been elected to the Football League's Management Committee. But he was losing his grip on the club. Once work on the stand commenced in 1922, the scale and elaboration of its design, its mosaics, moulded stone flourishes, stained glass windows, x-ray machines for the players and a restaurant – the first ever at a football ground – prompted increasing scrutiny. Worse still, the work was dogged by delays, partly caused by wet weather, but also by strike action.

As the 1922-23 season wore on, the costs rose. And rose. So did the club's borrowings.

And yet when finally complete, The New Pavilion, as it was first called, was magnificent, and quite obviously the best in football at the time. Holding 6,500 seats (all tip-ups), with an enclosure for 11,000 standing, it brought Villa Park's capacity up to 80,000. Were the rest of Leitch's scheme to be implemented, claimed Rinder, this would rise further to 150,000 – an unlikely figure, but then Wembley Stadium had just opened and his agenda was patently clear.

On the day of the stand's official opening on January 26 1924 all seemed well. The Duke of York attended, a real coup for Rinder, and was introduced to Archie. Three months later they all met again when Villa reached the FA Cup Final at Wembley.

But Villa lost that match, and worse was to follow. After more work on concreting the remaining terraces, plus sundry other fixtures and fittings, Leitch sent in his final bill in January 1925. It came to a staggering £87,335. More than twice the estimate put forward three years earlier.

Irate shareholders accused Rinder of 'squandermania'. Leitch was quizzed. But there had been no fiddles. Instead, all eyes pointed to Rinder. He had lost control of the project. He had been swept up by his dream.

In June 1925 he resigned from the board, humiliated and seemingly friendless. He was not even offered a seat in the stand.

Like Henry Norris at Arsenal, he found himself excluded from the ground he had helped create.

But there is a happy ending. Of sorts. Bogged down by debt, Villa's fortunes plunged after Rinder's departure. By 1936 they were in the Second Division.

Rinder saw his chance, got back onto the board – he was then aged 78 – and amazingly, helped turned the tide by appointing a brilliant manager, Jimmy Hogan.

And still he could not resist. As soon as Villa's return to the First Division was assured, he dusted down Leitch's plans and plotted out the second phase.

Exactly 25 years after the scheme had first been unveiled, work started on the expansion of the Holte End terrace.

Alas, Fred Rinder did not live to see the work even start. He died in late 1938. Leitch died four months later. The Holte End expansion was overseen by Leitch's son, and when finished in April 1940 cost a rather more manageable £14,000.

It was not the last football commission Leitch's company would undertake. There were other minor works in the late 1940s. But the Holte End was the last of Archibald Leitch's designs ever to be constructed.

Villa Park's Trinity Road Stand was quite unlike any other. Its flat-topped, elongated roof gable was larger than any other Leitch design. Its balcony, identical to Leitch's other criss-cross steelwork balconies, was encased in moulded wooden panelling, painted in claret and blue. Its main entrance and flanking walls – such as the north wall shown above – were decorated by five sumptuous mosaics, created by immigrant Italian craftsmen working for the firm of Marbello & Durus, tilemakers of Birmingham.

Engineering Archie 143

Aston Villa

Although shareholders in the mid 1920s castigated Rinder for his extravagance, future generations of Villa fans, and visitors from all over the world, held the Trinity Road Stand in great affection – as did this author, who watched his first match from the upper tier (*far right*) in 1962. It is no surprise that Leitch was keen for the directors of Glasgow Rangers to see the stand before he drew up plans for the equally opulent South Stand at Ibrox, built five years later. The quality of detail in the Trinity Road Stand, particularly the use of stained glass and the curved panels formed over the balcony, were unlike anything seen in a football stand before.

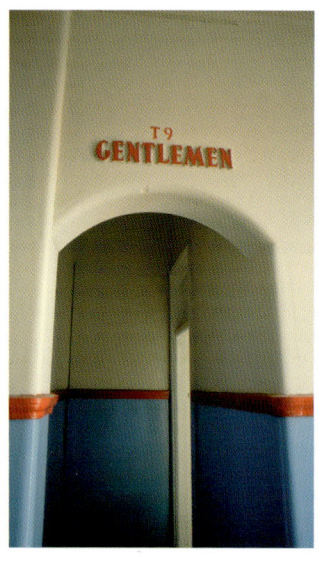

◀ Magnificent to look at but costly to maintain, the Trinity Road Stand proved to be a heavy burden on a struggling club, as Aston Villa were for most of the 1950s and 1960s.

Thereafter it was refurbished on several occasions. Seats and executive boxes were added to the lower tier in the early 1970s.

Another major refit was ordered in 1992 (*shown left*). This saw the glazing in of the central balcony (which for some reason had never been opened to fans on match days), the reseating and reflooring of the upper deck, and the addition of two protruding brick bays, either side of the central stairway.

On the pitch side of the stand the roof was reclad and extended over the lower tier and floodlight gantries attached to the gable (which had lost its original ironwork finial long before, it is thought during the Second World War).

Although not all the work completed was sympathetic with the original – the replacement windows in particular – the 1992 refit seemed like a worthwhile price to pay for the stand's retention. Like the original construction, it also cost nearly twice the original budget, a total of £2.4 million.

Yet despite this expenditure, eight years later, the stand was demolished.

The club wanted more seats, more boxes, more restaurants, larger dressing rooms and lower maintenance and running costs.

They did not feel, as did Rangers with their Leitch stand at Ibrox, that they could extend or modernise the stand any further in a cost-effective manner.

The same was true of the Holte End. That too was demolished, in June 1994, exactly 80 years after Messrs Rinder and Leitch had embarked on their Aston adventure.

Engineering Archie **145**

Dundee

Grounds
Dens Park, Dundee 1921–22

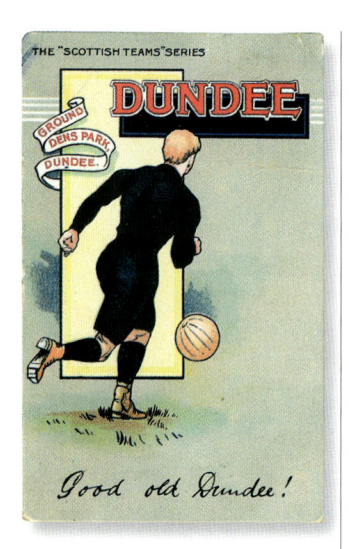

After the 'Light Blues' of Rangers and the 'Jam Tarts' of Edinburgh, now it was time for the 'Dark Blues' of Dundee, the city famous for its three chief industries; jam, journalism and jute (a coarse fibre imported from the Asian subcontinent and used in textile manufacture). Almost half the local workforce was employed in jute mills, two of which bordered Dundee's Dens Park ground.

After four years of slaughter, and with spasms of industrial and social unrest in some urban centres threatening to sour the peace, by 1919 Britain may not have been a land fit for heroes. But it was certainly ripe for diversion.

For Archibald Leitch, newly moved with his family from Liverpool to London, a surge in attendances at football matches in the immediate post-war period boded well for business. The professional game, now 35 years old, had never been more popular.

Dundee FC's needs were straightforward, and immediate.

In 1920, despite acute unemployment in the city, they drew 34,000 spectators for a Cup tie v. Celtic, the largest football crowd ever seen on Tayside.

But their Dens Park ground, established in 1899, was rented, had two basic wooden stands and a pavilion, and the owners of the neighbouring jute works were angling to buy part of the ground for expansion.

For the football club's charismatic and indulgent chairman, the dapper Willie McIntosh – owner of one of Dundee's most popular watering holes, the Opera Bar – it was time to act. Private investors were found, Dens Park was purchased for £5,000 and, no doubt based on advice from fellow committeemen at the Scottish FA (where he was the treasurer), McIntosh hired Leitch to plan for a bright new future.

Apart from the site's sloping levels, the commission was simple enough. But Dens Park did possess one unusual characteristic.

Since the 1880s a series of clubs playing at a number of grounds had sought to establish themselves in the rapidly expanding city. By 1919, only two remained in contention, Dundee at Dens Park – members of the Scottish League since 1893 – and Dundee Hibernian, the latest of several clubs started up by the city's sizeable Irish community.

As a city Dundee was much less defined, or blighted by the sectarianism which characterised Glasgow and, to a lesser extent, Edinburgh (where Leitch worked with Rangers and Hearts, rather than Celtic and Hibernian). Even so, by an extraordinary quirk of fate, Dundee had ended up with a ground on the very same street as their rivals. Less than 150 yards separated Dens Park from Hibernian's Tannadice Park.

Even in Britain's often eccentric sporting landscape, this close proximity was unique.

As shown opposite, Leitch proposed raising and terracing three sides of Dens Park, though not to uniform heights, and without providing shelter. A 4,500 seat North Stand would become the new club headquarters, as part of an increased capacity of 45,000.

Although incomplete, the revamped Dens Park was formally opened on 17 September 1921.

'It was pleasing in these depressing times,' Lord Provost Spence declared, 'to know that there was one body of men in the city who had faith in their future prosperity.' At a time when employment was 'badly wanted', the directors had provided work for a large number of men.

'It is up to us,' he added, 'to rally round. (The club) will require

146 Engineering Archie

bumper gates... to meet the expenses incurred.'

But there was still more work to be done. Three months later, the sole remaining structure from the original ground – the wooden South Stand – burnt to the ground.

How the Opera Bar must have buzzed with rumour. The rickety stand was in any case due to have been dismantled to allow for the south bank's expansion, and had of course been recently insured.

One Dundee player, Jimmy Guthrie – later boss of the players' union – harboured no doubts. In his memoirs Guthrie recalled how the groundsman, rather than being praised for trying to save the burning stand, had been sacked.

Several years later there was a further casualty. The expense of redeveloping Dens Park put such a strain on Dundee's finances that by 1935 McIntosh had to plead for funds from the city's wealthy jute merchants. They responded by easing poor Willie off the board.

McIntosh could not function without the game, however, so in high dudgeon he decamped next door, and over the next few years helped lay the foundations for the success that his former neighbours, now renamed Dundee United, would eventually lord over the Dark Blues in the post war period. Indeed while Dens Park hardly changed until the 1990s, Tannadice developed into one of Scotland's finest grounds.

Yet the fact that both clubs survive at all is remarkable, more so since Dundee racked up debts of over £20 million by 2003.

Some would consider the two rival clubs' refusal to merge, let alone even share, as foolhardy.

But one happy consequence of this longstanding impasse is that Dundee's North Stand is now one of only eleven Leitch stands still surviving. If only the Opera Bar were still around for a toast.

A classic, though unsigned pen and ink drawing from Leitch's office. The ground was developed more or less as planned, though without the ornate ironwork on the ridge of the stand roof.

Dundee

◀ Leitch's **North Stand** rises above and behind its wooden predecessor (b.1899), as Dundee face Third Lanark in August 1921.

This method of phased building was common. It allowed the existing stand facilities to be used during the construction period. The clearance of the old stand then allowed the new enclosure to be completed in the space made available.

Standing guard in front of Dundee's goalkeeper Willie Fotheringham was Davie Raitt, transferred to Everton in 1922 to help defray the costs of the new stand. Several other Dundee favourites would follow as the Depression set in.

The stand's corrugated sheeting (*above*), seen here before being reclad in the 1990s, was typical of Leitch's more utilitarian stands.

148 Engineering Archie

▶ To keep down costs when the **North Stand** was first built, Leitch specified prefabricated concrete risers only, infilling the treads with compacted cinders from local coal mines. As can be seen, Dundee's treads were later infilled with tarmacadam.

Another typical Leitch feature was the sinking of the front section of terracing to below pitch level.

This allowed for greater numbers of spectators to be accommodated on the enclosure with a shallower rake, thereby also improving sightlines from the seating deck.

It also meant that the height of the stand could be kept to a more cost-effective minimum.

One further advantage was that groundstaff could gain easier access to the pitch's undersoil drains.

Even the North Stand's characteristic angled, or cranked plan, was dictated by practical considerations.

Although this form provided improved sightlines for those in the wings (compared with the more usual rectilinear stands), it was adopted here – as at Blackburn, Everton and Wolves – simply to follow the angled line of the adjoining Sandeman Street. For all their popular appeal, football clubs in the pre-war period were still not sufficiently powerful to have roads re-aligned for their convenience.

In the 1990s, partly to meet the requirements of the Taylor Report, partly to prepare Dens Park for greyhound racing, the North Stand was completely reseated and reclad, and its enclosure divided into two halves; one with seats, the other becoming a flat concourse for bookmakers in front of hospitality lounges inserted under the seats.

The greyhound experiment failed to catch on, but the £1 million refit at least ensured that Leitch's stand would survive into the current century, albeit with an upper tier capacity reduced to 3,528 (down from the original total of 4,500) and the enclosure now holding just 400 seats, instead of 5,000 standing spectators as before.

Resplendent in their war paint and distinguished by just one letter of their postcodes, Dens Park and Tannadice Park defy reason to form one of the most eccentric juxtapositions of Britain's sporting landscape. Apart from the addition of the cover on the south bank (*right*) in 1959, Leitch's 1921 masterplan for Dens Park more or less survived until stands were completed behind each goal in 1999. From a peak of 43,000, Dens Park now holds 11,856. For the record, Tannadice holds 14,223. The former Densfield Jute Works (*centre right*) is now small industrial units and offices.

Engineering Archie **149**

Newcastle United

Grounds
St James' Park, Newcastle 1921–29

St James' Park in the 1960s, with Leitch's terrace cover at the near end being the only part of his 1926 scheme (*shown opposite*) put into place. The Leazes Terrace – a Georgian terrace as opposed to a football terrace – is in the upper left corner, hence the absence of cover on the east side. In the right foreground is the 1905 West Stand. Although similar to Leitch designs of the period, it was in fact the work of a rival engineer, Alexander Blair. In the 1940s St James' Park's wide open terraces were frequented by a Newcastle schoolboy, Peter Taylor, who went on to become Lord Justice Taylor, the judge who recommended the abolition of terracing after the Hillsborough disaster of 1989.

Archibald Leitch may have suffered the odd run-in with district surveyors and council officials, but he never had to deal with the myriad planning controls that face stadium builders today. If he had, at least half a dozen of his major works would never have left the drawing board.

But in Newcastle-upon-Tyne Leitch was to draw an almost complete blank. After eight years of work on behalf of Newcastle United, the only tangible results of his labour were improvements to an existing stand, upgraded terracing and a single terrace cover of no particular note.

The root of Archie, and United's frustration was twofold.

Firstly, within a few yards of St James' Park's eastern boundary stands the Leazes Terrace. Built between 1829-34 by the town's great speculative builder, Richard Grainger, this classic Georgian terrace, now Grade I listed, has acted as a constant buffer to the club's development plans.

No other football ground in Britain possesses such an illustrious neighbour, which explains why even today there is only a narrow, low stand on the east side of St James' Park, a mere bungalow next to the high rise behemoths forming the other three sides of the ground.

But there was another, more serious impediment to United's desire to develop St James' Park, and that was the obstructive attitude of United's landlords.

Castle Leazes, the site on which the ground was laid out, was, and remains part of a much larger landholding known as Town Moor, which had for centuries been managed on behalf of the townsfolk by the Freemen of the City. Ownership of the Moor, however, has since the 19th century been shared with Newcastle Corporation. (In fact, the latter owns the actual land, while the Freemen retain the 'herbage' or grazing rights, which is why, bizarrely, one still sees cattle in fields overlooked by the modern stadium.)

From the very moment United became tenants at St James' Park in 1892 – though it had been used by other clubs since 1880 – they encountered obstacles.

Their first permanent structure at the ground, the West Stand, was erected in 1905, under the supervision of Alexander Blair of Glasgow, the engineer responsible for drawing up the masterplan of the new Hampden Park (*see page 170*), a few years earlier.

The stand's steelwork (*see page 42*) was also entrusted to a Glasgow firm, the Clyde Structural Iron Company, with whom Leitch had himself often worked, building factories and, more recently the new stands at Bramall Lane and Ayresome Park. Leitch, however, was not involved at Newcastle at this time.

Immediately the stand opened Leazes Terrace residents appealed to the Freemen to 'compel the Club to remove all the erections placed on the ground.'

St James' Park in 1908, with Leazes Terrace on the far right. One of Leitch's roles in the 1920s was to oversee the relaying of the ground's notoriously heavy pitch.

150 Engineering Archie

They must have been apoplectic when the following December a record 56,000 crowd packed St James' for a derby v. Sunderland.

But if United's landlords did not accede to the residents' protests, nor did they make life easy.

As Paul Joannou's detailed history of the ground relates (see Links), Leitch arrived on the scene in 1921, just as his football work was starting to pick up after the war. (His other clients then were Dundee and Aston Villa.)

His first task was to install Leitch patented barriers to replace the wire-rope variety specified by Blair in 1905. Also used at Hampden (see page 29), they were by then largely discredited.

Leitch was also asked to sort out the West Stand. Two poorly located stairways leading from the front of the stand up to the centre seats were removed. The players' route from the dressing rooms, which required them to run the gauntlet of crowds through the enclosure, was also replaced by more secure tunnels. (One can just imagine Archie tut-tutting these mistakes. If only United had hired him in the first place!)

United, meanwhile, made their first attempt to buy the freehold. The Freemen expressed a willingness, but the Corporation remained adamantly opposed. Moreover they refused to extend United's lease beyond seven years, while insisting that all structures erected would automatically become the property of the Corporation, a stance they would maintain for the next 50 years.

Truly, there was not a club in the country operating under such restraints. Yet United were the toast of the 'Toon'. In 1927 they won their fourth League title. Before then they had appeared in six Cup Finals, winning two of them. They were one of the best supported clubs in Britain, yet still they had only 4,650 seats and not an inch of shelter on the terraces.

In 1926 Leitch and the club therefore tried again, with the scheme shown above.

And once again they failed, except in one respect. In 1929 the Corporation did eventually approve the erection of a terrace roof which covered the north, or Leazes End terrace. This provided shelter for 15,000 spectators, in an overall capacity which peaked at 68,386 in 1930.

And so St James' Park remained for the next forty years – one of the most basic grounds in top flight football – until in 1971 United were finally granted a 99 year lease, freeing them to begin the redevelopment of the ground.

Leitch would not be the last designer thwarted at St James'. Masterplans drawn up and then abandoned, or part-built but then superceded from 1967 onwards, included ones by Ove Arup and Faulkner Brown. Even now, the concrete and steel fortress that is the modern St James' is a necessary compromise.

As for Leitch's efforts, his terrace cover was demolished in 1978, while the West Stand survived until 1987. And as for relations between United and their landlords, pleased to report that since the 1990s, after a century as tenants, both 'Toon' and Town finally seem happily reconciled.

Newcastle, United, at last.

The one that got away – Leitch's scheme for St James' Park. Only the north section of terrace cover behind the far goal was built, leaving the east and south sides uncovered until the 1970s. On the other hand, Leitch's functional style hardly complemented the ground's more illustrious neighbour on Leazes Terrace.

Crystal Palace

Grounds
Selhurst Park, London 1923–24

By 1923, as work on the new Empire Stadium at Wembley proceeded, Leitch had worked at one time or another for five of London's eleven League clubs. Crystal Palace were the sixth.

They were at the time playing in the Second Division, having become inaugural champions of the newly formed Third Division in 1921. But they needed a new home.

And therein lies a tale, for as their name suggests, Palace's origins were somewhat unusual.

After the 1851 Great Exhibition in Hyde Park, Paxton's 'Crystal Palace' was re-erected in south London, as the centrepiece of a large amusement park in Upper Sydenham. It was there that staff formed the first Crystal Palace FC in 1861 and became founder members of the Football Association, two years later.

The club we know today was a later creation, formed in 1905 as a professional outfit. But it too was based at the Palace grounds.

The Glaziers, as the team became known, played in a huge, turfed bowl of an arena, which had been laid out east of the formal park, in 1895, and which from then until 1914 provided an unlikely venue for FA Cup Finals.

(With his football connections Leitch must surely have visited this predecessor to Wembley and seen for himself its appalling inadequacies. It somehow managed to fit in 120,000 spectators for the 1913 Cup Final, less than half of whom would have been able to follow the match.)

Palace attracted rather more modest crowds, but in any case were forced to leave when the arena – now the site of the Crystal Palace athletics stadium – was commandeered for the war effort.

By 1919 Palace were renting a small ground on Selhurst Road, quaintly called The Nest (previously the home of the area's leading club, Croydon Common, known as 'the Robins').

Stay put and they might have coasted along as a lower division club indefinitely. But find a suitable alternative and a world of possibilities might open up.

Why so? Because, apart from Millwall and Charlton to the east, there were no other senior clubs in the whole, vast suburban swathe south of the river Thames, nor any, for that matter, between The Nest and the south coast. For Palace, a new ground offered the chance to become the Arsenal or Chelsea of south London.

As it happened, suitable land was soon found only a short distance from The Nest. Owned by the London, Brighton and South Coast Railway, the 12 acre site was a sunken hollow, having once been a brickfield. It was, furthermore, within easy distance of three railway stations and was a snip at £2,570. (Arsenal paid £46,000 for the freehold of their 10 acres in Islington three years later.)

To help fund the ground's costs, estimated at £30,000, Palace's directors issued, and sold, £6,000 worth of Ground Bonds, priced at £10 or £50 each, offering five per cent interest. These were to be honoured only after Humphreys – the contractors with whom Leitch frequently worked – had been paid, via a levy on gate receipts. This was common practice.

Leitch's plans were hardly elaborate; a single, basic,

Two London clubs are named after buildings, Arsenal and Crystal Palace, although strictly the latter was a nickname, coined by *Punch* magazine. It referred, of course, to Joseph Paxton's iron and glass halls built for the 1851 Great Exhibition. Crystal Palace, the football club, were themselves originally nicknamed the Glaziers, hence this cartoon character, Mr Glazier, drawn by Herbert Godfrey for the club's 1913-14 yearbook. The figure was based on one of the Palace's prominent water towers.

corrugated stand seating 4,500, with standing in front for 1,500, plus three sides of open terracing, on a site with excellent access and little need for major earthworks. The task should have been routine.

But although Humphreys started work in December 1923 by the following August the stand was unfinished and only twelve steps of terracing on the other three open sides had been completed. Bad weather and a seven week building strike were the main culprits.

Nevertheless, after Leitch shrewdly wined and dined the press before taking them on a conducted tour a week before the opening day in August 1924, high hopes were expressed.

In one of many glowing reports, Tityrus of *Athletic News* gushed, 'In area it is the largest ground in London, and when the bank opposite the ground is fully terraced it will be, I understand, more immense than the… Spion Kop at Chelsea. I wandered around this place until fatigue overtook me, but it was evident that there (is) space for 100,000 people with the site fully equipped.'

The following year Palace were relegated. Selhurst Park never was fully equipped as planned. The stand did not gain its standard Leitch pediment, and it took over 30 years to finish the terracing.

In fact, few changes occurred at all until 1969, since when, apart from the extension and recladding of the Leitch stand, the transformation has been been total; three new stands and a supermarket at one end, and regular visits from the likes of Arsenal and Chelsea. South of the river, meanwhile, there are still no League clubs between Selhurst and the south coast.

Selhurst Park in 1924 (*above*), with just twelve steps of terracing concreted. The upper, unterraced sections remained notorious as mud slides for years to follow. Though much altered, Leitch's stand is still identifiable today (*left*). At its peak Selhurst held 51,482, in 1979. Its current all-seated capacity is 26,400.

Engineering Archie 153

Twickenham

Grounds

Twickenham, London 1924–32

Twickenham's 1927 East Stand, shortly before its demolition in 1992. The famous weathervane was designed in 1950 by Kenneth Dalgleish and depicts a winged Hermes delivering a perfect pass to a colleague under the posts. The East Stand and its opposite West Stand (b.1932) were almost certainly Leitch designs. With the North Stand being definitely one of his, it suggests that English rugby's HQ was thus one of Archie's highest profile venues.

Considering that Archie was a football man, it is ironic that while he was not involved in the design or construction of the original Wembley Stadium, the national home of English football, opened in 1923, he did work at the national grounds of the Welsh Rugby Union (mainly the terracing at Cardiff Arms Park), the English Rugby Football Union at Twickenham, and possibly also the Irish RFU at Lansdowne Road in Dublin. (Strangely, the Scottish RFU at Murrayfield never hired him, as far as we know.)

Then, as now, professional football operated at a quite different social level from rugby union. But if, to borrow a phrase from Charlie Sutcliffe of Burnley, the RFU were more public school than public house, it was all work for Archie. The design issues were essentially the same for rugby as they were for football.

The idea of a national home for English rugby is attributed to a referee and former MCC cricketer, Billy Williams. It was he who identified a market garden site by the River Crane in 1907.

Billy's 'Cabbage Patch,' as Twickenham was subsequently dubbed, opened in 1909. It had two stands each holding 3,000 seats, and a total capacity of 30,000, less than most senior football grounds at the time.

It was also located a fair walk from the nearest railway station, along narrow streets, and, in the eyes of one critic, was 'fearsomely remote from Piccadilly Circus.'

As for Leitch involvement, we know that in 1924, at the same time he was finishing off Selhurst Park down the road in Croydon, he designed a new North Stand for the RFU. This was a standard Leitch double decker with seats for 3,515 and a terrace for 4,800.

Opened in the presence of the Prince of Wales and Prime Minister Stanley Baldwin in January 1925, it cost, together with improvements to the east and west enclosures, in the region of £13,000.

But this was only the beginning. Despite unease that monies spent on Twickenham would mean less going to grass roots clubs (as the RFU was both the ground's owner and the sport's govening body), some £135,000 was spent over the next seven years on redeveloping the other three sides, to create London's third largest stadium, after Wembley and White City, with a capacity of 72,500. That the RFU was an entirely amateur organisation shows the extent of its clout with the banks.

The question is, were these later developments the work of Leitch?

In appearance, both the East Stand (erected in 1927) and the West Stand (1932), closely resemble Leitch double-deckers. Each featured his trademark balcony. Moreover they were built by Leitch's friends at Humphreys, who also built the North Stand.

And yet there are no records of Leitch being the architect.

So was Twickenham – as it existed between 1932 and 1990 (when the North Stand was demolished and the current redevelopment started) – really a Leitch ground, through and through, as were Goodison Park or Molineux, for example?

In the absence of written evidence, we must let the images be our guide.

154 Engineering Archie

▲ Twickenham's **North Stand** (*behind the far posts, above*) as crowds gather for its inaugural match, England v. New Zealand, in January 1925. The 60,000 crowd was the largest ever to have seen a rugby match in Britain at that time.

Note the lack of crush barriers on the south terrace, a sure sign that Leitch had not, by that stage, been involved in its design. Or was it that rugby's bowler-hatted fans were less prone to surging forward?

A corner of the North Stand is also visible in the later image (*left*), which records a rare moment of unity between the two football codes, as crowds before an England v. Ireland match in February 1958 pay silent tribute to the victims of the Munich air crash.

The stand shown here is the **West Stand**. Built in 1932 with seats for 12,000 on the slightly cranked upper deck, it certainly appears to be a standard Leitch double-decker, as did the East Stand, built in 1927.

Note the piled-up straw, used for protecting the pitch from frost.

Engineering Archie **155**

Portsmouth

Grounds
Fratton Park, Portsmouth 1925

League football finally arrived on the south coast in 1920, when Brighton, Southampton and Portsmouth, all previously members of the Southern League, became founder members of the Third Division.

Over the next 30 years, Pompey were to have, as one souvenir booklet put it, an 'adventurous career.' Promoted to the Second Division in 1924, then to the First in 1927, they reached three Cup finals and won the League twice in a row, in 1949 and 1950.

Never have Fratton Park's famous Pompey Chimes – 'Play Up Pompey, Pompey Play up' – tuned to echo the peels of the Town Hall bell, rung out so joyously.

Fratton Park had opened in 1899, and in 1905 gained a corner pavilion at least as impressive as Leitch's at Craven Cottage, also completed that year. On occasions the ground had accommodated up to 30,000 fans. But there had been some unpleasant moments.

As JE Pink, the club's financial advisor wrote to a bank in 1924, 'Unfortunately the Stand... at Fratton Park has accommodation for 1,000 people only, and in consequence considerable revenue has been lost to the Company. This Stand has been overcrowded directly the gates have been opened and a very large number of the better class supporter, being unable to obtain a seat, stays away from Matches.'

His next sentence may not come as a surprise.

'The directors have therefore called in Mr Archibald Leitch of 18 Victoria Street, Westminster SW1, the eminent Architect for Football Grounds.'

In fact it was Leitch's idea that Pink write to the bank, as the club was then £4-5,000 in debt and, based on the tenders already received, needed a further £20,000 to build the new stand he was proposing. It would appear that Leitch often played this role; using his contacts to help clubs find funding, while in the process keeping his own order book full.

Based on 21 home matches per season, and 'putting the estimate at a very very low figure indeed,' Pink's letter continued, 'the extra revenue for the new Stand would be, on average... £2,100 for the season, a sufficient amount to meet the interest charge and repayment of prinicipal.

'Personally, I can recommend the business to the bank. Fratton Park is situate in the centre of the town, in a very thickly populated neighbourhood and is within 5 minutes walking distance of the Fratton Railway Station. It is of four and a half acres in extent and would always command an excellent price for building purposes. Apart from this point, however, I consider it will always be required as a Sport Arena.'

Although it no doubt helped that each of the club's eight directors signed personal guarantees for the loan, the bank was clearly persuaded, because the following May, Humphreys the builders moved in on site.

The first steel column went up on June 17 (as a plaque would later record), and on August 29 1925, the Football League President, 'Honest John' McKenna of Liverpool, declared the stand open before Pompey's match against Middlesbrough.

From a 1950s card series issued by the Chix Bubble Gum Company, Jimmy Dickinson sports the distinctive crest of Portsmouth. Based on the city's coat of arms, the star and crescent moon derives from the seal of the crusader king, Richard I, who granted Portsmouth its charter in 1194.

156 Engineering Archie

Rarely during the mid-1920s had any of Leitch's commissions been concluded in such a speedy and straightforward manner.

No delays with steel delivery, no strikes, and no wet weather. Plus the added bonus of being able to pop down to the docks and study the ships, one of Archie's other great passions since his early days as a marine engineer.

There were two people at Fratton Park whom Leitch must also have been keen to please.

The Portsmouth chairman, Robert Blyth, was an Ayrshire man and former footballer whom Archie might well have seen playing for Rangers in the 1890s.

Portsmouth's secretary-manager at the time, meanwhile, was none other than John McCartney, who had occupied the same role at Tynecastle ten years earlier when Leitch got into such hot water with Hearts' new McLeod Street Stand.

In the close-knit world of football, no man could afford too many slip ups.

Having said that, Pompey's new South Stand was a routine commission. It was a standard Leitch double decker; similar to one he was designing for Twickenham at the same time but on a smaller footprint and with a line of houses immediately to the rear limiting its height and access points. It held 3,961 seats, with space for 6,685 standing in front.

Eighty years later it is still in regular use.

Reclad in modern profiled sheeting and with seats on its lower terrace, it is indeed one of only eleven Leitch stands remaining, and one of only three to feature the classic Leitch balcony detailing (the two others being at Ibrox and Goodison).

At Fratton Park, alas, this balcony detailing has been hidden for several years behind advertising hoardings.

But, the good news is that the stand seems likely to last a few more years yet.

Or at least, half of it will.

After decades of trying to find an alternative site, in 2004 Pompey decided to stay put, but rebuild three sides of Fratton Park as part of larger residential and commercial development.

As explained overleaf, half the South Stand will be retained in this new set up, and as half a Leitch stand is better than none, it must be hoped that what remains of the balcony will be uncovered for future generations to enjoy, as so many have done before.

Photo by Stephen Cribb, Southsea.

THE NEW STAND, FRATTON PARK.

Interior of the new Stand at Fratton Park, and playing pitch.
Photo by Stephen Cribb, Southsea.

Taken by photographer and club director Stephen Cribb, these early views of Leitch's South Stand show the extensive use of glazing to cast light not only on the seating deck but on the stairs and passages below. These had only a few windows because the stand backed onto the gardens of terraced houses behind.

Engineering Archie **157**

Portsmouth

▲ Before it became commonplace for clubs to focus all their day-to-day football business at training centres, players spent much of their working lives at the ground itself.

They trained there, not only on the pitch but also by running up and down the terraces. They met there socially – Leitch's designs usually included billiard and card rooms – and as apprentices they often swept away the litter after matches. In the summer some players even earned extra cash doing odd jobs, such as concreting the terraces or painting the stands.

They would have known the nooks and crannies of their home ground – particularly those corners where they might skive off for a crafty fag – better than any of their modern contemporaries.

Seen here are Portsmouth's team gathering in 1948 to hear tales of old from Jimmy Stewart, who was Pompey's trainer when the club formed 50 years earlier in 1898. His talk must have worked, for that season Portsmouth won the League for the first time in their history.

Note the complete absence of any barriers in the South Stand's enclosure.

▲ No mention of Fratton Park is complete without reference to its homely main entrance, tucked in at one end of Frogmore Road. Neither of the half timbered buildings above were by Leitch, but they deserve mention all the same.

The Pompey Shop was originally the Pompey public house, opened in 1902 by the Brickwood brewery, whose owner happened also to be the first chairman of Portsmouth, when Fratton Park opened in 1898.

The pub's designer also had a football connection. Arthur Cogswell, a prolific architect who designed *inter alia* seven other pubs in the city – characterised by their gambrel roof turrets, known as the 'witch's hats' – was one of the founders of an earlier Portsmouth football club which formed in 1884. (Playing in goal for that team, incidentally, was a certain Arthur Conan Doyle, though he played under the name AC Smith).

The half timbered gatehouse (seen to the left of the former pub) is all that remains of a pavilion built by the club in 1905. This pavilion had a witch's hat of its own, in the form of a clock tower, facing the pitch and paid for by Sir John Brickwood.

When Leitch remodelled this corner of the ground to make room for his South Stand in 1925 the clock tower and pavilion balcony had to be sacrificed, unfortunately (for they were rather splendid). But the rear section survives and forms part of the club's offices.

After 2005, Fratton's **South Stand** (*above right*) will take on a new lease of life as part of a major redevelopment of both the ground and its surrounds.

The plan, to be carried out by the Scottish contractors, Barr Ltd – who have been almost as active in football as were Humphreys in Archie's day – is to turn the pitch by 90 degrees from its present axis (*right*), so that the South Stand will be behind one goal.

Two new stands and the extension of the modern Fratton End Stand will result in a capacity of 28,000, rising to 35,000 if certain conditions can be met. A residential 'Pompey Village' on the site of the former railway goods yard next to the ground will help fund the redevelopment.

Engineering Archie **159**

Wolves

Grounds
Molineux, Wolverhampton 1925–39

Football souvenirs come no more wondrous than this special edition linen tea towel, produced by a local department store, Beatties, to celebrate Wolves' third League Championship in 1959. Images of Molineux, a town centre ground with four distinctive sides – each designed by Leitch, each burnished with the club colours of 'old gold' – featured strongly in the iconography of the Wolves. Once seen, Molineux was never forgotten.

In late April 1923, just days after the opening of Wembley Stadium, Wolverhampton Wanderers became the first of the Football League's twelve founder members to be relegated to the recently created Third Division.

Their humiliation seemed complete. Not only was the team poor, but their ground was so antiquated that the players had to change in a glorified shed, while the directors preferred to meet in rented rooms in the Molineux Hotel, a converted Georgian town house which overlooked the site and from which the ground's name was derived.

Once one of the Midland's finest ornamental gardens and pleasure grounds, Molineux had been turned into a sports ground in the 1880s. It had staged an international match in 1891, and four FA Cup semi-finals since. Wolves were themselves twice Cup winners and twice losing finalists. They were one of the great names of early professional football.

But as the Black Country town's motto puts it so nobly, 'Out of darkness cometh light'.

In July 1923 the old club was wound up. Shares worth £30,000 were issued in a new company, and the fightback began.

While the team soon restored pride on the pitch, the new board showed its own intent by buying the five acre ground from its owners, the Northampton Brewery Company, for £5,607.

A bargain it was too. Firstly, it sat conveniently in the dip of a steady incline, with a sizeable natural slope offering the perfect embankment for spectators at the southern end of the ground.

Secondly, it lay within a stone's throw of the town centre and main railway station, and was therefore connected with the town and its everyday life in a way that was rare for a football ground, even then.

In more prosperous times such a prime piece of urban real estate might well have been beyond the purse of an average Third Division club. But the reborn Wolves were determined to make up for lost time. Even before the deeds were exchanged, in December 1923 the club's adviser, a local architect called Marcus Brown, was instructed by the board to get in touch with Archibald Leitch.

Thus began a 16 year liaison which would transform Molineux into one of British football's most charismatic arenas.

Leitch's first task was to design an affordable Main Stand for the west, or Waterloo Road side. Plans for a two-tiered stand, similar to the one Leitch had completed for Dundee three years earlier, were seen and approved by the town's mayor in January 1924.

By the time the tenders came in Wolves had regained their place in the Second Division and attendances were recovering.

160 Engineering Archie

Boswell & Co. of School Street put in a tender worth £8,416 for the building work. For the steelwork, Herbertson & Co. of Lever Street were to charge £3,371, plus another £67 to move the old cover on the Waterloo Road side to the Molineux Street side (where it was blown down by a gale the following January).

Wolves offered a further £650 to buy a house on Waterloo Road (just visible in the drawing below, by the bus in the top left corner) whose owner was furious about the construction of a urinal backing onto his property.

As was common in the 1920s there were costly delays. (Two of Leitch's other clients at the time, Crystal Palace and Aston Villa, suffered similarly). In April 1925 the club also complained to Leitch – a familiar tale this, too – that Boswell's bill was now considerably over the contract price and that the finish of the stand left much to be desired.

By now the new company was over £6,000 in debt and only £8,000 of the shares had been subscribed. However, when the stand, which cost £15,000 in the end, was finally opened by the League president John McKenna in September 1925, Wolves were already on their way back.

Leitch was next called upon in the early 1930s to redevelop the North Bank (which fans continued to call The Cowshed). This was followed by the construction of the Molineux Street Stand (*see page 164*), opened in 1932 to coincide with the team's triumphant return to the First Division.

Throughout this period the vast South Bank terrace was extended and concreted, until it filled the entire 63 yard long incline leading up to the bowling green of the Molineux Hotel and held an estimated 30,000 spectators. Had Wolves been able to buy the green and square off the terrace it would have easily become the nation's largest terrace. (Instead, Aston Villa's Holte End, another Leitch design, just eclipsed it.)

The South Bank was covered in 1935 (*as illustrated on page 49*) but Leitch's company continued to work on at Molineux for the next four years, mainly on improvements to the main stand.

At a board meeting on August 31 1939 the directors authorised a final payment of £100 to Archibald Leitch and Partners. Archie himself had died in April that year. Neither his business, nor the world, would ever be the same again. The meeting ended with a resolution 'that arrangements be made to camouflage the stands.'

This grainy image, taken from the cover of one of the Wolves programmes of the 1930s, is the only surviving reproduction of Leitch's scheme for Molineux, before the covering of the massive South Bank in 1935. An earlier Leitch drawing, referred to in the club minutes in 1924, has never been found. Apart from the covering of the South Bank, this is how Molineux was laid out when it recorded its highest ever gate of 61,315 for a Cup tie v. Liverpool in February 1939, two months before Archie Leitch died. His firm was still undertaking minor works at the ground at the time.

Engineering Archie **161**

Wolves

▶ Viewed from the roof of the Molineux Hotel in 1920, this is how **Molineux** appeared when Archibald Leitch was entrusted with the task of transforming it from a typical late Victorian sports ground into a functional 20th century football stadium.

A stretch of the original running and cycle track can still be seen on the Molineux Street side (*right*). The players' changing rooms were in a modest pavilion in the far corner (behind the white fence). The ground's 300 covered seats were in the small stand on the left.

The Molineux Hotel itself, now a Grade II* listed building, was built for a prominent ironmaster and merchant, Benjamin Molineux, in the 1720s, before becoming the hub of commercial pleasure gardens in the 1860s. In 1869 these gardens hosted the South Staffordshire Industrial and Fine Arts Exhibition. In the 1880s the boating lake was filled in to allow the sports ground to be laid out.

The bowling green, seen in the foreground, is now a car park.

The view on the right, taken in the 1960s, shows how comprehensively Leitch engineered the available space. The South Bank, a classic Leitch terrace, held half the ground's capacity. At its rear, under the roof, the steppings were timber, on a steel frame raised above the natural slope.

WVN 14   WOLVERHAMPTON. THE MOLINEUX GROUNDS

162 Engineering Archie

1899

1938

2005

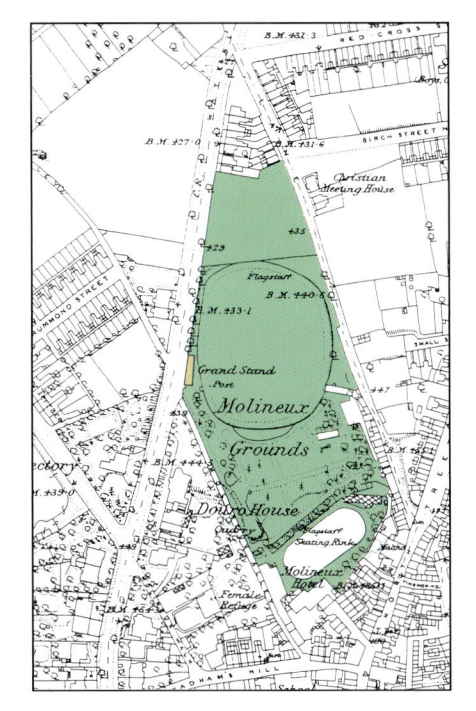

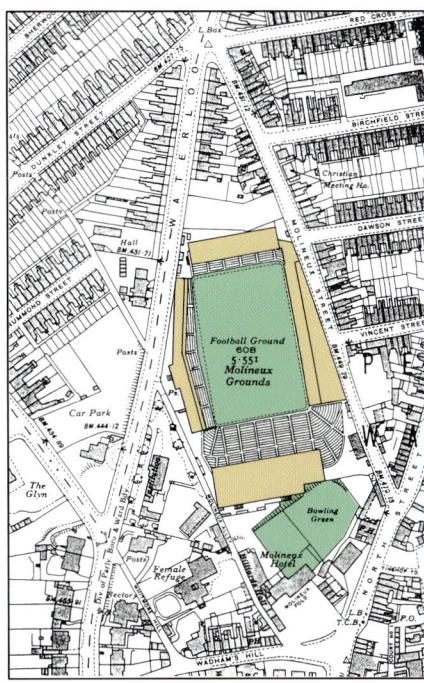

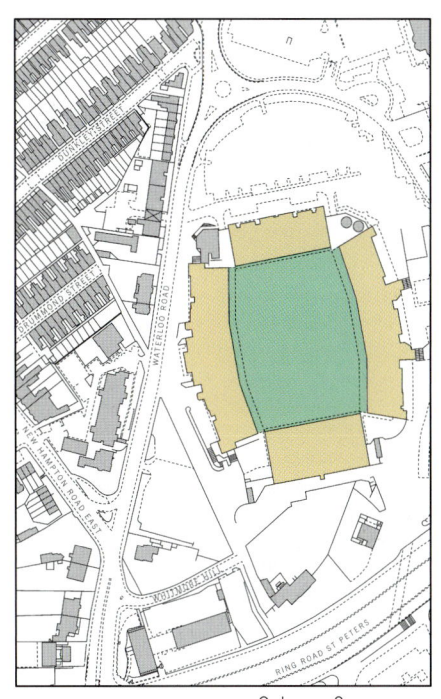

Ordnance Survey maps
© Crown Copyright. All rights reserved.
English Heritage, 100019088, 2005

▲ The three phases of Molineux's development over the last century can be clearly discerned from the 1889 Ordnance Survey map (the year that Wolves moved in); the 1938 Ordnance Survey map (shortly after Leitch's masterplan was completed), and the current Ordnance Survey map.

The early ground was informally enclosed and catered for various sports, including football, athletics, cycling, bowls and roller skating.

From 1925 onwards Leitch imposed strict boundaries, utilising every inch of the site to create a capacity of over 61,000.

In modern terms, his aim was the commodification of space.

Today, no trace of Leitch's work remains. The new Molineux, built between 1979-93, has spread eastwards, swallowing up over 70 houses and Molineux Street, for an all-seated capacity of only 28,500.

Within these new stands are shops, offices, restaurants and 23,000 sq ft of rented space. The modern, land-hungry football stadium has to earn its keep.

Similar mapped comparisons could be made based on several of the grounds featured in this book.

Engineering Archie **163**

Wolves

In the days before plastic seating, the use of colour was fairly limited at football grounds, not least because of the added costs of maintenance. Molineux's old gold was therefore highly treasured, and yet another factor in the ground's widespread popularity.

▲ Workers from Boswells the builders pose in front of the **Molineux Street Stand** during the summer of 1932. As factory architects Leitch's company would have designed many a multi-spanned, or saw-tooth roof of this ilk. Measuring 346 feet in length, the width of the stand's seven bays tapered from a maximum of 83 feet down to 31 feet at the north end. Costing £20,487, it held 3,450 seats, with an enclosure in front for 4,500 standing.

Given the site's irregular shape, and its incline, the adoption of such a solution made perfect sense.

Yet on the other hand, here was an exact contemporary of Claude Ferrier's West Stand at Highbury, a stand which embraced modernity and light. At the same time continental architects such as Pier Luigi Nervi and Paul Bonatz were experimenting with reinforced concrete cantilevered structures of grace and daring.

This is not to belittle Leitch's approach. The Molineux Street Stand cost a fraction of Highbury's stand, while the climate in the Black Country hardly allowed for artful canopies, column free or not.

Yet multi-spanned roof structures such as this one were notoriously top heavy and difficult to maintain. Indeed only four other examples from the period are known, of which two, at Old Trafford and Highbury, were Leitch's work a full two decades earlier, in 1910 and 1913 respectively. The former was destroyed during the Second World War. The latter was demolished only four years after Molineux's stand was completed.

But if the design did rather confirm that Leitch's company was rooted in the past by the 1930s, with its deep overhanging eaves, its old gold, advert-free gables, and its discreet central clock, the Molineux Street was nevertheless entirely emblematic of Molineux.

It was demolished in 1978.

164 Engineering Archie

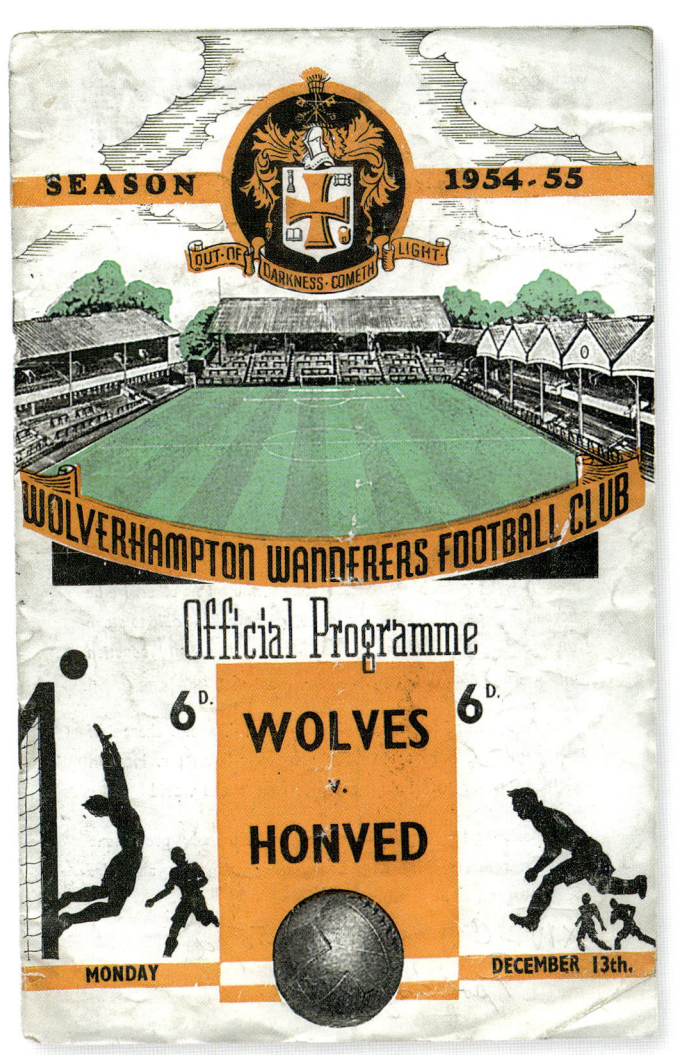

◀ To a whole generation of football fans in the 1950s, Molineux was a place of magic as Wolves – who between 1949-60 won the FA Cup twice and the League championship three times – staged a series of early floodlit friendlies against exotic foreign opposition.

The programme covers for these games, against the likes of Moscow Spartak, Racing Club of Buenos Aires, and Honved of Budapest (a match broadcast live on both radio and television), placed Molineux at the centre of this dazzling new era, expressing simply but affectionately the bond between a club and its ground, and by extension, between the fans and their home town.

But football's fortunes are fleeting, and by the 1980s Wolves were languishing in the Fourth Division watched by crowds of barely 4,000. While a stand built to replace the Molineux Street Stand in 1979 plunged the club into debt, the rest of Molineux crumbled and was nearly lost when Wolves went into receivership. The Waterloo Street Stand in particular (*above*) deteriorated rapidly after being closed on safety grounds.

Then once again, out of the darkness there came light.

A former regular on the terraces, Jack Hayward, rescued the club and lavished over £16 million on the ground's third makeover since 1889. Resplendent once again, the new Molineux re-opened in December 1993, appropriately enough with a match v. Honved.

Engineering Archie **165**

Grounds
Baseball Ground, Derby 1926–35

Formed in 1884, Derby County are one of several football clubs to have been formed by cricketers. County's nickname, the Rams, is thought to derive from the 95th Derbyshire Regiment. During the Indian Mutiny campaign in 1858 they captured a ram and adopted it as their regimental mascot. Its numerous successors – mostly drawn from flocks raised on farmland at Chatsworth – have been called 'Private Derby' ever since.

The story of Derby's tightly enclosed, no-frills Baseball Ground – four sides of which were redeveloped by Leitch – tells us much about the wider propensity of British sports clubs to develop facilities privately, at low cost, and in apparently unsuitable locations.

And yet it was exactly these factors which brought Leitch so much work.

The ground itself was first laid out in the 1880s by a philanthropic industrialist, Francis Ley, for the use of employees at his Vulcan Works foundry (Vulcan being the god of fire and metal forgers).

After a business trip to the United States in 1889 Ley set up a baseball club in one corner of the ground, and for a few short years, the American game vied with cricket as a summer draw. Four of the leading baseball teams were linked to football clubs (Derby, Preston, Stoke and Aston Villa), and in some cases, footballers were amongst the star players.

But as a succession of promoters of basketball and ice-hockey have found to their cost since, British sports fans are not easily diverted from their traditional allegiances. Ley's baseball league failed to prosper.

Meanwhile, beyond the sprawling locomotive works to the north, Derby County were keen to vacate the cricket ground they had used since 1884.

As this ground formed part of the town's racecourse, it meant that once a rental deal was agreed with Francis Ley, the football club, formed by cricketers, would move from the Racecourse Ground to the Baseball Ground – a veritable sporting trail if ever there was.

Ley lavished £7,000 on adapting his ground for County's arrival in 1895 (although baseball remained a summer attraction for a few years thereafter). But crucially, the ground's acreage shrank from twelve to four (of which just under two acres comprised the pitch).

On one side lay the clattering, steaming Vulcan Works. On the other three sides, streets were laid out for housing foundry workers.

Even by the standards of the day the Baseball Ground was caught in an iron grip, and so when, in 1923, Derby Corporation offered County an alternative, publicly-funded stadium – out in the wide open 'wilderness of Allenton' – the directors were tempted.

The context of this offer is worth noting.

A few years earlier another Derbyshire local authority, Chesterfield, had attempted to municipalise the town's football club, while on the Continent, a number of landmark stadiums were being built by socialist administrations, for example in Lyon, Frankfurt and Vienna. Sport, it was argued in the wake of the Great War and the Bolshevik revolution, belonged to the masses, and therefore so should the clubs and stadiums.

The year 1923 also saw the opening of Wembley Stadium, a project which led several cities to consider whether they might themselves create a 'Wembley of the North'.

Above all, stadium construction *per se* promised work at a time of acute unemployment (a factor which also led to the building of a network of lidos across Britain, during the 1920s and '30s).

166 Engineering Archie

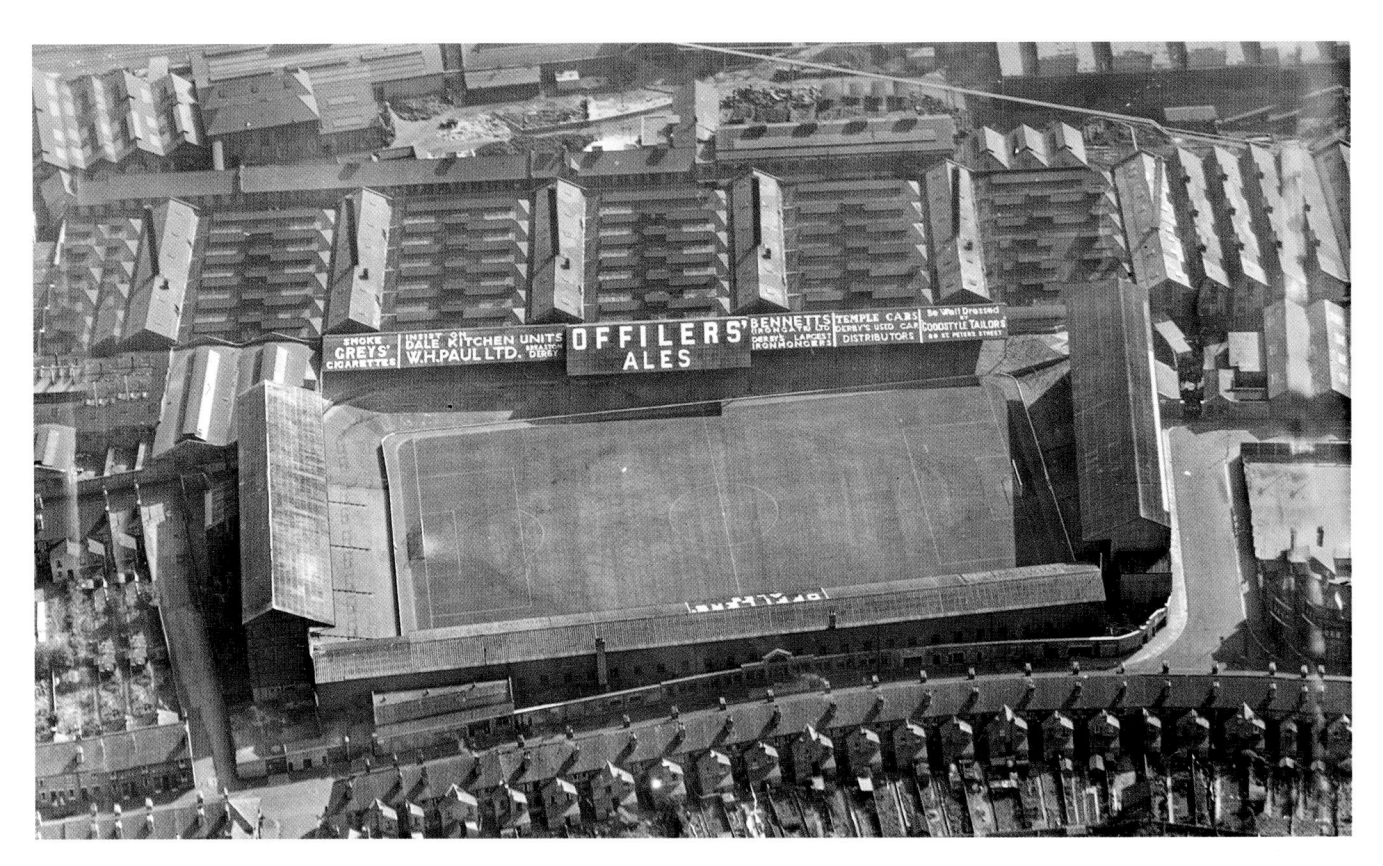

By current standards the Allenton site appeared ideal. It was spacious, accessed by one of the new generation of dual carriageways, and in an outlying district soon to be developed by social housing.

But although the Corporation offered to build a modern 4,000 seat stand with covered terraces for 20,000, and charge only £500 annual rent, after six months of negotiations County decided that the whole notion was too radical and uncertain for them to proceed.

This was a real blow to the Corporation, which had reportedly spent £63,000 on the scheme. To make matters worse, no other sports clubs were interested, leaving the barely developed site to be taken over by the Parks Committee and used for community sport alone, a role which continues today.

Back in the close confines of the Baseball Ground, Derby's directors now planned for their own vision of the future.

First, in July 1924 they paid the now Sir Francis Ley £10,000 for the freehold of the site.

Then they hired Archibald Leitch.

County were in Division Two at this point, and were managed by George Jobey, who, coincidentally, had been the first player to score at Highbury on its chaotic opening day in 1913 (see page 38). »

Football and factories, dreams and drudgery. Shown here in 1952, Ley's Malleable Castings Foundry (the sort of industrial plant Leitch had often designed himself) presses tightly up against the Baseball Ground's Popular Side, its parade of chimneys reminding all within of where the real power resided. There were no odd angles in the foundry, but plenty at the Baseball Ground. Helped along by pints of Offilers, a man could work, rest and play within just a few streets of this scene, for his whole life. And many did.

Engineering Archie **167**

Derby County

▲ While the groundsman sorts out the goalnets, select Rams pose in front of the recently completed **Normanton Stand** in the mid to late 1930s. They are George Collin, Ted Udall, Jack Nicholas, Jack Barker, 'Ike' Keen, Fred Jessop and goalkeeper Jack Kirby.

The stark, logo-free simplicity of their monochromatic playing strips – as black and white in reality as in this photograph – only accentuates the bald, functionality of Leitch's architecture. Even the balcony detailing was masked under a coating of matt green paint.

Not an advert, not a single piece of extraneous metalwork clutters the scene. Here was both austerity and dignity. Here, it was the game itself, and the crowd, which lit up the scene.

One section of the Normanton Stand (not visible here) which featured in many Leitch designs was a boys' pen. Called 'The Cage', a horizontal bar was positioned by its entrance. Any boy too tall to pass under it was refused entry.

In front of the pen a man in a top hat and suit would sell boiled sweets, swing a rattle and urge the boys to cheer on the Rams.

» As soon as the Rams secured promotion in May 1926, work started on Leitch's first phase, a new main stand – known originally as B Pavilion – on the narrow, west side.

The timing was not ideal. The General Strike had ended only two weeks earlier and striking miners were still holding up coal supplies. But then similar disputes had dogged Leitch's progress at Villa Park and Selhurst Park in the two previous years, and Derby's stand was, even by his standards, basic.

Constructed by a local firm, JK Ford & Weston, with steelwork erected by Rubery Owen, who worked on several other Leitch projects, including Molineux (see page 49), it held 3,300 seats, with a narrow paddock in front for 2,000 standing and a brick frontage onto Shaftesbury Crescent.

'On all sides could be heard expressions of delight at the appearance of the ground,' noted the *Derby Evening Telegraph* on its opening day in September 1926.

Three further stages followed. The Popular Side received the standard Leitch makeover; its banking lowered to below pitch level at the front, and concrete steppings with barriers installed. The roof was also extended to the full length, thus creating a shadowy, bunker-like enclosure backed by the wall of the foundry.

Derby were now flying high in the First Division. Average gates topped 18,000, and with success came a demand for more seats.

Two almost identical double-decker stands at either end answered this demand. First, in 1933, was the Osmaston End Stand (*illustrated right*). This did not extend the full width of the goal-line, leaving an uncovered section of terracing in the north

168 Engineering Archie

east corner, known as 'Catcher's Corner' (because it corresponded with the area behind the original baseball diamond's home plate).

The Normanton End Stand (*shown opposite*) followed in 1935.

Compared with the Art Deco bus station being completed in the centre of Derby at the same time (designed by Charles Aslin) both stands appeared almost primitive; illustrating not only how Leitch's designs had barely progressed, but also how little spare cash clubs like Derby had at their disposal.

During the ten year period that Leitch was involved, the Rams spent around £40,000 on four sides of the Baseball Ground – less than the likes of Spurs or Everton would spend on a single stand – to achieve a capacity of 38,000. The trouble was, they then carried on spending, mostly under the counter, trying to buy the success that would pay for the ground works. This resulted in five of the directors, including the chairman William Bendle Moore, a prominent Derby solicitor, and Jobey the manager, being suspended *sine die* by the Football Association in 1941.

In 1945 Derby Corporation tried again to persuade County to become partners in a new stadium scheme, this time a futuristic design by Maxwell Ayrton (who had worked at Wembley in 1923). Once again they were rebuffed.

Derby finally moved, in 1997, at the third time of asking. The ground's capacity then was 17,451.

Their new site, ironically, was not in the outskirts, but a former industrial area, closer to the city centre. As to the Baseball Ground, it was finally cleared for housing in 2004. Next to it, a modern industrial estate has replaced the foundry, which closed in 1986.

◀ Bunkerish in its depths, grim in its outlook; and yet in many ways the **Baseball Ground** – ironically, given its name – encapsulated much that was memorable and atmospheric about attending football matches in 20th century Britain.

It was buried in a maze of narrow streets and dead ends. Corner shops, chip shops and the Baseball Hotel pub filled the pavements with life and litter. Its floodlights, glowing above the neighbouring terraced houses, promised an illicit magic.

Inside, you could almost breathe on the pitch, so close were you to the touchlines. But that also meant the stands overshadowed the turf. Hence Derby and mud were synonymous in the football world.

In its heyday, after a stand was built over the Popular Side in 1969 – named the Ley Stand – it became only the fourth League venue to have seating and standing on all four sides. In December of that year the Rams recorded their highest ever attendance of 41,826.

But it was a creaking edifice all the same. By the end in 1997, the **Osmaston Stand** *(below)* and its neighbours, were a jumble of stairways, mismatched seats, coloured cladding and adverts.

Whatever raw dignity the stands once possessed was now sullied by the exigencies of modern survival.

Engineering Archie **169**

Queen's Park

Grounds
Hampden Park, Glasgow 1927–37

J. F. TEMPLETON, of the Queen's Park, is a half-back who plays with his brains. He feeds his forwards with discretion, and is a difficult man to pass. In 1902 he played for the Scottish League against the English League.

One of the great curiosities of football is that an amateur club, Queen's Park – formed in 1867 – should not only have built the world's largest stadium, as Hampden once was, but that they should also continue to play their first team matches there until the present day. In their heyday 'The Spiders' drew similar crowds to Rangers and Celtic. Now, in a stadium holding 52,000, their average gate is around 5-600.

Readers familiar with previous accounts of the work of Archibald Leitch, including those by this author, might well wonder why, at this relatively late stage in his career, we are returning to a ground he was thought to have worked on at around the time of its opening in 1903.

However, as mentioned in earlier chapters, a review carried out for this book of all the available evidence – including planning records, a 1920 history of Queen's Park (by Richard Robinson), plus sundry reports and photographs – leads to the conclusion that Leitch did not actually work at Hampden until 1927.

Even so, it is highly likely that Hampden's early development did influence Leitch's early career as a football architect, if for no other reason that it was laid out, between 1900-03, within a few hundred yards of where he was living at the time.

Leaping back in time for a moment, therefore, we recall that in 1894 the 29 year old Leitch, his wife Jessie and their three year old son, Archibald Kent, moved from Kinning Park to one of the tenements newly built for young professionals just like Archie, in Clincart Road, in the up and coming district of Mount Florida.

At the end of Clincart Road, across Cathcart Road, was the start of Hampden Terrace. Walking eastwards along this road, with its fine villas and views across the city towards the Clyde, Archie would have been able to look down the slopes of Mount Florida onto what was then home to Glasgow's oldest and most venerable football club, Queen's Park.

This, from 1884-1903, was Hampden Park, the second ground to have been named as such by Queen's Park. (Their first, laid out close by in 1873, had also been overlooked by Hampden Terrace, which is why they chose the name in the first place. The fact that the terrace itself had been named after an Englishman, the 17th century Parliamentarian John Hampden, did not seem to matter.)

Until the construction of Celtic Park in 1892, followed by the new Ibrox Park in 1899, designed by Leitch of course, the second Hampden Park was the best ground in Glasgow, holding at least 25,000 spectators and with a brick built pavilion, the first belonging to any football club in Scotland. 'Such matters were always done in good style by Queen's Park,' noted Richard Robinson. 'A new ground must have an ornate pavilion.'

But Queen's Park were tenants on only a short term lease, which hampered their ability to develop the ground further, and therefore crucially, to stay one step ahead of the rapidly emerging Rangers and Celtic when it came to acting as hosts of the lucrative annual Scottish Cup Finals and the even more profitable biennial internationals against 'the auld enemy' England. Queen's Park may have been amateurs, but the business stakes were high.

In 1898 therefore they turned their attention to a 12 acre plot a few hundred yards to the south, on the south side of Prospecthill and by chance even closer to Leitch's home. The purchase price, agreed in November 1899, was £10,240, on top of which a further £4,000

170 Engineering Archie

was spent preparing the site, which had a burn running through the centre.

(The second Hampden was, in the meantime, taken over by Third Lanark FC and renamed Cathkin Park, which it remained until the club went into liquidation in 1967. The pitch still survives, however, with remants of the old terracing eerily nestling in the overgrown slopes on two of its sides.)

Preparing the ground for the third Hampden Park took the best part of two years, from 1900-02, the period when of course Leitch was building up Ibrox's terracing using timber and iron, with such fateful consequences in April 1902.

But given the proximity of his home to the Hampden site, Archie must surely have wandered over to check on progress, and no doubt to ponder the wisdom of his methodology at Rangers.

Queen's Park's chief adviser during this period was an engineer and surveyor, Alexander Blair, of West George Street, five years' Leitch's senior and a key figure also in cycle racing. Blair would later go on to work for Newcastle United.

But he was only of several professionals amongst the club's membership. The club president, Arthur Geake, was described as an expert on sports ground construction. There was also at least one architect on hand to advise, plus the director of the engineering firm, McCreaths and Stevenson, who were awarded the contract to lay out the new ground.

In short, this was a well connected club representing the middle class elite of the city. They had no need of Archie, who was, in any case, a Rangers man.

Instead, in late 1902 when Queen's Park looked for an architect to complete the final phase of Hampden's preparation – the building of two stands on the south side, with a pavilion in between – they chose one of Glasgow's foremost architects of the day, James Miller.

It is a measure of Queen's Park's status that Miller was interested »

▲ Having spent some £20,000 on purchasing and preparing the third **Hampden Park** before its opening in 1903, Queen's Park did not find the extra funds to build a centre pavilion until shortly after this view was taken in 1905.

Each of the stands, designed by James Miller, held 2,200 seats, although a few hundred would have offfered restricted views of the pitch until a permanent centre pavilion was sorted in 1914 and the two stand roofs finally linked together. The postcard below, from 1908, shows a curious stop-gap pavilion, possibly by Alexander Blair, which served in the interim and was eventually sold to Dundee.

In 1909 Hampden was the scene of the worst football riot yet recorded, when Rangers and Celtic fans went on the rampage. In the process they burned down the fort-like corrugated turnstile block photographed above.

Engineering Archie **171**

Queen's Park

at all in the commission. By 1902 he had already completed a whole range of hotels, offices, houses, the famous Cranston's Tea Rooms in Buchanan Street, and, not least, in 1896, the fantastical, chateau-like St Enoch's subway station, located right in front of Leitch's office, in St Enoch Square.

That said, Hampden Park was not one of Miller's finest efforts.

The two stands, formed in brick and steel with hipped roofs, were substantial enough, but the pavilion he proposed was too ornate even for Queen's Park, and in the end the club decided instead to build a basic, low stand in the gap, as an interim measure.

After three years construction, the new Hampden Park finally opened its doors in October 1903, for a match between Queen's Park and Celtic. Its capacity then was 44,530 (although this would quickly rise to 80,000 by 1905).

Presiding over the ceremony was Sir John Ure Primrose Bart, the Lord Provost of Glasgow, who was more widely associated with Rangers. Also attending were the cream of Glasgow's civic dignitaries, plus the directors of several other leading clubs, Rangers included.

Whether Archie was there too we cannot say. A month earlier he had attended the opening of Ayresome Park, and he was soon to start work for Fulham. But if he was at the opening, his thoughts on the day can only be imagined. After all, despite its rather awkward, unfinished range of stands on the south side, Hampden was still the most substantial modern stadium yet seen in Britain.

It was certainly far superior to Crystal Palace. The Olympic Stadium at White City was still five years away, while neither the Germans, Italians or Americans would embark upon their first concrete superbowls of the century until the following decade.

So was Archie impressed? Or envious? Or was he fired with determination to do better, and thereby redeem himself after the Ibrox debacle?

In this final respect Hampden did offer Leitch an important model. Alexander Blair's system of radial and lateral aisles, dividing the terracing into sections, would become the basis of all Leitch's subsequent terrace design.

Another of Blair's ideas did not catch on however. This was his use of wire rope barriers and their arrangement in three-sided pens, a system eventually discredited in 1924 (*see pages 29 and 32*).

These were replaced by Leitch's own patented rigid barriers when his involvement with Hampden commenced in 1927.

Hampden c.1925, with newly aquired Lesser Hampden on the left. Still extant, this became the ground of Queen's Park's second XI, The Strollers. In the centre of the South Stand is the pavilion designed in 1914 by Baptie, Shaw and Morton, with its crow-stepped gable (later flanked by curved brick stairways in 1951). Leitch's first commission, starting in 1927, led to the addition of a further 15,000 places at the rear of the east terrace (*right*), and the replacement of all wire-rope barriers. Despite retaining its oval shape, and for many years a running track, Hampden never took on the mantle of a national stadium for athletics, a role now played by Edinburgh's Meadowbank Stadium.

172 Engineering Archie

▲ Hampden Park shown in the late 1940s after the second phase of works carried out by Leitch's company – though not Leitch himself, as he was now retired – in 1936-37.

Seating 4,390, the **North Stand** (*on the left*) was possibly the least attractive stand the company ever built. Its concrete facings rapidly became dirt-encrusted and streaked, while its brutally unadorned street elevation made no attempt to please its neighbours.

Even from pitch-side it was one of those buildings that looked the same in photographs, whether they were in black and white or colour.

There were therefore no tears when it was demolished in 1982.

In the foreground can be seen the castellated redbrick turnstile block by Baptie, Shaw and Morton, which replaced the corrugated structures destroyed in 1909.

Standing sentinel on the north west corner of Hampden, the block's deliberately defiant style (*also right*) was echoed by the firm's designs for the 1914 centre pavilion (*shown opposite*). As can be seen, the completion of that pavilion effectively linked the two original stands under a seamless roof.

The second part of Leitch's work in 1937 saw the extension of the South Stand at the rear, adding 948 seats, together with a major refit of the centre pavilion, to include new changing rooms, offices, hospitality areas and improvements to the 1914 rooftop press box. This box was destroyed by fire in 1945. (Its scarred skeleton is seen above).

As outlined overleaf, this series of works by Leitch – which cost £63,325 – helped make Hampden the largest stadium in the world.

But size is not everything.

Underfunded and increasingly outdated as the century wore on, Hampden suffered a second serious riot in 1980. And whilst Rangers and Celtic were starting to offer much better facilities elsewhere in the city, Hampden's future became a proverbial political football until a £24 million grant from the Millennium Commission helped complete a £72 million revamp, carried out between 1996-99.

None of the structures shown above survive, although three sides of the new bowl, seating 52,000, are formed on the original banking. A new South Stand also houses the offices of the Scottish FA, Scottish League and the Scottish Football Museum, which displays artefacts from the original stadium and a mock up of the old pressbox.

Engineering Archie 173

Queen's Park

◀ Behold the mighty Hampden! Until Rio de Janeiro's Maracana Stadium opened in June 1950, **Hampden Park** was the world's largest stadium.

Shown here in 1937, shortly after the completion of Leitch's North Stand (*on the left*) and the extension of the South Stand at its rear (*shown right*), Hampden's capacity was given on Leitch's plans as:

South Stand seats:	9,950
North Stand seats:	4,390
North Stand enclosure:	26,891
East and West terraces:	122,403
Press Box:	110
Disabled spaces:	38
Total:	**163,782**

Somewhat mischievously Leitch added that if standing in the passages were allowed (which, theoretically it was not), this would add 19,906 further places, creating a grand total of **183,688**. By comparison, the Maracana's initial capacity was given as 200,000.

In practice Hampden's true limit can be measured against its highest recorded attendance of **149,415**, for Scotland v. England on April 17 1937 (to which all reports added a further 10,000, at the very least, for those who snuck in).

Thereafter a more realistic level of **134,000** was established after the Second World War.

Engineering Archie **175**

Southampton

Grounds
The Dell, Southampton 1927–29

Another Write Away by Frank Reynolds, only this time with a message that Southampton fans know only too well. The club was formed in 1885 by a 'bunch of healthy minded fellows' at the YMCA in St Mary's. Despite playing on the other side of town for 103 years, at the Dell, they always remained 'the Saints'. And now they are back at St Mary's, in a new stadium, opened in 2001.

More than most nations, Britain seems to delight in choosing eccentric locations for its football grounds. Leitch himself had worked at a few of them: Goodison Park, with a church in one corner, Valley Parade, falling down a hill, and The Den, trapped in a web of railway lines.

And then there was The Dell.

A glimpse at the aerial view opposite should make the point.

Trapped in a parallelogram-shaped site in the midst of the quiet residential district of Fitzhugh, there were just yards to spare between two of the corner flags and the pavements outside.

To compound matters, in the north west corner stood a house, allowing just enough room for one line of spectators to stand between its side wall and the touchline.

And yet curiously, for all its constraints, when The Dell had first been laid out at a cost of £10,000, in a soggy dell with a brook running through the centre, in 1898 – the year before Leitch won his first commission in football – it had actually been the model of a very modern ground.

Well laid out, orderly, and with terraces for 20,500 spectators on its two, wedge-shaped ends, it had stands each holding 2,000 seats on both sides, a rare indulgence at the time, even at much larger grounds.

It was also apparent that its builder, a Mr Bunday, and its backer, a wealthy fish merchant called George Thomas, well understood the geometry of sightlines and the basics of crowd management. In short, had Leitch sought worthy examples to study early in his careeer, The Dell would have been strongly recommended.

After its inauguration, ground design inevitably moved on, and so after they bought the ground from George Thomas's widow in 1926, for £26,000, Southampton called in Leitch. Two years earlier he had designed a new main stand for the Saints' neighbours and rivals, Portsmouth.

In truth, little needs to be said of Leitch's work at The Dell.

The West Stand, erected in late 1927 after the clearance of the corner house, was a routine double decker, built by Leitch's old friends, Humphreys of Knightsbridge and his even older friends at the Clyde Structural Iron Company of Glasgow. It had 4,500 seats on its upper tier, lit generously with skylights, with an enclosure for 8,500 below, and the now standard Leitch balcony with latticework detailing.

Like most stands of the period its completion was delayed, and its £30,000 costs (which included other improvements at the ground) near crippled the club.

Then two years later, one night in May 1929, the old East Stand burnt down. 'East Stand Goes West' ran the memorable headline in the *Southampton Echo*. Within days Leitch was back and, with a £10,000 loan hurriedly secured, an almost mirror-image of the West Stand rose up during the summer, but on a narrower plan, allowing just 2,600 seats on the upper tier.

And there the two stands remained, to the end of The Dell's life in 2001; modified, adapted and tinkered with over the years but never more than routine examples of Leitch's work, in a ground that was always much more than the sum of its parts.

176 Engineering Archie

◀ When the popular contralto Miss Marion Knight sang out *Land of Hope and Glory* to mark the opening of the West Stand in January 1927 – a performance no doubt enjoyed by Leitch, who invariably attended on such occasions – it was said her voice, though unamplified, filled The Dell. But then, it was one of the most compact grounds ever to have staged first class football.

Patently that is what made it such an atmospheric stage, but also such a challenge to the succession of architects and engineers who, over the years, sought to eke out the most from its every nook and cranny.

For example, to add capacity after the war, three small pens of terracing were built on stilts over the Milton End, each holding 300 fans. They were dubbed, affectionately, the Chocolate Boxes.

The cleverly contrived single tier, triangular stand built in 1994 at the same end (*left on the above aerial view*), would, similarly, have intrigued Archibald Leitch, and most likely The Dell's original builder, Mr Bunday, too.

By comparison, Leitch's **West Stand**, shown here in 1989 (*above left*), before the Taylor Report, and afterwards in 1994 (*centre left*), was utilitarian and even anonymous. It had no distinguishing gable. Nor did it help that for most of its life its balcony was concealed behind hoardings and its roof cluttered with platforms and floodlight gantries.

The same was true of Leitch's **East Stand** (*below left*), which was narrower and backed on to a line of houses and a church hall.

At its peak The Dell held 31,044 for a match in 1969. On its final day in May 2001 it held just under half that, as an all-seated venue.

It had to go of course. The Saints needed more seats, more space, and less hassle. But if the two Leitch stands need hardly be mourned, English football's collective landscape is undoubtedly poorer for The Dell's demise.

Flats and town houses now occupy the site.

Engineering Archie **177**

Grounds
West Ham Stadium, London 1928

Not to be confused with its near neighbour Upton Park (home of West Ham United), the West Ham greyhound and speedway stadium on Nottingham Avenue, E16, was the largest of fifteen purpose-built tracks opened in London during the period 1927-35 (not including Wembley, White City and Stamford Bridge, which also embraced these new track sports). It was also the only greyhound and speedway stadium known to have been designed by Leitch.

Greyhound and speedway racing were the two wonder sports of the inter-war period.

Driven by technology and commerce, their arrival in 1926 (from America), and 1928 (from Australia), respectively, sparked a frenzy of speculative stadium construction that, as noted earlier, might have led Leitch's company into a whole new area of the expanding leisure market.

Instead, as far as can be ascertained, Leitch designed only one of this new breed of stadiums, while scores of investors soon found themselves with loss-making arenas, only a quarter of which would ultimately survive.

Sited on a sports ground already known locally as a popular venue for whippet racing, the West Ham Stadium – known also as the Custom House Stadium (that being the name of the somewhat bleak docklands district in which it was located, between Becton and Canning Town) – appears to have been financed by a consortium of businessmen led by Sir Louis Dane, a former Lieutenant-Governor of the Punjab.

(Perhaps because of greyhound racing's roots in coursing the new industry was full of ex majors, captains and brigadiers, quite unlike the businessmen Leitch was used to dealing with in football.)

They certainly showed no lack of confidence. West Ham was by far the largest of the new stadiums, estimated to have a capacity of 100,000, as large as Wembley and larger than White City, both in west London.

'We wish it to be a stadium in every sense of the word,' promised Sir Louis, 'and so provide a great centre for all sports in a densely populated portion of the metropolis which has been sadly in need of such a place of recreation.'

Speedway, which opened the stadium on July 28 1928, attracted the largest attendances, the best of which was a remarkable, if unverified 82,400 for a Test Match against Australia in 1933. In the late 1940s reports of crowds of over 50,000 were also common.

The first greyhound meeting, on August 4 1928, drew an equally astonishing 56,000, followed by regular crowds of 15-30,000 in the years thereafter.

But football failed miserably. Foolishly, the stadium's promoters tried to launch a professional club, Thames FC, the 'Dockers', even though the stadium was barely a mile from West Ham United's ground and not much further from Clapton Orient, who were themselves struggling at the gate. Even more astonishingly, they somehow managed to get Thames elected to the Third Division of the Football League in 1930.

The venture lasted just two more years, during which Thames won fame as the worst supported team in the League. One match attracted an all time low of just 469. How beleaguered they must have felt in the vast enclosure.

Archibald Leitch, meanwhile, now aged 63, returned to what he knew best – football at the highest level – and in the latter part of 1928 was to be found finishing off what would prove to be his finest work of all, at the club where his true heart lay, Rangers FC.

West Ham Stadium was finally sold for housing in 1972.

WEST HAM STADIUM

ARCH° LEITCH & PARTNERS
18 VICTORIA ST LONDON SW
30 BUCHANAN ST GLASGOW

◀ A familiar Leitch balcony in the background in April 1964, as West Ham's John 'Budgie' Byrne (*left*), Bobby Moore (*centre*) and manager Ron Greenwood (*right*) prepare for a training session on the lush turf of the **West Ham Greyhound and Speedway Stadium**, which they hoped would offer conditions similar to those they were about to face in the Cup Final at Wembley.

The stand, which held 5,000 seats, can be seen in the foreground of the rather tattered impression (*above*), by MacDonald, Leitch's regular artist of the 1920s.

West Ham's greyhound track measured 562 yards, longer than any other in Britain, and was uniquely formed on Swedish matting laid on wooden boards, raised 12 inches above ground level. This apparently guaranteed fast times in all weathers and fewer cancellations.

Another new idea was that each of the traps (positioned on the starting line) were colour coded to make identification easier for punters in the stands.

But for all its innovations and scale, with no easy tube or rail connections close by, and with no chance of staging regular football, the stadium's chances of long term survival were always slim, as were those of a dozen other similar greyhound and speedway ventures dotted around the capital (including the New Cross Stadium, next door to Millwall's Den, *see page 120*).

Today only two London stadiums remain in business, at Walthamstow and Wimbledon.

Engineering Archie

Rangers

Grounds
Ibrox Park, Glasgow Part Two 1923–29

From the moment one crosses the threshold of Rangers' South Stand on Edmiston Drive, Govan, it is apparent that Ibrox Park is the headquarters of a football club with a deep sense of tradition. But more than that, Ibrox Park is central to our tale of the life and works of Archibald Leitch. Here, at the club he supported, amid the community in which he flourished as a young man, Archie was to experience his first break in football, his darkest hour in football, and ultimately, perhaps his proudest moment too…

The design for a new South Stand at Ibrox Park, Glasgow, was, in his later life, probably the one commission Archibald Leitch most wanted to secure.

As he approached his 60th year Archie could look on Rangers as his first major clients in the football world, back in 1899.

That commission had of course led to the trauma of April 1902, and to those two or three anxious months following the disaster, worrying whether Rangers would stick by him or not.

But they did, and now, over twenty years later, he was back at Ibrox for talks on his most ambitious project ever.

William Wilton, the Rangers secretary-manager – the man who did more than anyone to put Rangers on the map, and keep them there after the disaster, and the individual with whom Leitch had worked the closest both before and after the construction of Ibrox in 1899 – was no longer around when planning for the South Stand began in the early 1920s.

He had drowned in a tragic boating accident in 1920.

In his place there was a new figurehead at Ibrox, Bill Struth.

Although Struth was strictly speaking only the team manager, his influence permeated every nook and cranny of Ibrox Park for the 34 extraordinary years he remained in post.

He was no stranger to the world of construction either. In his youth he had been a stonemason.

Struth's iron command of Rangers was not to everyone's taste. He was a strict disciplinarian who insisted, bizarrely, on all players travelling to matches wearing bowler hats. For away games he also made the players walk, or rather march purposefully, from the station to the ground of their opponents, so that all would know that the Light Blues were in town, and meant business.

But unorthodox as Struth's methods were, for many years they worked wonders. Under his eagle eye the Light Blues won 15 League Championships in 21 seasons and the Scottish Cup ten times.

It was this unprecedented success that financed what would be Leitch's largest, and most expensive grandstand ever – even more expensive than the massively over budget stand Archie was engaged upon at Aston Villa when

180 Engineering Archie

he started talks with Rangers for their new South Stand, some time around 1923.

When we left Ibrox Park in the earlier section (*see pages 64-65*), apart from the construction of the new terraced embankments during the years following the disaster, the South Stand and pavilion were much as Leitch had designed them in 1899.

At that time the club had been uncertain as to whether they would remain on the site for more than the original ten year lease. For that reason, and to keep down costs, neither structure had been built to a high specification.

Their replacement was therefore now a pressing matter.

Leitch's first known plans for the proposed stand are dated 1926.

However, in the two years prior to that Leitch was already putting into action an advanced phase. This involved the construction of an office and dressing room block on the land between the existing South Stand and Edmiston Drive.

Once these new facilities were ready, the pavilion was demolished.

The second phase began in 1928, just weeks after Struth had led the team to the club's first League and Cup double.

Though now close to retirement, on countless occasions Archie travelled up and down between London and Glasgow on the overnight sleeper, taking a close interest in every detail.

As the following pages reveal, this was one job he wanted to get absolutely right.

Ibrox Park's new South Stand was officially opened by the Lord Provost of Glasgow, Sir David Mason, before the Ne'erday match against Celtic on January 1 1929.

From that day until the 1970s Ibrox Park was the second largest football stadium in Britain, second only to Hampden Park (which of course Leitch also extended between 1927-36).

Its highest attendance of 118,567 (for a match v. Celtic, naturally), is an all-time record for a League match in British football, and was recorded on January 2 1939, a few months before Archie died. So at least he knew that his promise, made back in 1899 at the Trades Hall, that one day Ibrox would hold at least 100,000, was proven to be no idle boast.

Inevitably some fans decried its cost of £95,000 – more than had ever been spent on a single stand.

But Bill Struth knew a good building when he saw one.

'It is all good Welsh brick,' he told the doubters. 'Moreover, it will be here long after the others have gone.'

On which point, happily, he was correct.

◀ Ibrox Park in the late 1940s, with Leitch's **South Stand** a dominant presence on Edmiston Drive. In the same season as its completion, 1928-29, Celtic opened their own new main stand, designed, ironically, by Leitch's former chief draughtsman, David Mills Duncan.

For all the two clubs' rivalry, Celtic fans must have harboured some respect for the Rangers manager, Bill Struth. Apparently he grew tomatoes in a greenhouse located behind the west terrace (*to the left of the South Stand*) which was otherwise known as the Celtic End (because that was where their fans always stood for derby matches). In all the time that it stood there not a single window pane ever needed replacing.

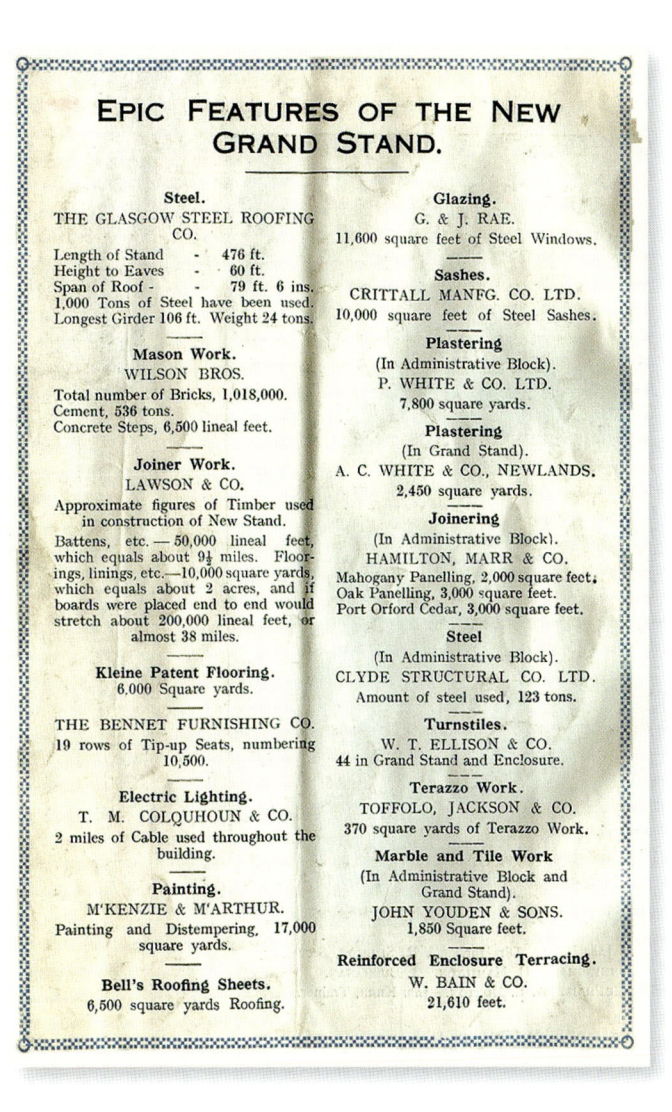

EPIC FEATURES OF THE NEW GRAND STAND.

Steel.
THE GLASGOW STEEL ROOFING CO.
Length of Stand - 476 ft.
Height to Eaves - 60 ft.
Span of Roof - 79 ft. 6 ins.
1,000 Tons of Steel have been used.
Longest Girder 106 ft. Weight 24 tons.

Mason Work.
WILSON BROS.
Total number of Bricks, 1,018,000.
Cement, 536 tons.
Concrete Steps, 6,500 lineal feet.

Joiner Work.
LAWSON & CO.
Approximate figures of Timber used in construction of New Stand.
Battens, etc.— 50,000 lineal feet, which equals about 9½ miles. Floorings, linings, etc.—10,000 square yards, which equals about 2 acres, and if boards were placed end to end would stretch about 200,000 lineal feet, or almost 38 miles.

Kleine Patent Flooring.
6,000 Square yards.

THE BENNET FURNISHING CO.
19 rows of Tip-up Seats, numbering 10,500.

Electric Lighting.
T. M. COLQUHOUN & CO.
2 miles of Cable used throughout the building.

Painting.
M'KENZIE & M'ARTHUR.
Painting and Distempering, 17,000 square yards.

Bell's Roofing Sheets.
6,500 square yards Roofing.

Glazing.
G. & J. RAE.
11,600 square feet of Steel Windows.

Sashes.
CRITTALL MANFG. CO. LTD.
10,000 square feet of Steel Sashes.

Plastering
(In Administrative Block).
P. WHITE & CO. LTD.
7,800 square yards.

Plastering
(In Grand Stand).
A. C. WHITE & CO., NEWLANDS.
2,450 square yards.

Joinering
(In Administrative Block).
HAMILTON, MARR & CO.
Mahogany Panelling, 2,000 square feet.
Oak Panelling, 3,000 square feet.
Port Orford Cedar, 3,000 square feet.

Steel
(In Administrative Block).
CLYDE STRUCTURAL CO. LTD.
Amount of steel used, 123 tons.

Turnstiles.
W. T. ELLISON & CO.
44 in Grand Stand and Enclosure.

Terazzo Work.
TOFFOLO, JACKSON & CO.
370 square yards of Terazzo Work.

Marble and Tile Work
(In Administrative Block and Grand Stand).
JOHN YOUDEN & SONS.
1,850 Square feet.

Reinforced Enclosure Terracing.
W. BAIN & CO.
21,610 feet.

The programme for the South Stand's official opening on January 1 1929 lists those companies and suppliers – several of them already familiar to us from his earlier commissions – who had worked under the 'Architect and Supervisor of Work, Archibald Leitch and Partners, Consulting Engineers and Factory Architects.'

Rangers

▲ Brick is not a material normally associated with civic or institutional buildings in Glasgow, and yet Rangers were as unlikely to have chosen stone for the façade of their new **South Stand** as Leitch would have been to suggest it.

More likely the directors were influenced by Villa Park's Trinity Road Stand (see pages 140ff), which Archie invited them to visit after its completion in 1924.

In addition to its red brick facings the South Stand shared with the Villa stand its arcade of segmentally arched openings, its pediments and its metal framed windows. On both end walls there were also mosaic crests, similar in design to those at Villa Park.

Otherwise the South Stand's treatment was far more restrained than its Birmingham counterpart, a reflection perhaps of the ultra-conservative – some might say dour – character of Bill Struth's Rangers during the inter-war period.

As to the extent of Leitch's personal involvement in the design of this façade, which in 1987 was listed Category B (the equivalent of Grade II), we shall never know.

And yet when compared with his one other listed building in Glasgow, the Sentinel Works (see page 35) it does possess a similar clarity and symmetry.

The curiosity is that whereas the stand's designs were first drawn up in 1926, those of the Sentinel Works date from 1903. One might easily imagine the chronology to be the other way round.

But then in the case of Ibrox Park, Leitch, the architect, was also Archie, the fan. If anyone understood the needs and character of the club, surely it was him.

▲ It could well be argued that Ibrox Park's **South Stand** perfectly exemplified the two sides of Archibald Leitch's professional persona.

On the Edmiston Drive elevation we see Archie the architect, and on this side – characterised by his trademark balcony detailing – we see Archie the engineer.

Where that leaves the somewhat fanciful rooftop press box, with its quirkily castellated facings, perhaps the reader is best left to judge.

(In fact Leitch's original drawings for the stand show only a simple pedimented gable, similar to those at Hillsborough or Craven Cottage, so it may well be that Rangers requested something a little more distinctive. If so, their inspiration, or Archie's, appears to have been the similarly eye-catching press box designed for Hampden Park by Baptie, Shaw and Morton in 1914, *see pages 29 and 173*).

But whatever its aesthetic merits, there can be no doubt that this was by far the largest single grandstand Leitch would design.

Its upper deck extended to 19 rows, offering a total of just under 10,500 seats. At the front, its deceptively capacious enclosure was able to hold 15,496.

The terrace was, of course, fitted throughout with patented Leitch barriers, as were the other three sides of Ibrox Park.

Leitch was 63 when the South Stand was completed in 1928.

Twenty six years earlier, just yards from this vantage point on the west terrace of Ibrox, his dream of building great stadiums had been shattered, it must have seemed at the time, forever.

And now this, his finest hour.

Engineering Archie **183**

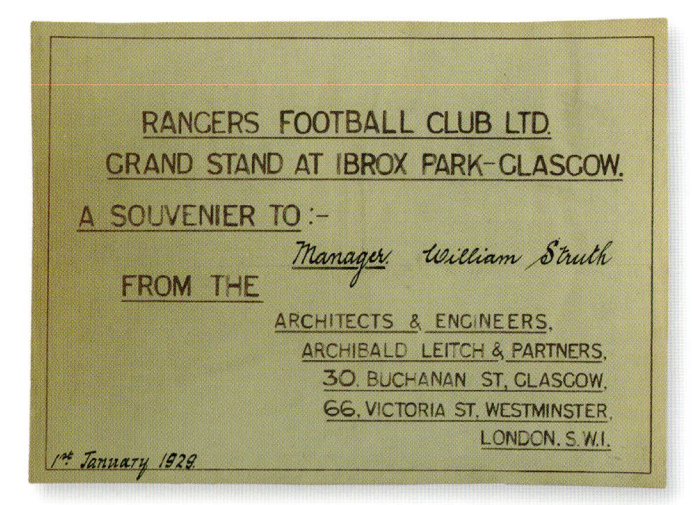

Rangers

RANGERS FOOTBALL CLUB LTD.
GRAND STAND AT IBROX PARK – GLASGOW.

A SOUVENIER TO :-
                        Manager William Struth
FROM THE
          ARCHITECTS & ENGINEERS,
          ARCHIBALD LEITCH & PARTNERS,
          30, BUCHANAN ST, GLASGOW.
          66, VICTORIA ST, WESTMINSTER,
                          LONDON. S.W.I.

1st January 1929.

▲ A measure of Archie's pride (if not of his spelling) was a leather bound souvenir photographic album he presented to the Rangers manager Bill Struth on the occasion of the stand's official opening on New Year's Day, January 1929.

All the images – some of them, alas, slightly marked – on these and the previous two pages, are reproduced from that album.

Above is the main first floor **concourse**, unusually bathed in natural light (compared with the gloomy passageways commonly found in other stands). On the right is the players' **warm-up area** behind the dressing rooms.

A sign suspended from the roof above the **upper tier** (*above right*) politely requests, 'Patrons please tilt your chairs when leaving.'

▲ The **manager's office** at Ibrox Park (*top left*) has changed remarkably little since this photo was taken for Archie's souvenir album. Even the desk is still used by the modern incumbent.

Bill Struth occupied this office for 26 of the 34 years he served as manager, before he finally stood down in 1954 at the age of 79.

Always a sharp dresser, he stored a supply of fresh suits in one corner. In another he kept a stray canary that had once flown in through the window (the hook for the cage is still there). On his desk was a sign saying 'The club is greater than the man.'

In the mornings Struth would stand by the window looking out for any player who dared to arrive for training improperly attired or with his hands in his pockets.

Also barely altered are the **dressing rooms** (*top right*), where the pegs are the originals, ordered specially by Struth so that the players could hang up their bowler hats safely before getting changed.

There was to be one later addition, however; a portrait of the Queen, displayed prominently on the wall to remind every man of where his loyalties should lie, for club and country.

The **secretary's office** at Ibrox (*above*) may not seem to offer much of interest, until one looks closely in the top right hand corner where a model of the South Stand can just be detected on the ledge.

Starting with Bramall Lane in 1901, Leitch often had models of his stands made, in order to sell the designs to directors and shareholders. It is a matter of great regret that not one of them is known to have survived.

Engineering Archie **185**

If much of the interior of Leitch's **South Stand** has changed little over the years, not so every other part within the stadium.

On January 2 1971 Ibrox Park experienced its second disaster. As fans exited at the end of a match v. Celtic, a crush on a stairway in the north east corner caused the death of 66 spectators.

The aptly named Stairway 13 had already been the scene of two deaths ten years earlier.

Whether the stairs were unaltered since Leitch's day is not known. But a simple amendment to their design, to create shorter flights with landings and changes in direction, would almost certainly have eliminated most of the risks.

Thus once again Rangers found themselves lambasted for negligence, and the football industry in general was found wanting in its regard for public safety and stadium management.

Unlike 1902, there was a public inquiry, and unlike 1902, and 1946 (when there was another disaster at Bolton), government action did ensue, with the passing of the 1975 Safety at Sports Grounds Act and the drawing up of the first edition of the *Guide to Safety at Sports Grounds*.

But for Ibrox Park, in the form that it had existed since Leitch's day, the 1971 disaster proved to be the last straw.

Between 1978-81 all three sides of banking were cleared (ironically most of the spoil being dumped in the now-disused railway cutting next to the ground from where much of it had originally come).

In their place arose three stands, forming, with the South Stand, a newly rectangular Ibrox (*right*).

The significance of this radical redevelopment was twofold.

Firstly, the stands were designed by a combination of the engineers Thorburn and Partners, and the Miller Partnership architects.

Both Glasgow firms would later play a major role in the redevelopment of grounds in the wake of the 1989 Hillsborough disaster; Miller in particular inheriting Leitch's mantle as the most prolific designers of new stadiums in Britain (such as Millwall, Middlesbrough, Derby and Southampton, each of which replaced Leitch-designed grounds).

Secondly, the three new stands were all-seated, requiring from Rangers fans a complete change in their traditional spectating habits.

Ten years later the rest of the football nation found itself following where Rangers had led.

▲ Having had their overall capacity drastically reduced by the redevelopment of Ibrox Park – from 65,000 in 1977 to 44,000 in 1981 – when Rangers emerged as a newly powerful force under the ownership of steel magnate David Murray in 1988, they might have been expected to demolish Leitch's South Stand in order to gain the maximum possible number of extra seats (as Aston Villa were to do in 2000 by replacing the equally historic Trinity Road Stand).

Instead, Rangers pursued the more challenging, and ultimately far more costly option of retaining the South Stand's listed frontage, and extending the stand upwards with an additional tier, covered by a new column-free roof.

Designed by architect Gareth Hutchison and the engineering firm of Blyth and Blyth, and built by the contractors Fairclough, the £13 million redevelopment required the insertion of 476 piles under the existing foundations, plus the addition – unfortunate but necessary – of four steel columns through the existing seating deck.

A massive 146m long roof truss was then raised onto two supporting towers at each end of the stand by two of the world's largest cranes (one of which was shipped over from Argentina).

Since then the two northern corners of the stadium have been filled in, to create a new capacity of 50,444.

This radical remodelling of Ibrox may have compromised Archie's original stand, and yet, such were the complexities of the engineering operation, which took four years to complete, that without question it would have fascinated him too.

Engineering Archie **187**

Rangers

▶ Ibrox Park is the only stadium where one can go on a conducted tour of an Archibald Leitch stand.

Among the delights that await is the marble floored **entrance hall** (*top right*) with its Art Deco lights. The portrait on the far wall is of Alan Morton, 'the Wee Blue Devil', one of Rangers' star players at the time of the stand's construction.

Another well preserved part of the stand is the **Blue Room** (*below right*). The polished oak panelling was fitted by carpenters from the shipyard belonging to John Brown – a regular in the directors' box – who were working on the Queen Mary ocean liner at the time.

As can be seen from this room and the boardroom Leitch fitted out for Blackburn 20 years earlier (*see page 56*), football club directors maintained conservative tastes.

In the far corner of the room is the piano Bill Struth used to play in order to wind down after games.

▲ Ibrox Park and Leitch's South Stand are barely recognisable from the ground as it appeared at the start of this chapter.

The stand now has seats for 5,267 on its former enclosure and 7,820 on its upper deck. The new third tier adds 7,283 seats above.

Its balcony is, of course, the original – mercifully kept clear of advertising – as are the gates (*left*), which were supplied to Leitch's specifications in 1928.

There is no need to guess why Ibrox is nowadays often referred to as 'The Blue Heaven'.

And, as this is the final stop on our own tour of the works of Archibald Leitch, where better to leave his soul to rest.

Engineering Archie **189**

Others

Grounds
Other Commissions 1899–1939

Before the opening of Wembley in 1923 it was common for new grounds to be touted as a potential home for the Cup Final. Stamford Bridge and Highbury, both Leitch grounds, were two such candidates. Another was The Valley, the cavernous home of Charlton Athletic, laid out in a disused chalk pit in 1919. When Charlton applied to join the League in 1921, Leitch was reported as saying that in his estimation The Valley would be capable of holding 150,000. There is no evidence that he did any designs for it, however. Humphreys were the contractors though, hence the similarity of the stand with that of Highbury (*see page 129*).

Trying to ascertain the exact 'authorship' of an old building is often difficult.

Previously mentioned examples of this are the stand built by the Clyde Structural Iron Company 'to designs drawn up by Archibald Leitch' at **Rugby Park**, Kilmarnock, in 1899, and by Humphreys at **Twickenham** in 1927 and 1932 (*see pages 154-155*).

The task of identification is made harder owing to the fact that many stands were the work of building contractors, using either in-house designers, anonymous engineers, or plans 'borrowed' from existing examples.

Some Leitch works may never therefore be positively identified.

Equally, some of the work featured on the previous pages may turn out not to be attributable to Leitch solely.

But what of his other clients?

Two locations where Leitch works can be positively identified are **Windsor Park**, Belfast, the home of Linfield FC (the South Stand, built 1930 and still extant), and **Dalymount Park**, Dublin, home to Bohemians (the Main

The Park Royal ground in north west London (on what is now Johnson Way, by Western Avenue) was a speculative venture financed by the Great Western Railway. An exact clone of Ayresome Park, it was home to Queen's Park Rangers from 1908-15 before being taken over by the army. Leitch was patently involved, but to what extent is not known.

Stand extension plus terrace works in around 1931).

Much of the work Leitch's company undertook was limited to the construction of terraces.

Just a few of the grounds where Archie's patented crush barriers or typical Leitch covers appeared were **St Andrew's**, Birmingham City; **Saltergate**, Chesterfield; **Firhill**, Partick Thistle; **Cardiff Arms Park**, home of the Welsh Rugby Union and **Celtic Park**, Belfast, home of the now defunct Belfast Celtic (possibly the only overtly Catholic club for which Leitch worked).

Leitch's name has also been associated with **Filbert Street**, Leicester (after the collapse of a crush barrier in 1907); **Boundary Park**, Oldham (1913-20), and the **Kursaal**, Southend (in association with Humphreys in 1920).

Then there are several stands which resemble Leitch's designs, but for which no evidence can be found to link him. Among these are the Main Stand at **Oakwell**, Barnsley (1904); the Main Stand at **Elm Park**, Reading (by Humphreys, 1926), and the **Mayflower Stand**, Home Park, Plymouth, built in 1952 but with a balcony truss very similar to a standard Leitch double-decker. If Leitch's company was in any way involved – and the company did continue trading under Leitch's son until 1955 – then it would be the last Leitch stand ever constructed.

Finally, and intriguingly, references have also been found to visits by Leitch to the **Kielstadion** of Beerschot in Antwerp, Belgium, before the stadium hosted the 1920 Olympic Games.

The main stand and general layout of the **Bosuil Stadion**, home of Royal Antwerp, opened in 1923, also look remarkably like typical Leitch designs. But then so do several other examples around Europe and the Commonwealth.

One thing is for sure. Following the publication of this book, the list will no doubt grow.

190 Engineering Archie

◀ Not all Archibald Leitch's stands were grand.

But then, nor did many serve for as long as did this one he designed at **Douglas Park**, the home of Hamilton Academical FC, in 1913. It remained in use until 1994, a total of 81 years.

Seating 1,221 spectators, the stand's most notable feature was its timber cover, built in a style known as a Belfast Roof.

Such roofs were commonly used for large sheds, warehouses and barns, and had the advantage of being lightweight yet robust.

Other grounds to feature them included, appropriately enough, Windsor Park, Belfast, where Leitch also designed the South Stand in 1930, and Leeds Road, Huddersfield (*illustrated on page 123*), erected in 1929.

Huddersfield fans called their new shelter the Cowshed.

Particularly after being treated during the close season the roofs would often give off a reassuring whiff of creosote. They also absorbed the sounds of crowds gathered under their timbers.

For the record, 22,000 attended the Accie's big day, William Wilton's Rangers winning 1-0.

A week later, Leitch was in north London for another opening, where a rather larger stand had yet to be finished at the new Arsenal Stadium in Highbury.

Legacy

Chapter Nine
Legacy

'A playing field becomes like a friend,' noted the *Scottish Umpire*, on the occasion of Rangers' final match at the old Ibrox Park in December 1899, 'and the wrench at parting is a bit stiff.' So too at The Dell in 2001, at Roker Park (*above*) and the Baseball Ground in 1997, at Ayresome Park (1995), at Leeds Road (1994), at The Den (1993), and at Bradford Park Avenue (1972). Still to come, farewell to Highbury in 2006.

When the English Football Association made its bid to stage the World Cup in 1966, the choice of venues was fairly straightforward.

In London it had to be Wembley (with White City as a back up).

Otherwise, the remaining six more or less chose themselves, apart from the north east, where Middlesbrough stood in for the original choice, Newcastle.

Ayresome Park was twinned with Roker Park. In the north west, Goodison Park and Old Trafford got the nod ahead of Anfield and Maine Road, and in Yorkshire and the Midlands, the choice of Hillsborough and Villa Park was uncontested.

In others words, a quarter of a century after the death of Archibald Leitch, the six venues deemed to be the best in the provinces were those that had either been laid out by him, or which featured his stands.

But his influence was wider still. Indeed from the early years of the century until its final decade, the landscape of British football was epitomised by Leitch's approach.

Apart from Wembley Stadium in 1923, and the Arsenal Stadium of 1932-36, in the absence of any trend whatsoever towards the new generation of classically inspired or modernist concrete super stadiums appearing across the Continent during the inter-war period, it was Leitch's almost retro-styled details – his rooftop gables and criss cross steelwork balconies in particular – that embodied the very modest architectural aspirations of those who ran the national game.

At the same time, the vast swathes of terracing that dominated the majority of grounds until at least the 1980s, many of them featuring Leitch's combination of concrete footings, sunken gangways and patented crush barriers, formed so familiar a backdrop as to be considered almost part of the natural order of football's existence.

The Leitch look was *the* look.

Of course no-one would have expected it to endure for ever, not least Leitch, who after all, was in the business of renewal – and profit – himself.

Moreover, one of the chief factors in his success was an ability to deliver at relatively low cost. And where every expense is spared, as was more often the case than not, long term obsolescence is the unavoidable corollary.

Indeed if Archie were around today to witness the level of affection in which his works have been held, though no doubt pleased, he might also be somewhat bemused.

Amused even.

The architect of factories and sheds would hardly expect such a fuss; even less a whole book on his life and work such as this.

No purpose is therefore served in overstating the quality of Archibald Leitch's designs.

Nor should the less savoury aspects of the predominant culture within which he operated be glossed over. The behaviour of many of his paymasters would hardly escape censure in today's world, while the prevailing mood on the terraces was not always one of tolerance and bonhomie.

As in all retrospective evaluations, context is everything.

192 Engineering Archie

As to the physical manifestation of Archie's legacy, apart from the listed structures featured earlier – the Stevenage Road Stand and Cottage at Craven Cottage, and the South Stand at Ibrox – there are no other football-related Leitch buildings which may yet warrant conservation. (The Sentinel Works in Glasgow is a case on its own, if no less important.)

Having said that, the planned retention of a section of Leitch's South Stand at Fratton Park is only to be welcomed, especially given the unlikelihood of the two remaining stands at Goodison Park surviving much longer.

Of the remaining structures, as of early 2005, the stand at Dens Park appears to be secure for the time being; the McLeod Street Stand at Tynecastle is living on borrowed time. Other remaining stands, at Anfield, Hillsborough, White Hart Lane and Selhurst Park have been altered to such an extent that only the closest of scrutiny reveals them to be Leitch's work.

Of those structures demolished in recent years, only one may be considered a significant loss.

Although this writer is hardly an impartial judge in the matter, the demolition of the Trinity Road Stand at Villa Park, in 2000, surely robbed Birmingham, and football, of one of its finest individual buildings.

As to Archie's wider legacy, the part he played in the remarkable rise of professional football in the 20th century is now as much absorbed within the popular memory as it is embodied by his actual buildings.

In effect, the lost world of Archibald Leitch, as encapsulated within these pages, may stand for the lost world of 20th century football as a whole. »

Patented Leitch barriers on the rotting terraces of Hampden Park (*above*), pictured in the 1980s, and at Craven Cottage (*left*), the failure of one such barrier during Fulham's Second Division match v. Millwall in October 1938. The match was the occasion of Craven Cottage's record gate of 49,335. Today the ground holds 22,000.

Engineering Archie 193

Legacy

Archie's people – the best seats in the house fill up in Leitch's South Stand at Ibrox Park before a Saturday match in October 1953. Smiling for the Picture Post photographer are the very sort of people amongst whom Archie worked and socialised within Glasgow's Protestant professional and business classes. These were, it might be said, members of his clan. In as much as any social group can be summed up in a few words, they were conservative, hard working, patriotic and God fearing people. The Rangers of Bill Struth, then nearing the end of his 34 years as manager, embodied much of their ideals and values.

» One of the more important elements of Archibald Leitch's legacy concerns the basic design standards to which he worked.

As has been stated earlier, because his work was so plentiful it inevitably bore a considerable influence on his successors in the post war period, and in particular on the specialist advisors who were tasked by the Home Office, in the 1970s, with the job of drawing up detailed guidelines on safety following the passing of the 1975 Safety of Sports Grounds Act.

This Act constituted the first ever attempt by any body, public or private, to regulate the design and management of British sports grounds, despite the fact that as early as 1924 the need for such regulation had been spelled out by a committee appointed to study the events surrounding the chaotic opening of Wembley Stadium.

Not even the deaths of 33 fans in March 1946, at Burnden Park, Bolton, prompted action by the government.

Instead, it took one further disaster, on the exit stairs of Ibrox Park in January 1971 – in which 66 people died – to finally force Parliament to intervene.

In addition to the 1975 Act, in 1973 the findings of the specialist advisors were summarised in the first edition of a publication called *The Guide to Safety at Sports Grounds*, familiarly known as the *Green Guide*.

So how well did Leitch's grounds measure up to that first bout of scrutiny in the 1970s?

And how do his standards compare with those that have subsequently been applied, following the revision of the *Green Guide* in 1997, as a result of the 1989 Hillsborough disaster (to which we will return below)?

A key element of all modern safety regulation concerns the rigorous calculation, and imposition of capacity levels.

After all, the best designed stand or terrace can still be rendered unsafe if too many people are allowed to occupy it.

In this respect there were two distinct sides to Leitch's work.

On one hand, when Archie was selling the idea of a new ground, to a club or to the press, he frequently talked up the figures, sometimes to an almost absurd level; 80,000 at Fulham in 1904 (*see page 77*), 100,000 at Selhurst Park in 1924 (*page 53*), and even 183,000 at Hampden Park in 1936 (*page 175*).

He was not alone in this.

Thoughout the 20th century, architects, club directors and occasionally politicians all around the world have tossed wildly exaggerated figures around in an attempt to impress. For many years every stadium had to hold at least 100,000 to pass muster.

However, from studying those surviving Leitch plans on which calculated numbers are stated, we know that he actually made quite detailed calculations.

For terraces he allowed a width of 16" per person, packed to a density of approximately 58 persons per 10 square metres.

The first *Green Guide* in 1973 recommended a maximum of 54, providing certain conditions were met (regarding barrier configurations, barrier strengths, underfoot conditions and so on).

The latest *Green Guide* reduced this maximum to 47.

But of course Archie's figures were meaningless if not accompanied by strict controls of the numbers actually admitted.

The invention of the Rush Preventive turnstile with an in-built counting mechanism, in 1895 (*see page 59*), should, in theory, have enabled clubs to exercise that control. But in practice the counters were used merely to check takings against the numbers of entries recorded.

Only when a section of the ground appeared to be full to bursting would stewards post up signs saying 'Full'.

And in any case there was widespread corruption, which meant thousands entered free of charge, or by paying turnstile operators to allow them to slip over or under the barriers.

In this respect, the grounds of Archie's era were hardly managed at all, a situation which has only been satisfactorily resolved since the Taylor Report, with the advent of all-seater stadiums, ticketed admission only, and computerised counting mechanisms.

For details of how Leitch's terrace and crush barrier design compared with later standards, see Chapter Three.

As for seating, where individual seats were fitted in Leitch's stands, Archie allowed a width of 18" or 460mm per person.

This, it was noted in 1914, when specified for Aston Villa's proposed Trinity Road Stand, was three inches more than was then the standard set for seats on an omnibus or train.

Surprisingly perhaps, the modern minimum recommended by the 1997 *Green Guide* is also 460mm (although in practice many stadium architects now work to a more generous 500mm).

On the other hand, the average British person has grown in height since Archie's day – one estimate puts it as four inches since the late Victorian period – meaning that a seated individual needs more leg room than in the past.

The simplest method of judging the amount of leg room that an average spectator might expect – although there are other factors involved, such as the design of the seat and the rake of the tier – is the measurement of the actual tread over which the seat is fixed.

In all Leitch stands from 1899 onwards, this tread depth was set at 26" or 660mm.

Once again, this turns out to be same standard that was still being applied in stands up until the 1980s. In some cases – in Old Trafford's new stands, for example, built in the 1990s – it continues to be used, much to the discomfort of anyone of more than average height.

As a result, today's recommended minimum is 760mm.

Concerning sightlines – that is, the ability to see the action above or between the heads of the people immediately in front – accurate comparisons are not available.

What we can say is that whereas there have been several modern stands built in which the sightlines have proved inadequate – in certain instances partly because no proper calculation was made – it is clear from Leitch's drawings that he was aware of the issue. It is unlikely he used much more than lines – he called them eye-lines – drawn from the front and back rows of each stand or terrace down to the touchlines.

But that in itself confirms that he did take sightlines into account, as well as related issues such as clearance heights of upper decks above terracing.

In consequence, few if any sightline problems have been encountered in Leitch stands.

What he did not avoid was the restrictions caused by columns.

Although cantilevered, or column-free roofs were starting to appear in Europe and South America from the 1920s onwards – the first one in Britain being at the Northolt Park Racecourse in 1929 – throughout his career Leitch stuck to the tried and tested method of post and beam construction.

On lower tiers, especially those converted from standing to seating – at Goodison Park for example – this has resulted in as much as 10 per cent of all views being classed as restricted.

So Archie was not perfect. But he did at least work to a method, and one which is still used today, albeit with the aid of computers.

The Leitch look at Ayresome Park – a factory architect catering for spectators who worked in factories and lived in their shadow.

Engineering Archie 195

Legacy

196 Engineering Archie

▲ **Archie in the news** – **Bradford Park Avenue** was a popular venue for the annual meetings of the Bradford Schools' Sports Association. Here in 1968 we see the cricket side of the Main Stand, the first to feature his familiar criss-cross balcony steelwork.

The stand was demolished seven years later, although the cricket ground remains in use today.

Shown opposite (*far left*) Welsh fans look on as one of their number scales the posts in front of Leitch's North Stand at **Twickenham** in February 1970. The stand was demolished in 1990.

At **Roker Park** (*top left*) the once prolific striker **Brian Clough**, steps out pensively in August 1964 as he attempts a comeback following a serious injury two years earlier. He managed only three more games before becoming the country's youngest manager a year later. The stand in view was demolished in 1997.

Fratton Park (*lower left*) in November 1948 is the scene as **Field Marshal Montgomery** greets the players on the occasion of Pompey's Golden Jubilee. The South Stand shown is still in use.

Engineering Archie

Legacy

The 25 victims of the 1902 disaster, remembered at modern day Ibrox Park. Since that fateful day in Archie's life there have been four major disasters at British football grounds, plus countless more minor incidents in which one or two deaths have occurred. Thousands more have been injured in routine accidents. Apart from the disaster at Valley Parade, Bradford in 1985 – caused by a fire in a wooden stand – all the other tragedies have taken place either on terraces, or in the entry and exit routes leading to them.

▲ To all intents and purposes, the world of Archibald Leitch came to an abrupt end at **Hillsborough Stadium** on April 15 1989.

A complete breakdown in the management of crowds at an FA Cup semi-final led to the deaths of 96 Liverpool fans at the Leppings Lane End.

In his report into the disaster, Lord Justice Taylor made the terse point that despite no fewer than eight official reports into crowd safety and behaviour since the first one appeared in 1924, there still existed fatal gaps in the regulation of the nation's football grounds.

The 1975 Safety of Sports Grounds Act offered a useful basis, but unless its implementation by local authorities was properly monitored, there was little chance of it being applied with any rigour or consistency across the country.

Too much depended on local interpretation and on local resources, while the clubs had more or less handed over crowd control to the police.

In short, the whole business of safety management was to be professionalised and regulated, with a new body, the Football Licensing Authority, acting as a watchdog in the public interest.

Taylor's 74 recommendations covered a wide gamut of issues.

But the one which did more than any to revolutionise the design and management of grounds – and in the process render much of Leitch's work obsolete – was the phasing out of all terraces at senior British grounds by August 1994.

The social and cultural effects of this abolition have been discussed at great length in other forums, and cannot be easily summarised here.

For the infrastructure of football as a whole, however, the effects have been dramatic.

Over a billion pounds has been spent on new stands and stadiums.

Thousands of cubic metres of banking – much of it found to have been contaminated industrial spoil – have had to be cleared.

A whole new stadium industry has arisen, in which not one company like Leitch dominates, but dozens of specialist firms of architects, engineers, contractors and other building service professionals now operate.

Many aspects of the old order may well be mourned, and with good reason. But football is well rid of the complacency and negligence which, over the course of the 20th century, turned the staging of matches in Britain into an accident waiting to happen.

◀ The Kop at Anfield; the Mauretania Stand at Goodison; the Shelf at White Hart Lane and the Cowshed at Leeds Road – all gone in the blinking of an eye.

The wholescale redevelopment of British football's infrastructure since 1990 has brought with it many painful partings, not least the loss of much-loved buildings such as the **Trinity Road Stand** at Villa Park (left), the great masterwork of Archibald Leitch and his co-conspirator, Fred Rinder.

Even without the Hillsborough disaster many of Leitch's works would not have survived the inevitable march of progress.

Spectators today expect not to have to watch matches with columns in their way. They demand better food outlets, more toilet facilities – or in the case of women at some grounds, any toilets at all.

To pay for all these changes, and to feed the demands of the game's ever more cash hungry players, the stands of today have to be brimming with boxes and lounges, shops and offices. Anything to bring in income, seven days a week.

But for the fans, whatever their modern form, football grounds are still likened to cathedrals. Still they speak of 'sacred turf', of 'hallowed ground'. Of the stadium as a shrine.

Here at **Goodison Park** (*left*), Leitch's stands look down not only on the living.

Engineering Archie 199

Legacy

▲ It has taken the world of football a long time to appreciate the value of heritage.

For whilst tradition is writ large on the game's front door, outside the back its bins have overflowed with the treasures of the past.

How often one hears of cupboards being cleared, of records being 'lost', and even, here and there, of books being burnt.

In one of those infernos, the story goes, one of Archie's models met its fate one spring cleaning day in the 1970s.

In more recent times, fans have been able to make a difference, such as with the Stevenage Road Stand at **Craven Cottage**, fought for and then cared for by campaigners at Fulham (*above*).

Elsewhere, in the car park of the **Stadium of Light** in Sunderland, proudly on display are two sections of Leitch's balcony truss (*above right*), cut down from the old Main Stand at Roker Park, when the ground was levelled in 1997.

How big, how heavy and how rudimentary they appear close up.

Truly, engineering as art.

At **Ewood Park**, Blackburn, the 'Rovers FC' sign that used to adorn Leitch's turnstile block on the corner of Kidder Street (*below*) now forms part of a memorial to Jack Walker, the steel man who forged the club's revival during the 1990s.

The sculpture (*right*) is by James Butler. Campbell Driver Partnership and Griffiths & Griffin designed the setting.

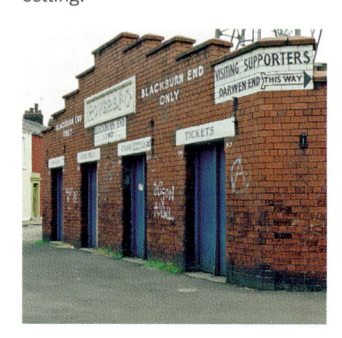

200 Engineering Archie

▲ On a modern housing estate a football sits oddly adrift by the roadside, inviting passers-by to give it a thwack. On the wall of a garden, the word 'enclosure' is sandblasted in cryptic capitals.

Elsewhere, a scarf, cast in bronze, is draped over railings. A pair of boots is rooted to a step.

The objects are the work of artist Neville Gabie.

The estate – its roads named The Turnstile, The Midfield and The Holgate – occupies the site of what, from 1903-95 was **Ayresome Park**, the first complete stadium built in England by Archibald Leitch.

The bronze ball marks one of the penalty spots. (The other is in front of a sofa in one of the resident's living rooms.) The scarf hangs where there was a corner flag.

Close by, studs in the road pick out the centre circle, while a bronze puddle in a garden marks the spot where North Korea's Pak Doo Ik scored the goal that knocked Italy out from the 1966 World Cup.

Supporting Gabie in this subtle remembrance were Cleveland Arts and Wimpey Homes.

The echoes of the crowd come courtesy of the wind.

Engineering Archie 201

Legacy

◀ Artist **Charles Cundall** was captivated by crowds. He painted vivid panoramas at Lord's, Wembley, Epsom, and here at **Stamford Bridge**, during a match between Chelsea and Arsenal.

    The Pensioners v. the Gunners.
    West London v. north London.
    The contrivance of Gus Mears v. the conceit of Henry Norris.

    Cundall chose his match well. It was the autumn afternoon in October 1935 that a record 83,000 souls packed into the stadium of which, it was predicted, when opened thirty years earlier, would 'stagger humanity'.

    And in the midst of this humanity, a peanut seller touts his wares, schoolboys perch on the fence, while beheld by the multitude, a leather ball is caught bobbing in midfield.

    The painting was exhibited at the Royal Academy in 1937, two years before Leitch's death, so it is just possible that Archie saw it.

    He would surely have approved, even if, in parts, like many of the views expressed within this book, it paints a somewhat idealised view.

    As 20th century football's designer-in-chief, Archibald Leitch was, at heart, a practical man.

    A blacksmith's son. An engineer.

    But he was also a builder of dreams; of powerful men's dreams and of little men's dreams alike.

    And if, in the reveries of those who dream on, Cundall's groundscape is how we choose to recall the world that Archie did so much to shape, it is a game as good as any.

Shadows fall upon the turf
A steam train on the line
The warm press of the terraces
And Archie's grand design

Archibald Leitch 1865-1939

Engineering Archie **203**

Links

Where no publisher listed assume self-published by club or author

Where no date listed assume published on final date within title, ie. 1860-1960 means published 1960

Football grounds
Guide to Safety at Sports Grounds HMSO (editions in 1973, 1976, 1990 & 1996)
Inglis S *The Football Grounds of Britain* Collins Willow (1996)
Report of the Departmental Committee on Crowds HMSO (1924)

History general
The Book of Football Amalgamated Press, London (1906)
Hutchinson J *The Football Industry – The Early Years of the Professional Game* Richard Drew Publishing (1982)
Inglis S *League Football and the Men Who Made It* Collins Willow (1988)
Mason T *Association Football & English Society* 1863-1915 The Harvester Press (1980)
Briggs Prof A *Mass Entertainment: The Origins of a Modern Industry* The Griffin Press (1960)

Glasgow
Hall Sir P *Cities in Civilization* Pantheon Books (1998)
Lauder J *The Glasgow Athenaeum*, 1847-97 (1997)
Moss MS & Hume JR *Workshop of the British Empire – Engineering and Shipbuilding in the West of Scotland* Heinemann (1977)
Stenhouse D *On The Make – How the Scots took over London* Mainstream (2004)
Wright H *Supporting the City: the Influence of Engineering in Glasgow's Buildings* Latheronwheel (1999)
www.theglasgowstory.com

Ibrox 1902 Disaster
Shiels R *The Ibrox Disaster 1902* Judicial Review 230 (1997)
Weir J *The 1902 Ibrox Disaster* Scottish Football Historian (63)

Arsenal
Soar P and Tyler M *Arsenal 1886-1986* Hamlyn (1986)
Watt T *The End* Mainstream (1993)

Aston Villa
Inglis S *Villa Park 100 Years* Sports Projects (1997)

Blackburn Rovers
Jackman M *Blackburn Rovers, Official Encyclopedia* (1994)
www.cottontown.org

Bradford City
Arnold AJ *A Game That Would Pay – A Business History of Professional Football in Bradford* Duckworth (1988)
Along the Midland Road Bradford City AFC (1997)

Bradford Park Avenue
Hartley M & Clapham T *The Avenue, Bradford Park Avenue Pictorial History* Temple Nostalgia Press (1987)
Hartley M & Clapham T *All About Avenue* Soccerdata (2004)

Chelsea
Benson C *The Bridge* Chelsea FC (1987)

Derby County
Wilson M *The Baseball Ground – 1895-1997* DCFC (1997)

Dundee
Price N *Up Wi' the Bonnets – Centenary history of Dundee FC* (1993)

Everton
Keates T *A History of Everton FC* (1929)

Fulham
Turner D & White A *Fulham, A Complete Record 1879-1987* Breedon Books (1987)
Turner D *A History of Fulham Football Club* Fulham FC (1979)
Turner D (ed) *Cottage Chronicles,* Northdown (1994)

Hearts
Speed D, Smith B & Blackwood G *Hearts – A Pictorial History 1874-1984*

Huddersfield Town
Binns GS *Huddersfield Town 75 Years On* HTAFC (1984)
Thomas I *Leeds Road – Home of My Dreams* HTAFC (1994)

Liverpool
Kelly SF *The Kop – The End Of An Era* Mandarin (1993)

Manchester United
Green G *There's Only One United* Hodder & Stoughton (1978)
McCartney I *Old Trafford Theatre of Dreams* Yore Publications (1996)

Middlesbrough
Paylor E & Wilson J *Ayresome Park Memories* Breedon (1995)

Millwall
Murray J *Millwall Lions of the South* Indispensable & MFC (1988)

Newcastle United
Joannou P *Fortress St James* NUFC/Ballast (2000)

Queen's Park
Robertson F and Ross D *The First 100 Years of Hampden* First Press (2003)
Robinson R *History of the Queen's Park FC 1867-1917* Hay Nisbet (1920)
Queen's Park FC Souvenir Pictorial (1949)

Rangers
Allan J *The Rangers Story* (1996)
Mason D *Rangers, The Managers* Mainstream (2000)
Murray B *The Old Firm, Sectarianism, Sport and Society in Scotland* John Donald (1984)

Sheffield United
Clareborough D & Kirkham A *Sheffield United: A Complete Record of Sheffield United FC 1889-1999* SUFC

Sheffield Wednesday
Dickinson J *100 Years at Hillsborough* Hallamshire (1999)

Southampton
Juson D & Bull D *Full Time at the Dell* Hagiology (2001)

Sunderland
Sunderland AFC – The Official History 1879-2000 SAFC

Tottenham Hotspur
Soar P *And The Spurs Go Marching On* Hamlyn (1982)
Wagstaffe Simmons G *History of Tottenham Hotspur FC 1882–1946* Tottenham Hotspur FC (1947)

Twickenham
Harris E *Fortress Twickenham; Home of England Rugby* Sports Books Ltd (2005)

West Ham Stadium
Belton, B *When West Ham Went to the Dogs* Tempus (2002)

Journals and publications
Architects Journal; Athletic News; Bradford Telegraph & Argus; The Builder; Building News; The Croydon Advertiser and Surrey County Reporter; Croydon Times; The Daily Telegraph; Dundee Courier; Edinburgh Evening News; Football Chat; Glasgow Evening Times; Glasgow Herald; Glasgow Weekly Mail; Groundtastic; Illustrated London News; Kilmarnock Standard; Lotinga's Weekly; Liverpool Echo; Manchester Guardian; The Scotsman; Scottish Sport; Sheffield Independent; The Sketch; Southampton Daily Echo; The Sphere; Sporting Life; West London & Fulham Times; Yorkshire Daily Observer; Yorkshire Post

Modern stadiums
Who are the Archibald Leitchs of the early 21st century? Numerous engineers and architects currently specialise in sports ground design, among them *Engineering Archie*'s sponsors HOK Sport (*Galpharm Stadium*, *Reebok Stadium*, currently responsible for the new *Wembley Stadium*, *Emirates Stadium*, *Ascot* and *Wimbledon*). The Miller Partnership has worked at over 20 locations around Britain (including *Millwall*, *Middlesbrough*, *Derby*, *Leicester*, *Southampton* and *Coventry*), and like Leitch is based in Glasgow. Also active in the field from Scotland is Barr Construction Ltd.
For further reading see:

www.hoksve.com
www.millerpartnership.com
www.barr.co.uk
www.acpractice.co.uk
www.afl-uk.com
www.arupassociates.com
www.kssgroup.com
www.tth-architects.co.uk
www.wardmchugh.demon.co.uk
www.anthonyhuntassociates.co.uk
www.bianchi-morley.com
www.burohappold.com
www.grandstands.net
www.mottmac.com

Played in Britain
for more information on English Heritage's *Played in Britain* series, see www.playedinbritain.co.uk

Published titles
Played in Manchester
Simon Inglis *(2004)*

Engineering Archie – Archibald Leitch, football ground designer
Simon Inglis *(2005)*

Liquid Assets – the lidos and open air swimming pools of Britain
Janet Smith *(2005)*

A Load of Old Balls
Simon Inglis *(2005)*

Played in Birmingham
Steve Beauchampé & Simon Inglis (2006)

The Best of Charles Buchan's Football Monthly ed. Simon Inglis (2006)

Future titles
Played in Liverpool Ray Physick (2007)

Great Lengths – the indoor swimming pools of Britain Dr Ian Gordon (2007)

Uppies & Downies – Britain's traditional football games Hugh Hornby (2007)

Played at the Pub Arthur Taylor (2008)

Bowled Over – the bowling greens of Britain Hugh Hornby (2008)

Played in Glasgow Ged O'Brien (2008)

Played on Tyne & Wear Lynn Pearson (2009)

Played in London Simon Inglis (2011)

Credits

Photographs and images
Please note that in the credits listed here, where more than one photograph appears on a page, each photograph is identified by a letter, starting with 'a' in the top left hand corner of the page, or at the top, and continuing thereafter in a *clockwise* direction.

Special collections
The family photographs and letters of Archibald Leitch and his family are reproduced by permission of Hilda Brew: 2, 36a, 52, 54, 57. The letter of Archibald Leitch of June 19 1902 which appears on page 25 is deposited at the National Archives of Scotland, ref JC26/1902/46. The plans of Bramall Lane on page 62 are reproduced with permission of the Head of Leisure Services, Sheffield City Council, and are located in the Sheffield Archives, Document no. CA206/05725. Charles Cundall's painting of Stamford Bridge on pp 202-03 is © The Artist's Estate/The Bridgeman Art Library.

The publishers also wish to thank the following sources for permission to reproduce original materials:
British Library (Patents Department): 30, 31; Glasgow City Archives: 17, 18 and 24ab; Glasgow University Archive Services: 12, 14; Hammersmith & Fulham Archives and Local History Centre: 28, 74abcd; London Borough of Haringey, Building Control: 111ab; Liverpool City Council: 46ab, 59c, 87, 88, 89c, 102a; London Metropolitan Archives: 71, 81, 82ab, 130ab, 131ab; National Football Museum: 55, 90, 98, 122, 128, 153b, 166; National Monuments Record © Crown Copyright. NMR: 75, 92a; National Monuments Record of Scotland © Crown Copyright: RCAHMS; 148a, 149a, 180a, 188b; Ordnance Survey © Crown Copyright: 163abc; Rangers FC: 20, 33, 65b, 181, 182, 183, 184abcd, 185abcd, 186-187, 187b, inside back cover; Scottish Football Museum: 29b; 48, 174-5; Trafford Borough Council: 114b, 115, 117a, 119a.

Agency, press and commissioned photographs
Action Images: 1; The Annan Gallery: 11, 36b; Ian Baxter: 200c; Bradford Telegraph & Argus: 96a; Colorsport: 39a, 56a, 85a, 102b, 129b, 142, 162a, 164b; Tony Davis: 169a; Empics: 4, 77a, 80b, 105, 112b, 113c, 121ac, 145b, 155ab, 164a, 180b, 188c, 189ab, 190a, 192, 196a; Neville Gabie: 201ab; Getty Images: 26, 32a, 38, 39b, 45b, 59b, 83, 104c, 110a, 112b, 123b, 131c, 137b, 179a, 193b, 194, 196c; Adrian Gibson: 56c; Illustrated London News Group: 21; Simon Inglis: back cover abd, 6, 8, 9, 35, 40, 44b, 47abc, 58, 68b, 70a, 77bc, 78abc, 79b, 80a, 85c, 106bcd, 107, 108a, 113abde, 121d, 127abcd, 135bc, 136, 138ab, 139ab, 143bc, 144abc, 145a, 154, 156b, 159ab, 160a, 165b, 169ab, 173b, 177d, 188a, 193a, 195ab, 198a, 199b, 200abd, 205, 208; Bob Lilliman: 93ab, 120a, 121b, 126, 177ac; Manchester Evening News Syndication: 119b; Mirrorpix: 56d, 172a; The News, Portsmouth: 50c; Colin Peel: 199a; Popperfoto.com: inside front cover, 32b, 50bd, 51abc, 56b, 86a, 106a, 114a, 117b, 158, 196b; Sheffield Newspapers: 63b; Simmons Aerofilms: 63a, 79a, 84, 91, 95a, 103, 123a, 129a, 159c, 167, 177b; DC Thomson: 51d, 149b; TopFoto: 76, 179b, 198b; Winter Collection: 168.

Libraries and local archives
Bradford Local Studies Library: 197; Brent Archive: 190b; Croydon Local Studies Library: 42b, 49b, 153a; Institution of Civil Engineers: 89a; Lewisham Local Studies & Archive: 120b; Liverpool Local Studies Service: 101; Mitchell Library, Glasgow: 10, 13ab, 15, 41b, 42a; Newham Archives & Local Studies Library: 178; RIBA Library Photographs Collection: 29c, 45a; Sheffield Libraries, Archives & Information; Local Studies: 27.

Private collections
Geoff Allman: 161; Tim Clapham: 94, 95b, 96b, 97abcd; John Dewhirst: 50a, 99abc; Alan Dick: 191; Jason Dickinson: 134; Clino d'Eletto: 41c, 61, 64c, 65a, 111c, 150b, 171b; David France: 44a; Harry Greenmon: 66, 68a; Simon Inglis: 53, 140; Mike Jackman: 92b; Paul Joannou: 151; Ian King: 152; Paul Macnamara: 60, 64a, 124, 132a, 176; Jack Murray: 171a, 172b; Richard Owen: 156a, 157ab; Andy Porter; cover flap, 34, 108b; Norrie Price: 148b; Stéphane Renauld: 125, 162b; Iain Robertson: 100, 146, 170; Dennis Turner: 70b; The Yorkshire County Cricket Club: 41a.

Football Club archives:
Aston Villa FC: 141, 143a, Dundee FC: 147; Everton FC: 104ab; Heart of Midlothian FC: 137a; Huddersfield Town AFC: 43abd; Kirklees Stadium Development Ltd: 7; Liverpool FC Museum: back cover c, 89b; Manchester United Museum: Cover, 37, 59a, 118; Middlesbrough FC: 67, 69; Newcastle United FC: 150a; Sheffield Wednesday FC: 43c, 132b, 133, 135a; Wolverhampton Wanderers FC: 49a, 164c, 165a.

Books:
The Book of Football: 22, 29a, 72, 73; Football and the Fine Arts: 85b; History of Tottenham Hotspur FC 1882 – 1946 (G Wagstaffe Simmons): 109, 110b, 111d.

206 Engineering Archie

Acknowledgements

Engineering Archie has been a delight to write and research. It would appear that there are a lot of Archibald Leitch enthusiasts out there, many of whom have been more than willing contributors to this book. I would like to thank in particular Rod Sheard of HOK Sport for his invaluable support for the project; Rob Richardson at English Heritage publications and Malcolm Cooper for their belief in the *Played in Britain* concept; Doug Cheeseman and family for their patience and commitment to Malavan Media; David Mason and Sandy Jardine at Rangers Football Club for their generosity and support; Hugh Hornby at the National Football Museum, Richard McBrearty at the Scottish Football Museum, Mark Wylie at the Manchester United Museum and Stephen Done at the Liverpool FC Museum, for access to their collections; Duncan McLean at the Miller Partnership for help at the Glasgow end; Bill Reid for explaining the arcana of engineering terms; Robert Shiels for his knowledge of the 1902 Ibrox disaster; Forrest Robertson for his knowledge of Scottish football and Glasgow; John R Hume for his knowledge of industrial history in Glasgow; Keith Moore at the Institute of Mechanical Engineers; Carol Morgan at the Institute of Civil Engineers; Mark Fenton at English Heritage for mapping skills; Clino d'Eletto, Stéphane Renauld and Jack Murray for access to their wonderful stadium postcard collections; Paul Macnamara for access to his equally wonderful collection of football memorabilia; Esther Sclare for her hospitality and inside knowledge of Glasgow; Ranald MacInnes and Richard Emerson at Historic Scotland, and Iain Paterson Glasgow City Council Development and Regeneration Service for background information; the staff at the Glasgow Mitchell Library for their patience and expertise; and finally to the people of the city of Glasgow who were unfailingly helpful, humourous and supportive.

In addition to the individuals credited above and opposite, the following club historians and collectors have been of immense assistance:
Arsenal: Ian Cook; Aston Villa: Bernard Gallagher; Bohemians: Peter Miles; Bradford Park Avenue: Tim Clapham and Malcolm Hartley; Chelsea: Colin Benson; Crystal Palace: Rev Nigel Sands, Ian Weller; Derby County: Mike Wilson; Dundee: Bob Hynd, Norrie Price, Tim Stobbs; Everton: Alan Bowen, David France, Gordon Lock; Fulham: Mark Collins, Dave Piggott, Dennis Turner; Hamilton: Scott Struthers; Heart of Midlothian: Tom Purdie, David Speed; Huddersfield Town: George Binns, Ian Thomas; Kilmarnock; Richard Cairns, David Ross; Liverpool: Ged Poynton, Tom Preston; Middlesbrough: Rob Nicholls, Newcastle United: Paul Joannou; Portsmouth: Richard Owen; Sheffield United: John Garrett; Sheffield Wednesday: Pauline Climpson, Jason Dickinson, Bill Eastwood, Eastwood & Partners; Tottenham Hotspur: John Babb, Andy Porter, Gordon Roy; Twickenham: Ed Harris, Jed Smith; Wolverhampton Wanderers: Graham Hughes, Mark Eagle; Yorkshire CCC: Chris Hassell, Peter Learoyd.

On a personal note, Archie's grandchildren John Easton and Hilda Brew made available the family archives, and were an invaluable source of reminiscences. It is an immense regret that John, a charming and kind man who had particular childhood memories of attending Spurs matches with Archie, did not live to see this book.

Above Lest we forget – Archibald Leitch's Sentinel Works in Jessie Street, Polmadie, Glasgow, stands derelict and apparently unwanted.

Following page Nature does her best to swamp the ruins of Bradford Park Avenue's abandoned ground in Horton.

Engineering Archie 207